Rebuilding Canadian Party Politics

R. Kenneth Carty, William Cross,
and Lisa Young

Rebuilding Canadian Party Politics

UBCPress · Vancouver · Toronto

Printed in Canada on acid-free paper ∞

ISBN 0-7748-0777-6 (hardcover)
ISBN 0-7748-0778-4 (paperback)

Canadian Cataloguing in Publication Data

Carty, R. Kenneth, 1944-
    Rebuilding Canadian Party Politics

    Includes bibliographical references and index.
    ISBN 0-7748-0777-6 (bound); ISBN 0-7748-0778-4 (pbk)

    1. Political parties – Canada – History.   2. Canada –
Politics and government – 1984-1993.★   3. Canada – Politics and
government – 1993-   4. Canada – Politics and government –
1963-1984.★   I. Cross, William P. (William Paul), 1962-   II. Young,
Lisa.   III. Title
JL195.C34   2000   324.271´009´045   C99-911202-3

UBC Press acknowledges the financial support of the Government of Canada through the Book Publishing Industry Development Program (BPIDP) for our publishing activities.
Canadä

We also gratefully acknowledge the support of the Canada Council for the Arts for our publishing program, as well as the support of the British Columbia Arts Council.

UBC Press
University of British Columbia
2029 West Mall
Vancouver, BC V6T 1Z2
(604) 822-5959
Fax: 1-800-668-0821
E-mail: info@ubcpress.ubc.ca
www.ubcpress.ubc.ca

Contents

Figures and Tables

Acknowledgments

This book was conceived and work on it started when Bill Cross and Lisa Young came to the Political Science department at the University of British Columbia in the fall of 1996. Though we had originally thought that we might undertake a study of the upcoming (1997) general election, it soon became apparent that it was more important to explore and explain the far-reaching changes that were reshaping Canadian party politics. This is our version of the map that will order the country's politics as we enter the twenty-first century.

We have had a good deal of help with this study and we would like to express our thanks to everyone who has contributed to it. First, we are grateful to the many women and men actively engaged in party politics who have taken time to talk to us – in formal interview settings, in campaign offices, on the telephone, in convention halls, and via questionnaire forms. These are the individuals who make Canadian democracy work, and the fact that we study them and their handiwork is testimony to our admiration and respect for their commitment to our political system. Next, we extend our appreciation to the several individuals who have worked hard as our research assistants – Adrienne Nash and Jennifer Delaney, in Vancouver; Lawna Hurl, in Calgary; and Anamitra Deb, in Sackville. Though they might not get the public credit they deserve for ferreting out material and organizing our research, we know the extent to which they made our work both easier and more pleasant, and we are grateful. Finally, we want to thank the Political Science department at the University of British Columbia for bringing us together and providing us with a congenial home to begin the work on this book. Though it is almost certainly invidious to point to individuals, thanks are owed to Don

Blake, Munroe Eagles, and Tony Sayers for help and advice on this and other projects.

Someone has to pay for work like this, and in Canada that often means the Social Sciences and Humanities Research Council. The council provided postdoctoral fellowships that created the opportunity for Cross and Young to come to UBC; it also supported Carty with a standard research grant. We have all also had the support of our respective universities, and thank UBC, the University of Calgary, and Mt. Allison University for small research-grant support.

Three individuals need to be singled out for pushing this book to completion. Emma Cross took on the daunting task of wrestling with our early drafts and shaping them into an integrated whole. She did this with grace and tact, and we are much in her debt. Emily Andrew has been our editor at UBC Press, and we could not have been better served. Her enthusiasm for the project, and perceptive observations about what it needed, have been just what we needed. We recommend her highly. Finally there is Camilla Jenkins, who got us done. Authors are often surprised that the work doesn't stop with delivering a "final" manuscript, but Camilla has worked patiently with us at all stages of production to make this a better book, and we are very grateful for her care and caring.

Though the book was started in Vancouver, it soon became a trans-Canadian collaboration. While that has not always been easy, it has provided for stimulating working sessions in locations as different as Whistler, BC, and the Sheraton Gateway Hotel at Toronto International Airport, all supplemented by the magic of fax machines and e-mail. In the end we have produced a book that is the result of a genuine intellectual partnership, and have also become good friends, an unexpected personal bonus that has contributed in no small part to the co-authorship.

The (almost) silent partners in this project have been our spouses, and they are undoubtedly as glad as we are that it is done. In thanks, we dedicate this to *Elaine, Emma,* and *Mike.*

Rebuilding Canadian Party Politics

1

Party Politics at Century's End

Canadian party politics collapsed in the early 1990s. This book is about that collapse, about the end of a party system, with a unique pattern of party organization and competition, that had governed Canada's national politics for several decades, and about the ongoing struggle to build its successor. Our questions are simple: What caused the collapse of the party system? How is the new one going to differ from its predecessor? Although these question are simple, our answers take us into the ambiguities and uncertainties of a new Canadian party system for the twenty-first century: one that is still emerging. Although the final mould of this new party politics has yet to be cast, we can discern its emerging outlines in the forces that are giving it shape.

Making sense of Canada has always meant making sense of its party politics. That is inevitable in a country first put together, and then kept together, by party politicians who must compete in electoral contests to win support and office. We can trace the country's history through the shifting rhythms of its politics, and through the shocks to its party system, which has periodically been set off in new directions. Though the pendulum has swung, rather unevenly, between Liberals and Conservatives for over a century, the patterns of the wider party system have twice before been dramatically reconstructed. Long periods of rather predictable political alignments and party life have suddenly been overturned, and then rebuilt in new ways in the matter of a few years. Our argument is that the 1993 general election marked the beginning of one such convulsion, and the first step in the establishment of the fourth Canadian party system.

The very idea of a party system, and, more particularly, a series of them, focuses our attention on the character of individual political parties and the nature of their competitive relationships with one another. The most obvious characteristic of a party system is the number of parties and the nature of the issues that divide them. Together, these simple characteristics reveal much about the electoral choices that voters face, for the parties' most basic tasks consist of nominating candidates and conducting campaigns on their behalf. And on these grounds there is a superficial case for saying that the Canadian party system has changed rather little since Confederation, given that the country's first parties (the Liberals and Conservatives) have successfully persisted as little more than two great, sprawling, seemingly indistinguishable machines for vacuuming up votes. However, a portrait of the party system as little more than the alignment of electoral forces misses much that is important and revealing about a country's democratic life. How do the parties organize and operate? How do they provide individual voters with the institutions and opportunity to participate in their government? How do they conceive of their representational responsibilities? How do they mobilize support, and with what consequence for the underlying political equations that govern the nation's politics? How are they financed? How do they structure the communication necessary for democratic debate and choice? Answers to questions like these, to questions about the party's organization and activity as instruments of an active citizenry, reveal as much about the real essence of a working party system as do the number, names, and positions of the parties in it.

This much richer conception of a party system allows us to recognize the distinctive fashion in which parties respond to the complex set of political and governing challenges that distinguish particular historical eras. It also enables us to mark the great turning points in our democratic practice and experience. For Canada, as for the United States, this conception of a party system highlights the essential features of several sequential, and distinctive, party systems otherwise masked by the impression of unchanging continuity suggested by the dominance of the same old political parties.[1] Thus, Kenneth Carty, focusing on the organization and activity of Canadian parties; Richard Johnston, exploring the cycles of party mobilization of the electorate; and David Smith, approaching party politics from the perspective of how parties have gone about governing when in office, have recognized three distinctive political eras, three distinctive Canadian party systems that have marked the country's democratic experience.[2]

Parties exist to solve the organizational problems of linking society to state in electoral democracies. Canada's history of successive party systems is the story of how parties responded to the peculiar challenges of doing just that as both the character and the demands of Canadian society, and the responses and activities of the state, changed over time. This perspective provides us with both the theoretical and the historical framework for understanding the great party-system collapse in 1993. In their day, previous party-system crashes were just as dramatic, as they opened the system to new participants and forced the parties to invent new ways of doing Canadian politics. And, in important ways, each created a new Canada.

The first party-system collapse in Canadian history occurred during and after the First World War as the era of the historic parties of Confederation ended and a new, more democratic, more regionalized, party politics emerged. The Canada of regional brokerage that this second system served lasted until about 1960, when it, in turn, collapsed, and a new party system, driven by parties promoting their own national agendas, arose in a Canada riven by existential and constitutional angst while attempting to marry Keynesian policies with the practices of executive federalism. It is this third, pan-Canadian, system that has now reached the end of its natural life and has given way. Each of these party-system collapses was heralded by an enormous electoral landslide – Robert Borden's in 1917, John Diefenbaker's in 1958, and Brian Mulroney's in 1984 – that signalled the voters' openness to change and marked the beginning of a fundamental realignment of the electorate that would underpin the politics of the succeeding era. In each case, the Conservative party was the immediate beneficiary of the landslide; in each case, Conservatives paid a heavy price as the Liberals (and others) moved more quickly to absorb the lessons of the collapse, and to build new and different organizations able to create new coalitions and practise new politics. The result has been that the Conservatives have spent much of the twentieth century playing catch-up in the effort to recover from the effects of winning the three largest electoral victories of Canadian history. And this is how they are starting the twenty-first century.

The 1990s demise of the party system constructed in the 1960s is obvious. Its three parties – the Liberals, Conservatives, and New Democrats – between them commanded more than 90 percent of the vote for three decades, but suddenly this easy dominance ended as their combined vote-share fell to just two-thirds of the electorate, and two new parties – the Bloc Québécois and Reform – became major electoral forces and parliamentary players. Several factors set the stage for the implosion of this third party system, including: increased voter cynicism; declining public confidence in representative institutions, especially the political parties; a concomitant desire for more direct, unmediated public participation; a rejection of consensus politics; a desire for more effective representation of regional interests; and an increasing pluralism in a society being animated by a rights discourse fostered by the new Charter of Rights and Freedoms. Many of these same elements had been among the catalysts for change in earlier periods of party-system transformation, breaking down old patterns as well as setting the terms for new ones.

Seen from the perspective of collapse, the story of Canadian party politics in the 1990s has been that of the failures of the old parties to accommodate to the forces of political, social, and governmental change. From the perspective of rebirth, the story is very much that of two new parties doing politics in new ways and to new ends. Both Reform and the Bloc practise a very different style of politics from the pan-Canadianism of the 1960s, 1970s, and 1980s, and both drew their initial support from voters opposed to pan-Canadian politics. Their roots lie in the failure of the Mulroney Conservative government to find common ground between Western Canadian and francophone Quebec interests. Despite early success, the Conservatives' failures in terms of the Meech Lake and Charlottetown constitutional accords demonstrated the limitations of intraparty brokerage and exposed the growing displeasure in both regions with the traditional institutions of political representation. Pushed to the partisan edge when the Conservatives' brokerage wheel finally fell off, Quebec nationalists and Western regionalists found a new voice for their concerns in parties devoted primarily to advancing regional, rather than pan-Canadian, interests.

In 1993, and again in 1997, voters in three of the country's five regions[3] abandoned the traditional parties in large numbers, and in so doing propelled these new parties to centre stage as first the Bloc, then Reform, took a turn as the Official Opposition. Yet both of these parties represents a distinctive region of the country in the House of Commons, and is largely seen as championing the interests of that region. In the two general elections of the 1990s, the Bloc won in 98 constituencies without ever fielding a candidate outside of Quebec, while Reform was victorious in 112 constituencies, only one of which is east of the Ontario-Manitoba border. This success makes it unlikely that the three traditional parties will dominate party competition in the new system.

This growth in the sheer number of parties has coincided with a pronounced regionalization in party support. After the 1997 election, the governing Liberals managed to hold a majority of the seats in only Ontario, Prince Edward Island, and Newfoundland. For their part, the Conservatives have been virtually obliterated in Western Canada, their stronghold over the previous three decades; have barely held on in Ontario and Quebec; and have staged a modest recovery in Atlantic Canada, where they managed to claim thirteen of the region's thirty-two seats in 1997. The New Democrats have also been shut out of central Canada; furthermore, with the loss of most of its support in British Columbia, the party has largely been reduced to its historic Saskatchewan and Manitoba base. It is too early to know whether NDP 1997 electoral successes in Atlantic Canada are sustainable, though it would be consistent with the direction of the new party system if voters in those provinces were looking for a party to voice regional interests in the House of Commons. In short, as the country's politics became increasingly regionalized, the parties developed distinctive regional bases. Reform represents the West, in particular, British Columbia and Alberta; the Liberals are a party of Ontario, with small pockets of support tacked on across the country; the Bloc speaks for francophone Quebec; the New Democrats represent parts of Saskatchewan and Manitoba, and perhaps Atlantic Canada. The Conservatives may be something of an exception to this new imperative, for they have yet to find a regional stronghold that will translate their modest strength in terms of the popular vote into a comparable number of seats in Parliament.

However, a growth in the number of parties and the realignment of the partisan face of the country is not all there is to the transformation of the party system. As on previous occasions, more profound and far-reaching changes are altering the character of the parties and the manner in which they conduct national politics. Just as Macdonald's and Laurier's patronage-driven parties gave way to the Mackenzie King's ministerial-brokerage party, and it, in turn, to the Trudeau and Mulroney-style pan-Canadian party, so now the parties are experimenting with new forms as they wrestle with the increased fragmentation of the electorate, insistent calls for increased democratization of the parties themselves, and a greater diversity among parties, in their ideologies, their representational impulses, and their internal practices. In previous party-system transformations, the big old parties survived such challenges by reinventing themselves, possible because there was never much more to them than their electoral vocation. Whether they can perform this almost magical reincarnation a third time is still an open question. In considerable part, it will depend upon their responses to the new parties' challenges in winning over a volatile electorate demanding more participatory, clearly defined political organizations.

Increased regionalization in party-support patterns has been accompanied by a greater fragmentation of the electorate. Unlike the pan-Canadian election campaigns of the previous decades, federal elections in the 1990s have been characterized by parties targeting relatively small groups of voters with specially tailored messages. In the new electoral playing field, with five major parties, the vote-share needed for success is considerably smaller. After all, the Liberals have discovered that they could win two majority governments with an average of just over 39 percent of the popular vote, compared with an average of 45 percent needed by the winning party in the five previous elections that produced a majority government. The other four parties have even more modest electoral objectives, and so each is targeting a small fraction of the electorate in the hope of maximizing its yield of seats in the House of Commons. The working of Canada's first-past-the-post, single-member electoral system means that (up to a certain point) parties benefit from a regional concentration of their vote.[4] The result is a focusing of campaign efforts and the delivery of targeted messages to those electors in specific areas of the country where the party believes it can muster enough support to win in individual constituencies. The parties are increasingly able to rely on sophisticated new communication strategies to, first, identify and, then, target those voters crucial to its electoral success. With little national political dialogue, and an effective absence of some parties from the campaign in each region, elections have lost their capacity to engender a national political debate. Since in no region of the country do all five of the major parties vigorously compete against one another for electoral support, there is no longer any genuinely national party system.

The appeal of the Reform Party is not based solely on its attentiveness to the parochial concerns of Western Canada, but also on its ability to give voice to the increased support for the democratic populism long found in much of the country. As voters have become increasingly disenchanted with elite-dominated, consensus-driven politics, Reform has successfully positioned itself as a genuine grass-roots, democratic organization. Playing on sentiments that directly echo those responded to by the farmers' parties in the 1920s, Reform has championed a greater, more direct role for ordinary Canadians in both public decision making and internal party affairs. When the three old-line parties were allied in support of the elite-sponsored Charlottetown Accord, the door was effectively opened for Reform to differentiate itself as being more responsive and in touch with the concerns of average Canadians. The traditional parties have responded both to the steps taken by Reform and to public sentiment on this issue.[5] The most noticeable change has been in the area of leadership selection. Elite-dominated conventions are portrayed as relics of an old, unacceptable political era, and direct election of party leaders by the membership is increasingly becoming the norm. It is not accidental that, in each of the two earlier transition periods, the parties had responded to similar demands for more meaningful grass-roots participation in their internal affairs with an overhaul of the leadership-selection processes. The special pre-eminence that leaders have always held in Canadian parties ensures that any serious party reform involves rebalancing the relationship between the leader and ordinary party members.[6]

Voters in the new system are being offered more than just more electoral choice. Not only do they have more parties to choose from, but the parties are also increasingly staking out distinctive policy positions. Gone are the days when all the major parties agreed on the essence of all the major issues. Consistent with their desire for more direct, effective participation, voters are demanding that parties offer them concrete policy positions during election campaigns. And as the parties' policy positions are increasingly influenced by their membership, and tailored to specific segments of the electorate, we are seeing more divergence in their views than was evident in the previous elite-dominated, consensus-oriented system.

Supported by the Charter of Rights and Freedoms, Canadians have also been advancing new representational claims, in particular, those related to gender and ethnicity, that transcend the traditional divisions of region and language. The parties have struggled to find ways to accommodate these new interests. Their success has been modest. One result of the advancement of these new representational claims, and the inability of the parties to incorporate these interests effectively, has been a significant rise in interest-group activity and the invasion of the electoral process by these groups. Many of these groups devote themselves to single issues and attempt to force the parties to take concrete positions. This type of activity works to the advantage of parties such as Reform that take pride in having a clear and decisive stance on all issues. By contrast, it lays bare the traditional practices of the old-line parties, which too often try to accommodate competing interests on the same issue.

For all the changes that these forces are working on the nature and practices of Canadian parties, the parties' traditional electoral tasks of nominating candidates as well as managing and financing electoral campaigns remain. Canadian elections are fought in geographically defined, single-member districts, and the local constituency associations remain the fundamental organizational unit of Canadian political parties. It is in these associations, spread across hundreds of local communities, that most Canadians come into contact with party activity and much of the hard party work of electoral politics takes place. But it is also clear that, in the absence of any significant reform of the electoral system, this process has changed little over time; thus, its forms and practices provide an important element of continuity, anchoring the nation's political parties against the shifting tides of the successive party systems.

In the chapters that follow, we use a variety of materials and approaches to explore these issues and to provide an account of why Canadian party politics collapsed in the early 1990s and how it is being reconstructed. An analysis of past party-system transformations structures not only the story of the shifting electoral fortunes of the parties, but also our interpretations of past organizational and representational styles that made each period so distinctive. To understand the contemporary parties and their responses to the situations they find themselves in, we have attended many local and national party meetings; leadership, policy, and reform conventions; campaign kick-off rallies; candidate schools; and nomination meetings. We have also consulted party documents and public records; interviewed party elites, activists, and members; and surveyed local organizations. During the 1997 general election, we visited local campaign offices to observe the parties' grass-roots operations, and the links between local and national organizations. In the aftermath of the campaign, we conducted formal interviews with senior party officials, such as the parties' national presidents, national directors, national and provincial campaign officials, and also with the political professionals, such as public-opinion pollsters, media and advertising specialists, and leader-tour directors, who now play such an important role in the parties' electoral activity.

This book is not an encyclopedia of Canadian political parties. Instead, it provides an examination of the changes that are reshaping the parties engaged in national politics, and the system of competition that governs their relationships. We identify the tensions that resulted in the demise of the recognizably distinctive period of Canadian party politics that stretched from the early 1960s into the 1990s, discuss how the parties are adapting, and look ahead to what the defining characteristics of the new party system will be. We start by exploring the cyclical pattern of party-system transformation in Canada, and the rise of two new parties at the expense of the Conservatives and New Democrats. That leads us to a consideration of the ways the new and old parties are going about representing interests, organizing political life, and paying for politics. We then explore the patterns of both continuity and change in local and national party electoral campaigning. The final chapter returns to our larger themes, and the building of the fourth Canadian party system.

2
The Party Question in Canada

One of the greatest democratic electoral earthquakes ever recorded hit Canada in 1993. The governing Progressive Conservative party, one of the principal instruments of Canadian politics since the middle of the nineteenth century, was humiliated: it was reduced from 169 to just 2 seats in Parliament. The country's modest social-democratic party, the New Democrats (NDP), saw their vote and seat-share plummet to an all-time low. While the third of the established parties, the Liberals, did manage to return to office, they did so with just 41 percent of the vote, the lowest level of support ever commanded by a majority government in Canadian history.[1] Two new parties appeared on the political landscape, the Bloc Québécois and Reform, and between them they captured a third of the vote and a slightly larger proportion of the seats in Parliament. When the dust settled, the Bloc, a party advocating the break-up of Canada, became the country's Official Opposition.

These two new political interlopers succeeded by defining as the country's primary problem the patterns of Canadian party politics, which had informed competitive democratic practice for several decades. The Bloc, speaking for Quebec nationalism, argued against the very idea of maintaining Canada as a political entity; Reform, claiming that traditional representative and parliamentary processes were at the heart of most public ills, demanded that a new politics, driven by new kinds of political parties, be created. Neither of these was a new idea or a new political impulse. But, coming together as they did in the 1993 election, they shook the party system to its foundations.

Confident that their traditional opponents to the left and right had been eviscerated, and convinced that the new protest parties were not serious contenders for national government, the Liberals responded as they had in the past, settling into office in anticipation of another long run in power. They usurped much of the defeated Conservatives' policy agenda, adopted the most stringent budgetary regime in generations, and ran a cautious stay-the-course government. The biggest challenge to national politics appeared to lie in the separatist Parti Québécois government's referendum on independence in Quebec. Despite the narrowness of the federalist victory in the subsequent 1995 referendum, or perhaps because of it, the Liberal party had apparently re-emerged as the country's natural governing party, a position it had occupied for much of the century.

All the political parties realized that 1993 had produced a major shock. The traditional parties anticipated the next election, hoping that it would begin to restore normal politics. It didn't. In the aftermath of the spring 1997 election, all the parties had good reason to think that they had lost. Neither of the new parties was able to maintain the momentum it had generated a few years earlier. The Bloc remained the largest party in Quebec, but its vote-share declined and it lost seats. Reform gained a handful of seats, to take its turn as the Official Opposition, but it failed to achieve its planned breakthrough into central Canada and so remained locked into the role of a Western protest party. The Conservatives and New Democrats had counted on restoring their place as major national parties and, while both saw their vote-shares rise and their seat numbers grow enough to become recognized parliamentary parties, neither could be happy with the results. If the Conservatives had halted Reform's growth, they had not reversed it, and they ended up with only a third as many seats as Reform for about the same number of votes. The New Democrats staged a mini-revival in Atlantic Canada, but the party's failure to win a single seat in Ontario, the country's industrial heartland, was a major disappointment and ominous portent for the future. The Liberals returned to office, but with an even lower vote-share than in 1993, and by just five seats, rather than the healthy majority they expected when the election was called. They survived, but only by seeing their governing coalition shrink significantly: two-thirds of the new Liberal caucus came from Ontario, so that, for the second time in a row, the government could not count on a majority in Quebec or the West. Suddenly it was clear that the familiar party system had been destroyed in 1993 and that it was not going to be restored. National parties, national politics, and national electoral competition no longer existed in a Canada that was deeply divided and regionally fragmented.

How had this happened? What kinds of parties, what new patterns of political competition were emerging to replace the system that had been shattered? Does it matter? As it happens this is not the first time Canadians have smashed their party system and rebuilt the patterns of national politics.[2]

A Party Country

Canada, more than any other country, has been defined by its politicians, its political parties, and its patterns of party competition. Politicians created the country in considerable part to solve partisan deadlocks; they grew it through a series of deliberate political acts, adding provinces and territories on favourable political terms. The first common act of Canadians was to hold an election and, for that, and the Parliament it produced, political parties were needed.[3] Those parties were the institutions with the largest vested interest in the survival of the nation, and electoral competition between them came to be one of the few genuinely national activities involving Canadians. So it remains: three-quarters of the electorate told a 1991 national royal commission on electoral reform that, however much they dislike them, parties are necessary for democracy.[4]

This simple reality lies at the heart of one of the mysteries of Canadian history and public life. For it is a curious fact that when Canadians get really angry about national politics and the accommodations it demands, dissatisfied with public policy, or disillusioned with their governments, and decide to do something about it, their instinctive response is to start by attacking the party system. Not for Canadians institutional engineering, social chaos, or civil war: for them, relegitimating the national community or reshaping their social contract means rebuilding national political parties. The 1993 election signalled the beginning of the fourth round in the cycles that see Canadians overthrowing their political parties and creating new ones. Each turn of the wheel has seen parties with new and distinctive organizational forms come into being. Each has seen the emergence of new competitive dynamics reflecting the shifting political equations that underlie a continually changing political community.

The Roots of Canadian Party Politics

The first Canada was a society of small rural communities that gradually grew from the original four provinces of Confederation to nine (plus two northern territories) in the early years of the twentieth century. The politicians of Canada's first half-century were predominately local men who gathered cadres of partisan supporters around them at election time. Their principal political imperative was to respond to the insistent demands of their constituents for jobs and public works. Thus the politics of building the new state was so driven by patronage that it quickly became "a distinguishing characteristic of Canadian political culture."[5] The parties needed and built for this purpose were simple "cadre-style" organizations, classic electoral machines structured by the relationships that tied the local politicians together in networks of obligation and office-holding.[6] Eager to exploit all the opportunities for patronage available, the parties made little distinction between federal and provincial political life, and the party organizations served, and were served by, both indiscriminately. In this way the early political parties bound together and integrated the federal and provincial politics of the new state.

While local interests shaped politicians' responses to their electorates, the parties also struggled to represent and contain the linguistic and religious divisions of the new state.[7] They did so by attempting to build coalitions that accommodated individuals on both sides of the great social divides. This strategy inevitably worked to minimize the differences between the parties rather than polarizing them on big issues, a practice that led one contemporary foreign observer to note that, in comparison with those in other countries, Canadian political parties "differ very little really in their opinions on crucial questions" and that this "frequently deprives the electoral consultations of the people of their true meaning."[8] Distinctly Canadian issues sometimes divided the parties, but the ideological range seemed unusually narrow. Over the second half of the period between Confederation and the First World War, the geography of Canadian politics linked the Liberals to those parts of the country where Roman Catholics were most numerous, and continuing tensions on the religious divide began to erode the two old parties' capacities to contain all the representational impulses of the growing society.

From the beginning, strong leadership was a distinguishing characteristic of Canadian parties. Chosen by and accountable to their parliamentary caucuses, it was the leaders who were at the centre of the parties' organizations. It was they who enforced the discipline that gave their parties shape, and it was they who had a relatively free hand in determining matters of policy, which gave the parties their identity. With patronage both their raison d'être and organizational glue, the politics of these parties was inevitably expensive and steeped in corrupt practices. Despite the absence of any regulation of party activity, politicians were answerable for their electoral conduct: Sir John A. Macdonald, the country's first prime minister, had a government collapse in a railway financing scandal, while John Abbott, the third prime minister, was himself once unseated for corrupt electoral practices.

Two parties, Conservatives and Liberals, completely dominated the public life of that first party system, and the equation that governed the competition between them was straightforward. With both parties having a real presence in all parts of the country, and many of the small ridings decided by no more than a few hundred votes, these most parochial of party organizations created a system of real national competition. The result was a long string of majority governments that had the support of most members of Parliament (MPs) in a majority of the provinces. In this the parties were helped by the plurality electoral system, which ensured that the largest party of the day received more seats than a strictly proportional accounting would have provided.

Stable and effective as it was for fifty years, this traditional two-party system was unable to meet the demands of a rapidly growing and changing Canada. The West was filling up with immigrants from central Canada, the United States, and Europe, who resented the subservient position their region was accorded by Macdonald's National Policy, and who were not prepared to long support a party system built upon it. With new democratic ideas in the air, both women and men were challenging established norms and old party practices. The First World War intensified these demographic pressures and generated its own set of challenges to the parties. The cumulative impact of all this was to break the first party system. Civil service reform abolished patronage as the basis for political organization; the conscription crisis led a quarter of the Quebec electorate to abandon the Conservatives and turn the province into a Liberal fiefdom; the Progressive movement induced large parts of rural Canada to revolt against the existing parties and experiment with new political forms; and the women's movement generated a universal franchise necessary for a fully democratic politics.

The Brokerage Politics Era

The 1920s saw new party organizations and new patterns of political competition emerge as a distinctive second party system was created. This was to be the golden age of political regionalism in Canada. The dominant politicians of the period were regional political bosses articulating regional interests and carrying their regions with them as they practised a politics of accommodation that came to be known as "regional broker-age." The pre-eminent partisan structure of this era has been described by Whitaker as the ministerialist party – an organization run by powerful regional chieftains whose control of the cabinet offices of the national government allowed them to engage in the political bargaining necessary to maintain their electoral support.[9]

Responding to populist demands for a more open politics, the national parties adopted delegate conventions to choose their leaders, and created their first formal extraparliamentary organizations capable of reaching beyond the boundaries of a single electoral district and across the provinces. However, neither innovation seriously challenged the dominance of the professional politicians, and the small groups of men of money, power, and influence that made up the traditional party elites. The dominant Canadian party mould, cast in the first period, persisted: parties remained largely cadre-style organizations of electorally oriented local partisans gathered around a parochial politician and held together at the centre by leaders who enjoyed considerable autonomy in determining policy and setting their party's electoral agenda.

New regions and new voter alignments in old regions made for a new set of political equations in this second party system.[10] The Prairies, with a quarter of the electorate, now surpassed the Maritimes in electoral importance. As their part in demolishing the original party system, Prairie voters initially deserted both of the old parties, but skilful Liberal leadership recaptured many of them by co-opting their leaders and supporting regionally popular policies. In Quebec, memories of Conservative enthusiasm for conscription made the Liberals unassailable. In both regions, the electoral system exaggerated the Liberals' support and delivered large seat majorities, leaving the Conservatives with virtually no parliamentary representation from either region. With these two regional pillars of support, elections simply became occasions at which the Liberals renewed their mandate as the government party. In this system, the Conservatives assumed the permanent role of parliamentary opposition.[11]

Of course, not all Canadians were happy with a system in which elections could not hold governments accountable and national policy making was reduced to the bargains struck among a group of regionally focused Liberal cabinet ministers. This dissatisfaction led to the creation of the Cooperative Commonwealth Federation (CCF) on the left. Though nominally a socialist party, the CCF was in reality a complex federation also drawing on populist and social-democratic strains in the political culture.[12] The party assumed the forms and structure of European-style mass parties but never developed a mass membership and had no significant presence in the provinces east of the Ottawa River. Whatever success the CCF had at the polls was discounted by the electoral system, and only on the Prairies could it hope to elect many members. Thus, ironically, the one ideological party whose whole existence was a protest against the second party system's politics of regional brokerage was transformed into a vehicle of regional protest. By contrast, the Social Credit Party emerged and thrived as the voice of Albertans who believed their concerns were not being accommodated under the expansive Liberal umbrella. It was able to do so precisely because the electoral system rewarded its regional concentration of votes with most of the province's seats in the House of Commons.

Despite the Liberals' relatively easy dominance during the four decades after the First World War, the distinctive regional partisan alignments and the survival of minor parties meant that governments no longer had the support of a majority of the voters and were dependent on the electoral system to provide a parliamentary majority. And as these governments were based on regional coalitions, it was also true that governments could no longer count on having the support of a majority of MPs from a majority of the provinces, as they had in the first party system. This more obviously regionalized party politics was also reflected in the growing separation of federal and provincial politics.

Quebec voters decisively rejected the national Conservative party at the beginning of the second party system, but this left the traditional *bleus* of the province with a problem, for their label was so tainted that it could no longer be used in provincial elections. In one sense the problem was solved in the mid-1930s, when conservatives and dissident liberal nationalists in the population came together to create the Union Nationale. The new party was remarkably successful, winning all but one provincial election between 1936 and 1960, but it meant that the Conservative party no longer had any presence in Quebec provincial politics. Conservative supporters had to adopt split party identifications, which was bound to produce lower levels of party loyalty, and their organization could no longer depend on a healthy traffic in people, ideas, and material support between the two levels that had been a feature of the first great party era.

Much the same thing went on in the Prairie provinces. The provincial party systems of all three provinces were altered, and successful governments were formed by the Progressives in Manitoba (1922), the CCF in Saskatchewan (1944), and both the United Farmers (1921) and Social Credit (1935) in Alberta. Towards the end of the period (in 1952), Social Credit also worked a transformation of the party system in the West Coast province of British Columbia. In all these cases, the easy and natural symmetry that had existed between federal and provincial politics through the working of an integrated party system was broken. Canadians were coming to live in "two political worlds."[13] Well, not all Canadians, for the traditional pattern persisted to a considerable extent in Ontario and the Atlantic provinces. But this very difference was part of what distinguished the first and second party systems. Canadians' experience of party politics, the patterns of electoral choice they faced, and the partisan loyalties they formed were increasingly a matter of where they lived.

Regional brokerage seemed so much the essence of Canadian politics that it was difficult to imagine that this party system might end. But the same had been said of patronage and its role in the first party system, which had not long survived in the face of civil service reform and a realigned, energized electorate. Like the first system, this second pattern of party politics could last only as long as it was required to broker regional differences. By the end of the 1950s, a set of forces was gathering that would end it and launch the country's politicians on another round of building new kinds of party organizations and establishing new patterns of party competition.

The most important and far-reaching of the changes to the Canadian governmental world was the shift in national decision making to a process soon described as one of executive federalism.[14] With the rise of the welfare state had come an explosive growth in provincial government activity, and with it the advent of provincial politicians as the premier representatives of regional interests. Important national policy was increasingly debated and made in meetings of federal and provincial ministers rather than within the confines of the national governing party in Ottawa. As such meetings regularly included individuals from three or four different political parties, most social policies lost any strong partisan colour they might have had.[15] Regional brokerage was still important in Canada, but it had deserted the party hall for the federal-provincial conference room. Parties would continue to play at regionalism, just as they did with patronage, but it would no longer provided the animus and dynamic that organized and drove party life.

By the end of the 1950s, the sheer size and make-up of the electorate were beginning to overwhelm the parties and upset their capacity to represent the growing numbers of interests being articulated in Canadian society. The electorate had more than doubled from the beginning of the 1920s, and grown by an astounding 40 percent in the decade and a half after the end of the Second World War. This demographic explosion produced an electorate that was increasingly urban and more socially diverse than ever. Finding a way to politicize and mobilize these large numbers of new voters was an enormous challenge to parties locked into a politics focused on accommodating long-standing regional claims.

It was in this context that the second great voter realignment in Canadian politics got under way. Led by John Diefenbaker, a Prairie populist who had finally won the Conservative party's leadership on his third try, the Conservative party moved to defending the interests of primary producers while articulating a nostalgically British conception of the country.[16] The result was a major shift as large numbers in the Prairie provinces moved to support the Conservatives. In what seemed less than a moment, the region of the country that had been most hostile to the Conservatives over the life of the second party system became its partisan stronghold. The electoral system cemented this reorientation into place so strongly that the Conservatives were able to win every seat in Alberta over six straight elections, from 1972 until 1988.

Quebec was also in political turmoil. In the early 1960s, the Ralliement Créditiste emerged, espousing a simple form of social-credit doctrine in defence of the traditional rural Roman Catholic society, under attack from the Quiet Revolution that was quickly transforming Quebec society and politics. The party was not destined to last, but it temporarily broke the Liberals' hold on the province and contributed to a new political volatility. The Liberals were able to resume their place, and in the process leave the Conservatives weaker than ever in the province, but Quebec was no longer going to serve as a docile sheet anchor for any national party.

Like the 1920s, this new period of party transformation saw an upsurge in the populist impulses of the electorate. In considerable part, it was just such impulses that fuelled the Diefenbaker and Quiet revolutions. Nationally this was most obvious in voter turnout rates. The proportion of the electorate participating in general elections jumped by five percentage points in 1958 and stayed high until the middle of the next decade, when it fell back to earlier levels. Parties came under pressure to bring their finances, especially election spending, under public control, and for the first time in a century the state moved to regulate political money and the electoral activity it funded. Within the parties these same stimuli led to new organizational structures designed to create what Pierre Trudeau and the Liberals called "participatory democracy."[17] In an ironic turn of fortune, the first politician to fall victim to members' demands for greater control over their party organizations was Diefenbaker himself, when Conservatives, meeting in a national convention, asserted the right to remove as well as choose the party leader.

The Coming of Pan-Canadian Politics

Parties, no longer in the brokerage business of catering to the peculiarities of the country's various regions, soon found themselves engaging in what David Smith would perceptively call "pan-Canadian politics."[18] This was a politics dedicated to creating a Canadian community, and it became the task of parties in the third party system to define a national agenda and to mobilize Canadians, as individual participating citizens, in support of their competing visions for the country. It was a politics that required parties to present consistent and coherent messages to voters in all corners of the country and that inevitably reinforced the longstanding importance of the party leader's appeal in electioneering. This pan-Canadian approach to party politics was greatly facilitated by the emergence of two powerful tools of communication that allowed party elites to engage their supporters directly. Opinion polling enabled them to identify and define their electorate, while television gave them the capacity to speak to national audiences.

Both the Liberals and the Conservatives managed to survive this second transformation of the country's politics as they had the first, by reorganizing and reorienting themselves to meet the new political demands being made on them. The same could not be said for Social Credit, whose role as a regional protest party was superfluous now that the politics of regional accommodation no longer drove party competition. Its supporters quickly folded into the new Conservative coalition. The CCF chose a more radical course. Recognizing that it had not succeeded in restructuring Canadian politics, it opted to shut down the party so that its supporters could, in partnership with the Canadian Labour Congress, create a new party more closely tied to the trade union movement. Thus the emergence of the New Democratic Party was more than a cosmetic make-over. With a large affiliated union membership, it represented a serious attempt at building a party on the left that would appeal to and represent the industrial working class. If the CCF had been a party with an idea, the NDP emerged as the party of an interest. In this it was well placed to participate in pan-Canadian party competition over the national agenda, and its vote-share quickly grew to double what it had been in the party's CCF incarnation.

While the NDP's solution to the task of building a new party was to graft local union memberships on to its provincially based mass-party organization, the Liberals and Conservatives adopted a different strategy. They followed the NDP in trying to build a larger and more participatory membership, but they differed from them in ensuring that federal and provincial party organizations were increasingly disentangled.[19] These larger memberships, recruited as ever through the local constituency associations, which are vital to the parties' electioneering, were expected to participate in defining party policy and writing party agendas. Such direct participation would open the political process to all citizens, and provide the support and legitimacy politicians needed to implement partisan reforms.

Engaging large numbers in sustained policy debate and then creating coherent policy manifestos proved difficult. In part this goal was obstructed by the proliferation of interests demanding attention in an increasingly diverse society. But even when it could be achieved, party organizations, now with regular national conferences, multiplying numbers of committees, and expanding head offices, proved obtuse instruments for controlling elected politicians. Party members soon rediscovered an old truth of Canadian party politics: the most effective way to move the party agenda is not by passing resolutions but by removing (or at least challenging) the leadership. With members meeting regularly in convention, and leadership review now firmly embedded in party constitutions,[20] internal policy disputes could easily be turned into leadership conflicts, especially when the party was in opposition and the leader had limited resources with which to discipline. In this way, policy debate fostered and reinforced personal factionalism.

The history of the Conservative party, from the fall of Diefenbaker in the mid-1960s until the ascendancy of Mulroney in the mid-1980s, was marked by just such conflict.[21] In opposition, the Liberals experienced much the same thing when battles for the soul and future direction of the party were fought out by the leadership supporters of John Turner and Jean Chrétien after the electoral debacle of 1984. The consequence of focusing internal divisions, whatever their origins or meanings, so intensely on the leadership was to strengthen the pre-eminent position of the leader in Canadian parties. And because internal party conflicts were ultimately fought out at delegate conventions, it also ensured that national disputes would penetrate into constituency associations in every corner of the country. This mobilization of local partisans legitimized increased internal competition at the grass-roots level and in turn contributed to the ferocity and expense with which delegate-selection and nomination contests were fought in many constituency party associations.[22]

Another important aspect of these participatory parties was the dramatic change in their financial bases. For a century the large national political parties had relied on gifts from large corporations and wealthy individuals.[23] While those groups certainly didn't disappear, the legislation of a new election-expense and party-finance regime in the early 1970s increasingly put the parties into the hands two new groups – large numbers of partisan supporters making modest contributions, and the state. As contributors, the former could no longer be safely ignored by party organizers concerned with financing partisan activity. For its part, the state had now established a lever, as well as a claim, to regulate internal party life.

The second significant dimension of the new parties that emerged in the wake of the collapse of the brokerage parties was the disentangling of federal and provincial party organizations. At a minimum this meant that the national party was no longer managed by a coalition of regional party bosses. While leaders continued to designate colleagues as responsible for the political health of the party in their province or region, those individuals no longer held sway as independent power brokers. That task was taken up by the leaders of provincial parties, organizations whose agendas, driven by the particular political dynamics of their respective provinces, were increasingly at odds with those of their national or other provincial namesakes. The result was a process of formally separating the provincial and national party organizations. This went furthest in the Conservative party, leaving the national and provincial parties as quite separate organizations. The Liberals moved in the same direction, though formal separations took place only in the largest provinces, leaving members in the smaller provinces to continue as members of joint organizations.

If national parties were thus freed from the parochial pulls of provincial interests to pursue their national agenda, this also meant that they could no longer count on provincial-level parties to support them at election time. Indeed, provincial leaders would often seek to distance themselves from the national party while playing to their domestic audience. In some cases, this put national and provincial party organizations of the same name in opposing political camps. Perhaps the most dramatic example of this occurred during the 1988 general election, which focused on the Canada-U.S. Free Trade Agreement. The Quebec Liberal provincial government, led by Robert Bourassa, supported the agreement, and the premier made it clear that he would not countenance any member of his government supporting the national Liberal party, which was campaigning against the agreement. With Premier Bourassa effectively supporting them, the Conservatives won the election, Quebec being one of the two provinces to return a majority of Conservative members. Small surprise, then, that when, a decade later, the Quebec Liberal party needed a new leader, it could draft the Conservatives' national leader to take up the position. Canada's two political worlds – federal and provincial – had spawned distinctive and independent party worlds at the two levels of government.

The political equation of this third party system took on its own distinctive shape, one that was quite unlike the national competition of the first, or the Prairie/Quebec-based Liberal dominance of the second. The new political calculus flowed from the realigned electorate and important demographic shifts within it. The biggest change was the massive shift of Prairie voters to the Conservatives. Although the New Democrats could count on winning some seats in the region, it was now heavily Conservative, all the more so, given that the most Conservative province, Alberta, had grown from being the smallest to the largest in the Prairie West. With the Liberals still ensconced in Quebec, the electoral system now gave both of the old parties a solid base, which meant that, for the first time, Canadian elections were decided in Ontario. The Liberals could win if they married Ontario to Quebec; the Conservatives could win if they could marry enough Ontario seats to their Western base. Thus the centre finally came into its own, and the new pan-Canadian politics was inevitably very much Ontario-focused. The result of this new set of political balances was the most competitive period in Canadian electoral history. There were five minority governments in the 1960s and 1970s, and no majority government formed after 1953 was re-elected until 1988.

The Liberals rather uneasily resumed their position as the country's pre-eminent party. In part this shift occurred because they had a modest advantage in Ontario as a result of the demographic changes reshaping the province. Ontario had developed an urban industrial society, with its dominant political impulses now flowing from Toronto, whose share of the province's seats in the House of Commons doubled between 1950 and 1980. With the Conservatives tied to the rural electorate in the wake of the Diefenbaker realignment, the Liberals were well placed to recruit the growing urban, multicultural clientele. Their new organization, policy agenda, and skilful use of the Toronto-centred national media were all designed to allow them to exploit the privileged position of Ontario in the third party system.[24] As a result they managed to reassert their dominance of Canadian politics for two decades, beginning in the early 1960s.

Liberal success under Pierre Trudeau's leadership rested on an agenda that reflected the very epitome of pan-Canadian party politics. The Liberals appealed to the country to create a bilingual, multicultural society that was to be bolstered and institutionalized by a constitutionally entrenched Charter of Rights and Freedoms.[25] Dramatic economic initiatives such as the National Energy Policy were taken to assert the place of the national government in shaping the economic well-being of the country. On the one hand, this was a profoundly liberal politics, mobilizing individual Canadians who supported the program to support the party. On the other hand, this was a centralizing and nationalizing politics, for the partisan agenda of policy making was divorced from the imperatives of provincial and regional organizational interests. These two powerful influences ran in tandem, pulling the long-serving Trudeau government from 1968 to 1984.[26] Eventually the Liberals ran up against the communal and decentralized face of Canadian political reality, and the party suffered the worst parliamentary defeat in its history.

In 1983 the Conservatives chose a Quebecer as their leader for the first time in this century. One of Brian Mulroney's appeals to his party was a promise to end the Liberal's long-standing advantage in Canadian party politics by attracting Quebec voters to the Conservative party. Growing numbers of nationalists in Quebec, unhappy with the centralizing drift and constitutional policies of the federal Liberals, and smarting from their defeat in the 1981 constitutional "settlement," were looking for a new electoral option. At the same time, the Liberal party's replacement of Trudeau with the anglophone John Turner changed the calculation for Quebec voters wanting to support one of their own. Mulroney exploited this opportunity. He persuaded the province's voters to desert the Liberals and support the Conservatives, who were galvanizing an English-speaking Canada that was angry about or simply tired of marching to the

Liberal drum for sixteen years. The result was an overwhelming Conservative victory: for the first time in Canadian history, the electoral system returned a Parliament in which the governing party had a majority of the seats in every province.

The very magnitude of the Conservative victory soon became part of the new government's problem, for its excessive size and reach violated the basic political equation structuring the third party system. By winning everywhere, the Conservatives lost sight of their core constituencies and their interests. This left Prime Minister Mulroney free to try to achieve his long-time goal of rebalancing the party system by bringing his native province into the Conservative party. Mulroney worked assiduously throughout his first government to portray the Conservatives as sympathetic to the claims of Quebec. This positioning paid off in the short run, for, with the help of the Liberal premier, the Conservatives' greatest support in the 1988 election was in Quebec, the province that had been least supportive of them only eight years earlier.

The 1988 election was fought on the issue of the Canada-U.S. Free Trade Agreement, but it was also the first test of the Conservatives' ambitious attempt to restructure the third party system's political balances. The result was remarkable in a number of ways. The country voted against free trade but got it anyway, because the electoral system punished the anti-free trade forces for being split between the Liberals and the New Democrats. The Conservatives were re-elected, the first time the party had managed consecutive majority governments in the century, but with a sharply reduced vote-share. This victory was fashioned with a majority of seats in two provinces – Alberta and Quebec[27] – making it appear that the Mulroney Conservatives had indeed re-created the old Liberal second-party-system coalition, which had been so durable.

An overarching coalition between Western and Quebec voters may have been the essence of the brokerage party's practice of regional accommodation during the years of the second party system, but, ruled out since 1960 by the dominant alignments of the third period, it represented a major political risk. The problem was that it put together, in unbuffered fashion, francophones and francophobes, whose sensibilities had been rubbed raw by almost twenty years of identity claims and constitutional wrangling.[28] Within weeks of the election securing free trade, the heart of this coalition began to come unstuck. In Alberta, discontented voters deserted it for the fledgling Reform Party in a by-election held before the new House of Commons even had a chance to meet.

Months later, unhappy Quebec nationalists inside the Conservative government and caucus, distressed that the government was not able to deliver on the Meech Lake Accord, abandoned the party and created the Bloc Québécois. These developments exposed the incoherence of the Conservatives' agenda and the instability of the support base Mulroney had attempted to establish. They also threatened the working premise of the third party system, for neither of these new parties was prepared to offer a national agenda, or a full slate of candidates, to a Canadian electorate. Reform sought to speak for and to English-speaking Canada, while the Bloc urged French-speaking voters to support dismembering Canada in the interests of its two separate nations.

Disaffected Partisans

Our portrait of the changing patterns of electoral politics to this point has focused on the parties and the structure of competition among them. However, this is only one side of the picture, for elections involve voters as well as parties, and the Canadian electorate has been neither stable nor consistently committed to their parties. The electorate, like the country, has grown, often at rates far in excess of those in any other electoral democracy, which has posed enormous challenges to parties trying to organize it.[29] Initially a three-region, small-scale, rural society, Canada was, by the end of the twentieth century, a modern, five-region, urban one. Historically, the country's politics responded to and reflected the pressures of such a changing demographic base in a number of ways: Canadian elections were very volatile, with turnover rates greater than in Britain or the United States;[30] protest parties periodically appeared to represent new claims; at least twice the electorate underwent a major partisan realignment;[31] and whole new party systems had been built on three occasions. But, throughout, party had remained central to Canadian politics.

The media-intensive pan-Canadian politics of the third party system, and the frustrated promises of participatory democracy that citizens and engaged partisans were too often left with,[32] stimulated new sets of responses, and Canadians began to develop increasingly ambivalent attitudes towards politics in general, and their parties in particular. Through the years of the last Trudeau Liberal and Mulroney Conservative governments, there was a marked growth in popular cynicism towards the political process. Figure 2.1 traces two aspects of this. On the one hand, the number of people reporting that the government didn't care what people

Figure 2.1

Political cynicism in Canada, 1965–97

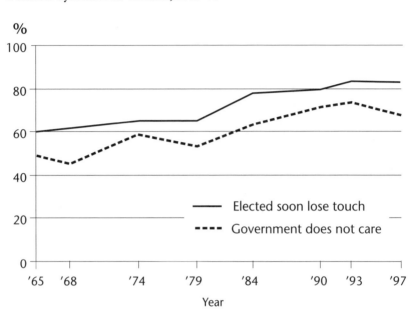

Source: Blais and Gidengil (1991); Canadian Election Survey 1993, 1997.

like them thought increased by almost 40 percent. When asked more specifically about the democratic face of government and the individuals elected to Parliament, even more had adopted a cynical perspective. By the 1990s over 80 percent of Canadians reported that they believed the party politicians in Parliament soon lost touch with the people who had elected them. This cynicism appears to have peaked in 1993, the year of the electoral earthquake.

Not surprisingly, these changing attitudes were mirrored by a sharp decline in the feelings Canadians held about the parties themselves. Figure 2.2 provides the average thermometer rating of the major political parties in general elections from 1968 to 1997. It reveals that, when asked to rate how they felt about the parties on a scale from 1 to 100, Canadians gave lower scores election after election until, by the beginning of the 1990s, the parties' average score was about 40, a failing grade. By the time of the earthquake election, Canadians held "decidedly unflattering images" of their established political parties, "negative judgements about

Figure 2.2

Feelings about parties, 1968-97

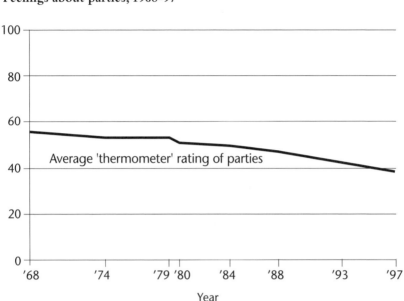

Source: Blais and Gidengil (1991); Canadian Election Survey 1993, 1997.

party performance were pervasive throughout the country," and there had been a downward trend in the number of voters who expressed a strong identification with any party.[33] One might have thought that those disenchanted with the old parties would have been happier after the appearance of the Bloc and Reform provided new alternatives for them. However, that was not the case. The general ratings of the two new parties were even lower than those of the three old parties, and these low public-approval ratings only contributed to the continuing steady decline in Canadians' views of their political parties.[34]

Canadians responded to this increasing frustration with their political parties in two seemingly contradictory ways. First, they did what they had historically done in previous periods of political decay, such as the early 1920s or the 1960s: they started more parties. Figure 2.3 traces the steady growth in the number of officially recognized parties contesting general elections. There were just four in 1972, but that number doubled by 1980, then almost doubled again, reaching a peak of fourteen in the earthquake

Figure 2.3

Candidates and parties, 1972-97

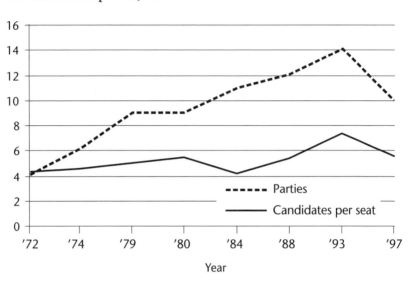

election of 1993. Along with this increase in the number of parties went a corresponding growth in the number of candidates contesting the average electoral district, so that, in the crisis election, voters typically had more than seven candidates to choose from. Both numbers declined in 1997, suggesting that the party system had passed through its shake-out, and that the process of building a new, fourth Canadian party system had begun.

If this growth in the number of parties and candidates suggested a vigorous electoral process, with Canadians keen to build new parties and reshape the patterns of party competition, the other side of the coin was not so bright. The reshaping of the party system in the early 1960s had been marked by record high levels of participation, but this new transition, despite the populism of the Reform Party, was very different. As Figure 2.4 reveals, the number of Canadians bothering to turn out and vote at general elections was in long-term decline from the high point of the Diefenbaker years. It fell sharply in 1993, and then dropped again in the 1997 election to the point where fewer than 60 percent of the voting-age population cast a ballot. While this drop in voter turnout might be attributed, in part, to difficulties with the new permanent national electoral register,[35] it does also seem to suggest a growing withdrawal of a

Figure 2.4

Election turnout, 1957-97

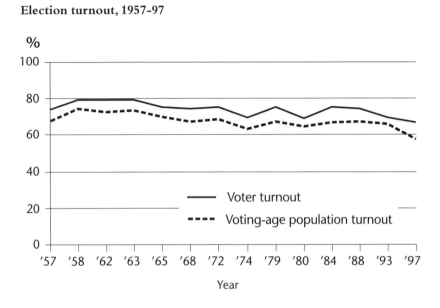

disaffected electorate from national party politics despite the arrival of two new major parties on the scene.

This apparent alienation of growing numbers of voters from the national parties and from participating in national elections inevitably threatens the legitimacy of governments. When only a quarter of the population of voting age supports the government, as was the case for the Liberals in 1997, then that government has, at best, a rather feeble mandate and cannot always count on carrying the population with them on major policy innovations. This challenge to the legitimacy of national governments means that, as in previous cycles, the party system needs to be rebuilt in a fashion that responds to changing democratic norms and practices, and that finds ways to incorporate the many competing interests clamouring to be represented.

After the Dust Settled
We started by observing that the 1993 general election was an electoral earthquake, a major turning point in Canadian democratic history, marking the beginning of a transition to a whole new system of party competition. To put this all into context, it is important to note just how

high on an electoral Richter Scale the 1993 Canadian election really registered, and to observe just how different are the political choices now faced by Canadians as compared with those previously on offer.

The extent of electoral change between elections can be measured by volatility, which simply calculates the net shift of voters from one party to another across successive pairs of elections. In a study of the 1993 election, Donald Blake and Lynda Erickson found that there was more voter movement in that election than at any time in the past. Voter volatility in 1993 was "nearly twice as high as that in 1935 ... and more than twice as high as the national vote shift associated with the Conservative victory in 1984."[36] But this dramatic election was more than just the most volatile ever in Canadian history. In an analysis of more than 300 national elections across a century of democratic experience in thirteen countries, the European scholars Stefano Bartolini and Peter Mair did not find a single case in which the electoral volatility was as high as in the Canadian election of 1993.[37] This suggests that it may well have been the greatest democratic electoral earthquake yet recorded. Ironically, it restored the

Figure 2.5

Party electoral support, 1988 and 1993

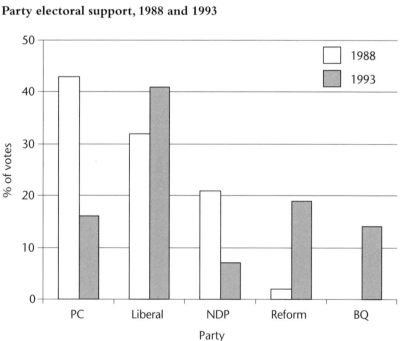

Liberals, Canada's traditional governing party, to office. Perhaps only in Canada could that have happened.

But, as is the case after all earthquakes, once the dust had settled, the landscape was transformed: two of the old parties saw their support base badly eroded, while two new parties captured the votes of a third of all Canadians. Figure 2.5 illustrates the shape of the party-system landscape before and after the 1993 election. Before, the Conservatives, Liberals, and New Democrats had managed a three-party system little changed for three decades. After, five parties commanded the field. Of course, the single-member, winner-take-all electoral system does not reward parties for the total number of votes they win, but, rather, for the number of constituencies in which they happen to come out on top. And, with five parties, the translation from votes to parliamentary seats becomes more unpredictable, with much depending on the geographic concentration of the parties' support. Figure 2.6 indicates just how dramatically different the parliamentary landscape was after the 1993 election.

The Liberals won a comfortable majority, but the Conservatives and New Democrats virtually disappeared from the parliamentary landscape, neither being large enough to be recognized as a party under House of

Figure 2.6

Party parliamentary strength, 1988 and 1993

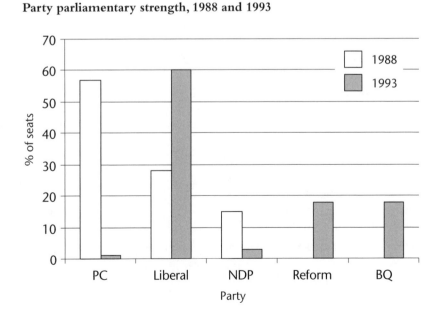

Commons rules.[38] So, despite the fact that the election had seen five parties compete for support, the new parliamentary party system offered three-party competition of a radically different kind from the one it had just displaced. While the Conservatives and New Democrats managed to re-establish themselves as parliamentary players after the 1997 election, they remained in supporting roles, unsure of the parts they would play in the emerging new party system.

It was not just the number and strength of the parties in the party system that the 1993 earthquake shook up. Throughout the third party system, Canadians had participated in a genuinely national system. The Liberals and Conservatives had national organizations with a presence in all parts of the country, and they were challenged by the New Democrats in the five provinces west of the Ottawa River. The 1993 political explosion tore up this pattern and left the country balkanized, with a set of regionally distinctive party systems. Canadians no longer faced a common set of electoral forces or political options. Instead, each region spurred its own distinctive party system and related to national politics in its own way. Quebec was now dominated by the Bloc Québécois and, though the Liberals and Conservatives both made a modest comeback in 1997, national politics in the province was reoriented around the federalist-separatist divide that structures its provincial politics. In Ontario, the right side of the political spectrum was divided between the Conservatives and Reform, leaving the Liberals with virtually all the seats and making the province (for parliamentary purposes) a one-party stronghold. Neither of the two new parties made the slightest dint in the political life of Atlantic Canada, though the New Democrats' 1997 success in the region suggested it, too, was abandoning its traditional patterns. Two Western provinces, Alberta and British Columbia, provided the electoral and parliamentary base for Reform, with the principal effective opposition being mounted by the Liberals. Finally, the midwest (Manitoba and Saskatchewan) was left with three-party competition, among Liberals, New Democrats, and Reform.

This fragmentation of national party politics into a series of distinctive regional party systems may have been intensified by the electoral system that rewards parties with regional concentrations of strength, but it reflects fundamental breaks in the national political community. The West, Quebec, Ontario, and Atlantic Canada all have different political agendas, all seek distinctive approaches to doing politics, and all have created new patterns of party politics. It is on this new landscape that Canadian politicians are struggling to build a new, fourth Canadian party system.

3
Challenging the Consensus:
Two New Parties

A primary manifestation of change in the Canadian party system is the entry of two new, regionally based, parties after the 1993 election. Although the Western-based Reform Party and the sovereigntist Bloc Québécois espouse vastly different social and political agendas, they have more in common than either would probably care to admit. Both are regionally based parties that emerged out of the breakdown of the Mulroney coalition, both were founded by charismatic leaders whose images were closely intertwined with that of the party, and both challenge certain fundamental elements of the Canadian confederation, albeit in different ways. In addition, the two parties have faced similar organizational and tactical challenges in terms of building extraparliamentary party organizations and in trying to reconcile their system-challenging entry into Parliament with the exigencies of parliamentary government. That said, the two parties have followed different trajectories since their formation in the late 1980s (Reform) and early 1990s (the Bloc).

Above all else, Reform and the Bloc represent a rejection of how politics was done in the third Canadian party system. While parties in the third system were united in their desire to hold the country together at any cost, the Bloc and Reform exist to articulate, and even exacerbate, ethnolinguistic and regional tensions. Both parties rejected the pan-Canadianism of parties in the third system, as well as the elite-driven approach those parties took to dealing with the national question. Where the old party system served to maintain the existing political structure, the Bloc and Reform challenge fundamental precepts of the party system and seek to reshape it radically.

In each of the transitions between party systems in Canada, new parties have formed, only to fade away later, leaving the Liberals, Conservatives, and, more recently, the New Democrats in place. During the transition between the first and second party systems, the Progressives emerged as a populist, anti-party party, with support in the West and, to a lesser degree, Ontario.[1] Similarly, nationalist precursors to the Bloc – notably the Créditistes, who won twenty-six seats in 1962 and continued to hold seats until 1980 – have emerged periodically in Quebec.[2] It is not yet clear whether either the Bloc or Reform will become a permanent part of the new party system. What is certain is that these parties will affect the shape of the new system. In the aftermath of the elections of 1993 and 1997, the Canadian party system cannot avoid responding to the increasingly regionalized pattern of party support, the renewed democratic ethos introduced by the Reform Party, and the citizen discontent that the two new parties signalled.

The parties that constituted the third Canadian party system were characterized by ideological flexibility and an overarching desire to maintain national unity by fostering accommodation among different regional, linguistic, ethnic, and other groups.[3] This was not merely a characteristic of parties in the third system; rather, it has been a perennial feature of Canadian party politics since Confederation. Unlike their predecessors, the Bloc and Reform are essentially ideological parties. Even though the Bloc is ideologically flexible on a range of issues, its staunch support for Quebec sovereignty qualifies it as an ideological party.[4] Independence for Quebec is the Bloc's raison d'être, and on this question it is unwilling to compromise. Given this stance, the Bloc has no interest in entering into a tacit agreement among parties to manage regional and ethnolinguistic conflict. Similarly, the Reform Party is firmly rooted in Western Canada and has not adopted the traditional parties' belief that national unity must be maintained at any cost. In the 1997 election, the party based its campaign on highly sectional claims designed to play on antipathy to Quebec among English Canadians. In this regard, Reform represents a significant departure from the pattern of partisan behaviour embodied in the third party system. Reform is also a relatively coherent ideological party; it has adopted an extensive set of policies reflecting its social and fiscal conservatism, and its populism. The parliamentary caucus is effectively bound by those policies. In an effort to win support from voters outside its traditional Western base, the party leadership has tried to moderate its ideological stance and attendant image. However, any efforts to follow the traditional parties in this regard have been profoundly constrained by the ideological commitments of its membership.

The Breakdown of the Mulroney Coalition

The Reform Party was formed in 1987, and the Bloc in 1991, but their stories begin much earlier. The politics of the third party system were epitomized by the lengthy Trudeau regime. Under Trudeau, the federal government worked to construct a Canadian identity as an alternative to regional identities. This involved implementation of bilingualism and multiculturalism as pan-Canadian policies to mitigate or replace provincial and regional political identities. These policies were by no means uncontested. In Quebec, nationalism emerged as a significant force, as reflected by the electoral success of the sovereigntist Parti Québécois (PQ) at the provincial level. In Western Canada, both the nationalizing policies of the Trudeau government and the elite-driven politics the government espoused served to heighten regional identities and resentment of the Canadian political elite.

The beginnings of the Bloc and the Reform Party can be traced to Brian Mulroney's effort to stitch together his electoral coalition in anticipation of the 1984 federal election. The Conservatives had formed a minority government for nine months in 1979 but had then been returned to their usual spot on the opposition benches. When Brian Mulroney was elected party leader in 1983, he was under great pressure to oust the increasingly unpopular Liberals and form a government. Mulroney set out to construct an electoral coalition of several disparate groups, employing precisely the kind of elite-level accommodative techniques for which the party system was best known. Western Canada already provided the Conservatives with a solid base of support, and the antipathy between many Westerners and the departing prime minister, Pierre Trudeau, served only to bolster that Conservative base. Parts of Ontario were reliably Tory blue, as were parts of the Atlantic provinces. But to form a solid and stable majority government that could govern effectively, Mulroney had to win a substantial number of seats in Quebec, long a Liberal stronghold.

In 1982, the Trudeau government had patriated the Constitution and adopted a Charter of Rights and Freedoms with the support of all the provincial governments – except Quebec. The original impetus for constitutional change had come from Trudeau's promise during the 1980 referendum on Quebec sovereignty to renew Canadian federalism. Mulroney promised a new constitutional initiative to bring his native Quebec back into the constitutional fold. This promise, coupled with the appealing prospect of unseating the Liberal government, allowed Mulroney to recruit former sovereigntists and soft nationalists as candidates, and considerably aided the party's electoral fortunes in the province. The result was the party's landslide victory in the 1984 election, winning 211 of the 289 seats in the House of Commons.

In the West, the Mulroney coalition began to erode in 1986, when the federal government awarded a contract to maintain CF-18 airplanes to a Montreal contractor, despite what was generally agreed to be a superior bid from a Winnipeg manufacturer. For many Westerners, this decision was taken as evidence that even a government in which the West was well represented would sacrifice the region's economic interests on the altar of Quebec politics. There was also an ideological element to the erosion of Conservative support in the West. Despite cries from opponents that the party under Mulroney was neo-conservative and intent on dismantling the Canadian state, once in government the party was unable to live up to the expectations of its more conservative supporters, many of whom were concentrated in the West. As Tom Flanagan notes, "the Conservatives in the 1980s adopted a number of positions shared by the Liberals and New Democrats: official bilingualism, multiculturalism, deficit spending, medicare and other social policies, and several waves of constitutional change ... that incorporated theories of group rights."[5] In short, the Conservatives had embodied the elite-centred national politics that characterized the third Canadian party system. These policies alienated the party's hard-core conservative supporters, who perceived the party to be drifting away from its ideological moorings. Coupled with perceptions that the government favoured Quebec, this led to the party's eventual demise in Western Canada and, arguably, in parts of Ontario.

By its very nature, Mulroney's coalition was fragile. Certainly, there were unifying elements: Quebec and the West were the two regions most supportive of the Free Trade Agreement (FTA) negotiated by the Mulroney government; thus, consolidating the FTA in advance of the 1988 election strengthened and prolonged the life of the coalition. In other respects, however, the coalition was tested by serious internal strains. The most notable source of tension was national unity. Mulroney walked a fine line between the Québécois nationalists who required constitutional recognition of special status for Quebec, and Westerners who resisted such special status and were suspicious of any apparent favouritism shown to Quebec.

In Quebec, the Mulroney coalition was maintained – at least in Western eyes – by a steady stream of government largesse directed at the province, and by the prospect of constitutional recognition of Quebec's special status through the Meech Lake Accord. The accord, which recognized Quebec as a distinct society, was signed by the eleven first ministers in 1986, but the agreement unravelled, as there was strong opposition to it in English Canada, which eventually made it impossible to receive the consent of all ten provincial legislatures. The Conservatives' base of support in Quebec was not seriously eroded until it became clear that the government could not fulfil its promise of constitutional reconciliation. Once the Meech Lake Accord failed, the Tories began to lose not only public support, but also several members of their Quebec caucus, who went on to found the Bloc Québécois.

The Formation of New Regional Parties

Although both the Reform Party and the Bloc grew out of the collapsed Mulroney coalition, the origins of the two parties took different forms. Reform was founded by individuals outside the party system, and gradually attracted disaffected Conservative voters and party activists in addition to mobilizing new supporters, including even former NDP voters. In contrast, the Bloc was formed by disaffected Conservative and, in two cases, Liberal MPs who left their caucuses to sit as independents. The organizational development of the Reform Party was essentially from the bottom up (or, perhaps more accurately, from the outside in), while the organization of the Bloc was from the top down (or, from the inside out). What the two parties had in common were charismatic founding leaders, able to motivate activists and to jump-start the process of party foundation.

The Reform Party

Despite its image as a populist party, Reform's roots are found in the Western Canadian business elite. In 1986, several pockets of influential business leaders and people connected with various think-tanks in Alberta and British Columbia were advocating the formation of a new, Western-based political party. In Calgary, a group of lawyers and oil executives disappointed with the Mulroney government's performance (including its failure to remove the petroleum and gas revenue tax immediately upon taking office) began to discuss the need for a new party. This group heard that Preston Manning, an Edmonton-based economic consultant and son of former Alberta Social Credit premier Ernest Manning, thought that the time was right to form a new, Western-based, populist political party. In Edmonton, Manning was gaining the attention of a group of wealthy business leaders. Meanwhile, a similar group of Vancouver business leaders was also discussing the need for a new political movement on the right. Just as Manning was emerging as the central figure in the Alberta network, Stan Roberts was taking the lead for the BC group. Roberts, a former Manitoba Liberal member of the Legislative Assembly (MLA) and former president of the Calgary-based think tank, Canada West Foundation, attracted start-up financial backing for the emerging movement in the form of a $100,000 contribution from Victoria millionaire Francis Winspear. With this financial base, Manning and Roberts formed the Reform Association of Canada. The new movement also enjoyed editorial support from Ted Byfield, publisher of *Alberta Report* and *BC Report* magazines. In 1987, these groups coalesced to sponsor the Western Assembly on Canada's Economic and Political Future in Vancouver.[6]

The emergence of Preston Manning as the organizational and tactical mastermind behind the party, and its unlikely charismatic leader, forestalled conflict among elite groups within the party. At the party's founding convention in Winnipeg in 1987, Manning's leadership bid was far better organized and more strategic than that of his only opponent, Stan Roberts. Although Roberts took his defeat with little grace, alleging dirty tactics and missing money, he had little support. Manning emerged from the Winnipeg convention as the undisputed leader and driving force behind the Reform Party. Manning directed and oversaw the development of party organization, paying personal attention to even the minutest of details. In fact, his reluctance to delegate or share power, and his insistence on directing all aspects of the party, have alienated some party stalwarts.[7] Nonetheless, his exerting that level of control did facilitate the development of a strong modern party organization.

With its roots limited to Alberta and parts of British Columbia, Reform had to work to develop a broader basis of support, first in the West, and then in Ontario. The party's support was initially concentrated primarily in Alberta, with half the party's members and half the delegates to party assemblies coming from that province. In the 1988 election, the party ran candidates in seventy-two of the eighty-six Western Canadian ridings, and won 7.3 percent of the popular vote in those four provinces. In Alberta, however, the party won 15 percent of the popular vote but no seats. Then, in early 1989, Reform candidate Deborah Grey won a by-election in an Alberta riding, becoming the party's first MP. The same year, when the Alberta government held an election to select a senator under a temporary agreement with the federal government allowing provinces to forward names for Senate appointments, Reform elected Stan Waters.

During the period from 1988 to 1993, the party had to establish a credible presence and organizational structure in the other Western provinces and grapple with the question of Eastern expansion. The organizational challenge faced by the party involved recruiting activists while repelling the advances of undesirable supporters. From its founding convention, Reform has attracted supporters from the extreme political right. These have ranged from Western separatists through linguistic bigots (members of the Alliance for the Preservation of English in Canada) to overt racists (including members of the neo-Nazi Heritage Front).[8] As the party began to lay the groundwork for its expansion into Ontario in 1990, concerns about being hijacked by extremist groups were even more pressing, as the national party office lacked a network of trusted activists and informants. Hoping to defuse public perceptions of the party as racist, Manning and national party officials tried to avoid having extreme groups capture fledgling Reform constituency associations. In advance of the 1993 election, the party's national office instituted a practice of requiring potential candidates to complete extremely detailed questionnaires, which the national office would vet prior to the nomination meeting. When a Vancouver constituency association ignored Manning's warnings and nominated Doug Collins, a columnist known for his extreme and arguably racist views, Manning used his prerogative under the Canada Elections Act and refused to sign the nomination papers, prompting considerable dissent among the party's grass-roots supporters. In a party founded on populist rhetoric, displays of centralized authority in defence of the party's image were unpopular, but were tolerated nonetheless by most party members, either in deference to Manning's leadership or in the long-term interest of the party.

The Bloc Québécois

The catalyst for forming the Bloc was the constitutional crisis surrounding the failure of the Meech Lake Accord. Mulroney had won considerable support in Quebec with his promise to bring the province back into the constitutional fold, healing the wounds of the "night of the long knives" in 1981, when the federal government and all the provinces except Quebec reached a deal to patriate the Constitution. To achieve constitutional reconciliation, Mulroney engineered a constitutional agreement that recognized Quebec as a distinct society. This accord, as well as the process by which it was reached, was highly controversial in English Canada, and by 1990 it appeared unlikely that it would receive the support of the ten provincial legislatures required for ratification. In an effort to save the accord, the government appointed MP Jean Charest to chair a parliamentary joint committee to study possible changes to the document. Many Quebec leaders considered the changes proposed in Charest's report to be an insult and a betrayal of Quebec.[9] Three Conservative MPs resigned from the party's caucus in protest. Among them was Brian Mulroney's Environment minister and close personal friend, Lucien Bouchard.

As the only prominent political figure to resign in protest, Bouchard was the natural leader of any new parliamentary block of nationalist MPs. Although initially resistant to the idea, soon after his resignation Bouchard began to prepare for the creation of a new political grouping within the federal Parliament. A month after their resignation from caucus, Bouchard and the other two defecting MPs met with a group of four sympathetic Quebec Conservative MPs. The four refused to leave the Conservative caucus until the fate of the Meech Lake Accord was clear, but appeared likely to defect if it failed.

Despite heroic eleventh-hour efforts to save it, the Meech Lake Accord failed in 1990 when it became clear that it would not receive the approval of the Manitoba and Newfoundland legislatures. In the dramatic days after the failure of the accord, three Conservative MPs from Quebec and one Quebec Liberal MP left their respective caucuses to sit as independents. Days later, Liberal MP Jean Lapierre joined the small band of independents, citing newly elected Liberal leader Jean Chrétien's opposition to the Meech Lake Accord as his reason. By June 1990, the six Conservative defectors had constituted themselves as an informal parliamentary grouping and had chosen Bouchard as their leader. By the end of July, Lapierre had joined the cause, and the Bloc was officially formed as a parliamentary grouping, although not a party. In subsequent months, the new entity began to take on the organizational attributes of a party.

The provincial Parti Québécois was an enthusiastic sponsor of all this activity. As early as 1988, PQ leader Jacques Parizeau had headed a small group of senior PQ officials and strategists planning a systematic approach to Conservative MPs with nationalist leanings. Their initial objective was simply to encourage these MPs to leave the Conservative caucus in an effort to harm the party's credibility in Quebec. According to Manon Cornelier, the PQ group approached more than thirty Conservatives, including cabinet ministers. Once Quebec MPs started resigning from the Conservative caucus, the PQ encouraged them to form a parliamentary grouping under Bouchard's leadership.[10]

The need to build a party organization confronted the Bloc soon after its formation. A by-election was called for a Quebec riding less than two months after the Bloc had declared itself a party. Parizeau, armed with poll results indicating that a Bloc candidate could easily win the riding, pressured Bouchard to run a candidate. Bouchard assented, and settled on Gilles Duceppe as the candidate. Duceppe relied heavily on local PQ activists and organizers to run his campaign, which he won with a striking 67 percent of the vote.

The question of party building was controversial within the Bloc caucus in its first year. Former Conservatives in the caucus wanted to create a properly organized party with ties to the PQ. The two former Liberals, along with party leader Bouchard and newly elected MP Gilles Duceppe, argued for building a non-partisan movement − a "rainbow coalition" without the formal organization of a party.[11] Gradually, however, the former Tory MPs started putting in place the foundations for a formalized party. They began to raise funds and maintain lists of potential candidates. By 1991, the Bloc MPs agreed to form a party. At the party's founding convention in June 1991, there were some Liberals and former NDP activists in attendance, but the vast majority of delegates were PQ supporters. The party's membership began to grow, from 12,300 in January 1992 to 25,000 by the time of the party's general council meeting in June of that year.

These party-building efforts were constrained by Bouchard's personal reluctance to commit himself to remaining in politics, and by his concern that all these efforts might be redundant if a referendum on sovereignty was held in 1992.[12] If the sovereigntist option prevailed, then the Bloc would be irrelevant.[13] This eventuality was pre-empted by the first ministers' eleventh-hour agreement on the Charlottetown Accord and the national referendum that ensued.

The Charlottetown Referendum
The national referendum on the Charlottetown Accord was a defining moment in Canadian political history and a pivotal moment for both Reform and the Bloc. The accord was a constitutional agreement reached

by the first ministers and Aboriginal leaders in 1992. It contained watered-down versions of most of the elements of the ill-fated Meech Lake Accord, but also included provisions to recognize an inherent Aboriginal right to self-government and to reform political institutions, including the Senate. Intended to offer something to everyone, the accord pleased few. When it was put to a national referendum, with all three major parties (and, indeed, most of the Canadian political class) endorsing it, it was defeated with a 54.4 percent "No" vote. The provinces where the accord received the least support were British Columbia (67.8 percent "No" vote), Manitoba (61.7 percent), Alberta (60.2 percent), and Quebec (55.4 percent).

The Canadian electorate's rejection of the Charlottetown Accord represented a repudiation of the Canadian political elite and foreshadowed the imminent demise of the third Canadian party system. Prior to the 1992 referendum, the Reform Party was still a ragtag band of alienated Westerners, another Western protest movement apparently unlikely to make a lasting mark. Bloquiste members were described in a *Le Devoir* editorial at the time as "a bunch of mediocre MPs" with an uncertain purpose and dismal future.[14] By the time the dust had settled on the national referendum, these two groups were poised to benefit from a profound disruption in the patterns of Canadian politics and a restructuring of the party system.

In Quebec, the debate over the Charlottetown Accord pitted federalists against sovereigntists. The governing Liberal Party of Quebec endorsed the accord, while the Bloc and the Parti Québécois opposed it. With the provincial Liberals facing off against sovereigntist forces, the idea that the Bloc could act as a non-partisan coalition including Liberals came to an end. Liberal defector Jean Lapierre quit the Bloc, thereby severing the already weak tie between it and the provincial Liberals. Bouchard and Parizeau joined forces to oppose the accord, cementing the relationship between the provincial and the federal sovereigntist parties. The referendum revitalized the Bloc, saving it from the doldrums of poor morale and limited financial backing. Having helped win the referendum campaign in Quebec, the Bloc emerged with new purpose, and a federal election to contest in 1993. Although reinvigorated, the party still lacked an autonomous organization. As Cornelier reports, with the split between Liberals and sovereigntists during the Charlottetown referendum, "the Bloc's hopes of creating a totally independent organization had disappeared, and the PQ was more than happy to fill the gap."[15]

In the rest of Canada, the political class united in support of the constitutional package. Every provincial premier and all three of the major parties aggressively defended the bargain struck in Charlottetown. The national "Yes" campaign was staffed by politicos seconded by the three parties, and MPs returned to their constituencies from Ottawa to sell the three-party line that the Charlottetown Accord was necessary to the survival of the country. Prime Minister Mulroney, in a fit of rhetorical excess that would come back to haunt him, declared that only the "enemies of Canada" would oppose the accord. Despite – or perhaps because of – this solidarity of purpose among the political class, substantial segments of the electorate were sceptical not only about the deal, but also about the process by which it was reached. The Reform Party emerged during the Charlottetown Accord as the voice for English Canadians who opposed the deal, and especially those who were angry at the country's political elite. Reform opposed the accord because it "represented change which [was] too great and yet unknowable; on the other hand, the status quo, even if not entirely satisfactory [was] still tenable."[16] By terming the accord "the Mulroney deal," Preston Manning was able to play on anti-elite sentiments, particularly in the West. The Charlottetown referendum campaign essentially gave Manning and the Reform Party an ideal pre-election opportunity to articulate two sentiments fairly widely held in the West: a dislike and distrust of Brian Mulroney, and a deep-seated resentment of the Canadian political elite, writ large.

When we study the actual effect of Reform's "No" campaign during the referendum, it becomes clear that Manning's stance in opposition to the accord did not directly affect many voters' decisions. In its extensive study of voting behaviour in the Charlottetown referendum, the Canadian Election Study research team found that Manning's intervention in the campaign did little to increase opposition to the accord. In fact, in both Ontario and British Columbia, Manning inadvertently helped the "Yes" side: "As voters who might otherwise have gone straight over to the 'No' side located the Accord relative to Manning, they paused, perhaps, and asked themselves if his was the sort of company they wanted to keep."[17]

This does not mean that the referendum was unimportant to Reform Party fortunes. Voters likely to be swayed by Manning's intervention were in all likelihood inclined to oppose the accord on its merits. Taken in this light, it is not at all surprising that Manning had a limited impact on the vote. What was important for the Reform Party through the Charlottetown campaign was not its ability to sway votes, but the opportunity

Figure 3.1

Charlottetown and the fragmentation of the vote in Quebec

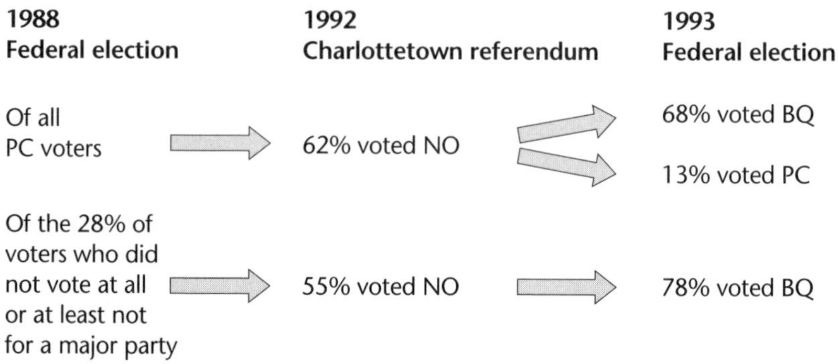

1988	1992	1993
Federal election	**Charlottetown referendum**	**Federal election**

Of all
PC voters ⇒ 62% voted NO ⇒ 68% voted BQ
13% voted PC

Of the 28% of
voters who did
not vote at all ⇒ 55% voted NO ⇒ 78% voted BQ
or at least not
for a major party

Source: Canadian Election Survey, 1993.

afforded the party to position itself as a prominent political force in Western Canada and as a voice articulating the popular discontent with the governing elites of the day.

If we examine the patterns of voting from the 1988 federal election, across the 1992 referendum, and then the 1993 federal election, we find evidence that the Charlottetown referendum shook up existing alignments and provided a springboard for the two new parties (see Figures 3.1 and 3.2). In Quebec, 62 percent of voters who had cast a ballot for the Conservatives in 1988 voted "No" in the referendum. Of that 62 percent, 68 percent went on to vote for the Bloc, and only 13 percent returned to the Conservatives. The Bloc also drew disaffected voters back into the system. Of the 28 percent of Quebec voters who did not vote in 1988, or who voted for a candidate not affiliated with the major parties, 55 percent voted "No" in the referendum, and 78 percent of them went on to vote for the Bloc in 1993.[18] In the rest of Canada, a majority of voters did not follow the lead of the party they had voted for in 1988 when they cast their ballots in the Charlottetown referendum. Among those who voted Conservative in 1988, 49 percent voted "No" (and 42 percent voted "Yes"). Among Liberal voters in 1988, 52 percent voted "No", as did 57 percent of NDP voters. In all three cases, those who voted "No" were less likely than those who voted "Yes" to support the same party in 1993. This pattern was most pronounced among 1988 Conservative voters: of those who voted "Yes", 40 percent voted Conservative again in 1993, and only

Figure 3.2

Charlottetown and the fragmentation of the vote in the rest of Canada

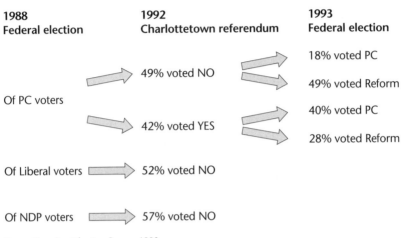

1988 Federal election	1992 Charlottetown referendum	1993 Federal election

18% voted PC

49% voted NO

49% voted Reform

Of PC voters

40% voted PC

42% voted YES

28% voted Reform

Of Liberal voters   52% voted NO

Of NDP voters   57% voted NO

Source: Canadian Election Survey, 1993.

28 percent voted Reform. Of those who voted "No", only 18 percent voted Conservative again, and 49 percent voted Reform.[19] It is difficult to know whether these voters had shifted their support away from the Conservatives prior to the referendum, or whether Reform won them over in its aftermath. Either way, the referendum was a watershed for Reform.

The 1993 Federal Election Campaign

The outcome of the Charlottetown referendum can be understood as a wholesale rejection of the Canadian political class and the elite-dominated nationalized politics that characterized the third party system. When the 1993 election was called, the electorate remained angry and cynical, and it was the Conservatives who suffered the voters' wrath most directly. As the Conservative coalition shattered, the Bloc and Reform were able to emerge as the second- and third-largest parties in Parliament, respectively. The enormous shifts in electoral support made the 1993 election the most volatile in Canadian history.

In mounting its 1993 campaign, the Bloc relied heavily on PQ organization and resources. It accepted staff lent by the provincial party, as well as data provided by the PQ's pollster.[20] Of the fifty-four Bloc MPs elected, at least thirty-seven had close previous associations with the PQ; only three had previous associations with the Liberals at either the provincial or the federal level.[21] At the mass-membership level, however, the Bloc did have a somewhat more autonomous cast. A comparison of Bloc and PQ membership lists for fund-raising purposes found that some 60 percent of Bloc members were not members of the PQ. In short, the Bloc maintained an organizational presence separate from that of the PQ, but relied heavily on its provincial counterpart for the kind of tactical and logistical functions a well-established party would usually be able to provide for itself.[22]

Despite its need to use a borrowed party machine on the ground, the Bloc swept the province of Quebec in the election. Winning fifty-four of seventy-six Quebec seats, the Bloc had become an important player on the federal political scene, and firmly established Lucien Bouchard as a leader within the nationalist movement. The Bloc's own analysis of its success noted the importance of public dissatisfaction with government and the desire to protest "politics as usual." According to Cornelier, the Bloc's assessment of its success identified several factors: "the leader's personality, the party's nationalist stance, but also a hostility to the old parties, a profound disillusionment that has led people to try something else. In short, there was a strong sentiment of frustration that favored a new party, and the Bloc simply gathered the protest vote."[23]

Reform also benefited from a substantial protest vote and made huge gains in the 1993 election, going from one seat in the House, to fifty-two. In part, Reform's success can be attributed to its ability to replace the NDP as the partisan vehicle for populist sentiment. Prior to 1993, voting NDP was a way to register protest against the system. In English Canada, Reform was able to capture 11 percent of the voters who had supported the NDP in 1988. This protest vote moved to Reform both in Western Canada and in Ontario. More significant, however, was Reform's ability to replace the Conservatives as the party of the right, particularly in Western Canada. Reform won the support of 38 percent of 1988 Conservative voters in English Canada, and 55 percent of Conservative voters in the four Western provinces.[24] Although its support stemmed more from its conservative ideology and populist stance than from its 1988 election slogan, "The West Wants In," Reform's support was heavily concentrated in Alberta and British Columbia, reinforcing its image as the party of Western Canada.

Growing Pains: Protest Parties in Parliament

Having harnessed the force of the electorate's disenchantment with politics as usual, the two new parties found themselves in Ottawa, facing a series of dilemmas. Committed to Quebec secession, the Bloc was expected to act as "Her Majesty's Loyal Opposition." Reform, an anti-politics party, had to find ways of being effective in Parliament without appearing to compromise its principles. Compounding this, both parties' caucuses were made up almost entirely of political neophytes. Of the fifty-four Bloc MPs, only six were former members of Parliament, and two were former members of the Quebec National Assembly (MNAs). In the fifty-two-member Reform caucus, only Deborah Grey had previously sat in Parliament, although Ray Speaker had experience as an Alberta MLA. Even the party's leader, Preston Manning, had never held elected office. Newly elected MPs invariably face a steep learning curve and a difficult process of adjustment. Almost overnight, they move to an unfamiliar city to begin a new job for which they have little or no training, and for which there is no clear job description. For new MPs in established parties, this transition is eased somewhat by experienced caucus members who can show them the ropes. But for parties where almost every MP is a newcomer, this kind of mentoring is unavailable.

The charismatic leaders of the two parties dealt with this problem in similar ways. Both refused to delegate meaningful responsibility within their caucuses, directed caucus affairs personally, and imposed strict discipline on caucus members. Bouchard was particularly concerned that his inexperienced caucus would discredit the sovereigntist movement through inappropriate behaviour, so he imposed strict rules: "Farcical behavior, attacks on MPs from other parties, insulting replies and unprepared questions [were] formally banned in the House of Commons," reports Manon Cornelier.[25] Because they were deeply committed to the sovereigntist cause, members of the Bloc caucus accepted this discipline with reasonably good grace. The only significant concession Bouchard made to his caucus was to expand the number of shadow-cabinet positions beyond the twenty that were initially assigned.

The Bloc was more successful than Reform in capturing media attention and performing the functions of an opposition party. In the first months of the new Parliament, the Bloc's efforts received positive reviews both within Quebec and from the rest of Canada. The Bloc appeared consistently better prepared than Reform and was able to capture media coverage of its efforts – a crucial element of opposition strategy. A persistent difficulty for the Bloc was the question of how a Quebec-based sovereigntist party could act as the country's Official Opposition. In his first speech in the House of Commons after the 1993 election, Bouchard set the parameters of the balancing act facing the party: "Bloc members will not forget that their commitment to sovereignty constitutes the real reason for their presence in this House ... For the time being ... members of the Bloc will seek to safeguard the future by averting present evils to the best of their ability. These evils include unemployment, poverty, lack of budgetary restraint, undue duplication, threats to our social programs, fiscal inequity and loss of confidence in our political institutions and leaders."[26] Despite a rhetorical commitment to act as a national opposition party, the bulk of the Bloc's attention naturally went to representing Quebec's interests. A *La Presse* survey of the Bloc's interventions in Question Period found that the Bloc's attention was largely on Quebec, and its focus on sovereignty increased after the PQ took power in Quebec in 1994, and again during the Quebec referendum.[27]

Preston Manning's efforts to control his caucus were somewhat less successful. Unlike the Bloc, Reform was elected on a platform emphasizing grass-roots democracy. This populist commitment contributed to the belief of caucus members that the parliamentary party should be run according to democratic principles and without discipline imposed by the leader. From the very beginning, the stage was set for clashes between Manning and his rambunctious caucus. At the first caucus meeting, Manning ignored the results of a straw vote for the election of caucus officers, instead offering his own slate for ratification.[28] In its first months in Ottawa, the party made every effort to appear to do politics differently, but most of these initiatives were doomed. Rather than taking the leader's traditional seat in the first row of the House, Manning sat in the second row, surrounded by his colleagues; he made a public show of eschewing the traditional perks of office, such as the car and driver assigned to leaders of official parties in the House. In practice, however, Manning maintained tight control of caucus operations, tried to avoid potential rivals from emerging from within his caucus, while accepting considerable benefits (such as an automobile allowance) from the national party. Before long, these contradictions sparked conflicts between the leader and national office, on the one hand, and the caucus, on the other. MP Stephen Harper was particularly outspoken in his criticism of Manning for accepting additional funds from the national party office to subsidize his wardrobe.

Throughout the period from 1993 to 1996, Reform was plagued by conflicts within its caucus, and between Manning and the grass roots. Discontent within the caucus, much of it in reaction to Manning's authoritarian leadership style, eventually resulted in the resignation of two caucus members. Manning's determination to expand Reform into a national party that could eventually form the government alienated many party members, as it appeared to involve renouncing the party's founding principles. Manning addressed this issue by allowing delegates to adopt policy platforms that positioned the party far to the right. At the party's 1996 assembly, where all of these conflicts came to a head, Manning "laid down the gauntlet ... in a closed-door meeting with constituency association presidents where he announced that he would remain leader and the campaign team that had already been assembled would stay in place."[29] After this confrontation, the party fell in line behind Manning and began to prepare for the 1997 election campaign.

Charismatic Leadership and Crises of Succession

Parties with charismatic founding leaders can face serious crises of succession when the leader steps aside or when the leader is ousted. Typically, such parties rely on the strong personality of the leader to unite party activists with a broad range of political perspectives. In some cases, the leader personifies the party, in the public's view, and is consequently essential to its electoral success. Both Manning and Bouchard played such crucial and central roles in the founding of their respective parties. Manning's unique ability has been to direct the party's strategy personally and keep its potentially unruly activist base under control. This has allowed him to shift flexibly among the three principal orientations of the party – populism, conservatism, and regionalism – as political conditions dictate. In this sense, Manning's primary effectiveness as a charismatic leader has been his ability to harness the energy of his activist base while muting those partisans whose views would constitute an electoral liability.

While Manning's charismatic leadership has been most effective inside the party, Lucien Bouchard's charismatic appeal was directed outwards, towards the Quebec electorate, which responded enthusiastically to his eloquent advocacy of Quebec sovereignty. Such was Bouchard's appeal that when the "Oui" campaign was floundering during the 1995 provincial referendum on Quebec independence, he was brought in to replace the PQ leader and premier, Jacques Parizeau, as the campaign's principal spokesperson.[30] Given his popularity in Quebec, Bouchard's leadership of the Bloc was never questioned.

When Bouchard stepped down from the leadership of the Bloc to become leader of the PQ and premier of Quebec, the Bloc floundered. After only ten months as leader, Bouchard's replacement, Michel Gauthier, stepped down amid considerable internal discord in the hope that a leadership race would reinvigorate the party. However, the leadership contest held in March 1997 did little to boost the party's chances in the upcoming election. The six candidates held similar views on most important issues, and none seemed equipped to replicate Bouchard's charismatic leadership. Even though the six candidates contesting the leadership differed little on policy questions, the competition for the leadership was acrimonious, and the fallout unpleasant. Gilles Duceppe won the leadership with the support of half the Bloc caucus, and 53 percent of the votes cast by party members in the mail-in leadership contest. The runner-up, Yves Duhaime, was slow to signal his confidence in the new leader, and Bloc MP Nic Leblanc left the caucus to sit as an independent. The leadership race did, however, create some interest in the party, with about 17,000 new members joining during the campaign.[31]

Reform has not yet experienced its crisis of succession, but it seems inevitable that it will. Manning has led Reform since it was founded in 1987, and has operated the party in such a way as to discourage the emergence of potential rivals or successors. His adamant refusal to allow provincial branches of the party to form has meant that provincial politics is less likely to serve as a source of potential replacements for Manning. Because Manning is so closely identified with the party, struggles over its future direction are likely to manifest themselves as battles over his leadership. It remains to be seen how long Manning can keep dissent within the party in check.

Here to Stay? The Bloc, Reform, and the Canadian Party System

After the startling electoral results in 1993, many observers of the Canadian political scene remained convinced that the Bloc and Reform would fade after the next election. The outcome of the 1997 campaign made it clear that the party system was undergoing a significant transformation. Both Reform and the Bloc performed relatively well and remain the second- and third-largest parties in Parliament, respectively. While it remains uncertain whether either party will remain a permanent feature on the electoral landscape, their impact means that the party system as a whole cannot revert to its earlier patterns.

The "B-Team"

As the Bloc launched its second electoral campaign in 1997, it was plagued by difficulties. Had events unfolded according to sovereigntist plans, the party would have already been dissolved after having helped secure a "Yes" victory in the 1995 Quebec referendum. Having fallen short of that objective, the party found itself in the somewhat uncomfortable position of running again, while still asserting that its ultimate objective was to disband. The party had lost its charismatic founding leader and suffered a serious crisis of succession in the months prior to the election call. Further compounding the Bloc's problems was the growing unpopularity of the provincial PQ government, under fire for imposing budget cuts.

The Bloc's ambiguous relationship with the PQ continued to present the party with difficulties. As Quebec journalist Lysiane Gagnon observed, "because the Bloc will never form a government, it attracts neither power-hungry activists nor people with a serious political or social agenda nor cabinet minister material. Its membership is older, less educated and less assertive than the Parti Québécois. This is the B-team – a party whose goal is its own disappearance (after Quebec secedes) ... And everybody knows where the real boss is: Quebec City ... [The new leader] will go on taking his marching orders from the founding father of the Bloc, Premier Lucien Bouchard."[32] This was illustrated very clearly during the election campaign. The Bloc had started the campaign with its own organizers in charge, but the first week of the campaign was disastrous for the party. Party leader Gilles Duceppe's bus got lost on its way to a campaign event, and Duceppe toured a cheese factory wearing a comical hairnet, all of which produced a great deal of negative media coverage for the party. After this inauspicious beginning, the managing director of the PQ was brought in to run the Bloc campaign. Two Bloc communications staffers were fired and replaced with officials seconded from the offices of PQ cabinet ministers. In addition, Lucien Bouchard sent a dunning letter to PQ members, soliciting contributions, during the Bloc's fund-raising drive.[33] Bouchard made several appearances on the Bloc's behalf during the campaign, as did former premier Jacques Parizeau.

These interventions may have been the Bloc's only hope for electoral success, but they served to illustrate its close and subsidiary relationship to the Parti Québécois. As a result, the PQ government's unpopularity apparently rubbed off on the Bloc, which won a disappointing 38 percent of the popular vote in Quebec, down from 49 percent in 1993. With forty-four seats, ten fewer than in the previous Parliament, the Bloc no longer formed the Official Opposition.

As it cannot develop an image and an organization distinct from the PQ, the Bloc will remain hostage to events largely beyond its control in Quebec. That said, it does not face any serious challengers at the moment: its electoral base consists of voters with varying degrees of commitment to the sovereignty of Quebec. If they vote at all in Canadian elections, those who remain most committed to the cause of Quebec independence will continue to vote for the Bloc. It is true that in some circumstances less committed, "soft" nationalists can be persuaded to desert the Bloc: about 21 percent of the Bloc's 1993 voters switched allegiance to the Jean Charest Conservatives in 1997.[34] Without a leader from Quebec, however, the Tories may not be able to retain those voters or attract others away from the Bloc. In this sense, the Bloc appears poised to remain an ongoing element of the emerging party system that will affect patterns of political competition in Quebec, but will not exercise an effect on the broader national party system.

Just Another Western Protest Party?
Preston Manning and his party are well aware that they risk suffering the same fate as other Western protest parties that appeared in the aftermath of previous party-system collapses: a brief period of influence followed by a lengthy decline. Certainly, this was the experience of the Progressives' and Farmers' movements; of Social Credit; and, to a degree, of the Cooperative Commonwealth Federation. Like Reform, all were protest-oriented parties founded on the Prairies, and all experienced considerable initial electoral success. The task facing Manning and his party is to avoid the fate of those earlier movements.

In the 1997 election, Reform's objectives were to consolidate its base in the Western provinces while making sufficient inroads into Ontario to establish a national presence for the party. These two objectives are not necessarily compatible, as the image and policies that have made the party so popular in Western Canada do not play nearly as well in Ontario. Efforts to appeal to Ontario voters alarm Reform's core supporters, who see such tactics as selling out the party's principles.

Nonetheless, Reform's ambitions to eventually form the government dictated the party's approach to the 1997 election. In the fall of 1996, Reform released the document that would serve as the foundation for its 1997 campaign: a Fresh Start for Canadians. Canadians were not the only ones promised a fresh start, as the document's release marked the beginning of the election campaign for a new and improved Reform Party. Just like the subjects of make-overs in fashion magazines, Manning and his party were put in the hands of professionals charged with the task of transforming them from dowdy, alienated Westerners into sophisticated, blow-dried political operatives. Manning personally underwent extensive cosmetic dental work; had eye surgery, allowing him to shed his glasses; acquired a new, blow-dried hairstyle, with a flashy wardrobe to match; and underwent vocal training to eliminate the squeak in his voice. The caucus was also made over by communications consultants who taught them the art of "messaging" and professionalized the caucus's Question Period performance. By the end of the make-over, Manning looked and sounded more like a traditional politician, and his caucus had been substantially reshaped into a traditional opposition party.

The party's electoral strategy called for it to distinguish itself from its competitors early in the campaign. Because the issue of deficit reduction, which was essential to Reform's success in 1993, had been stolen by the governing Liberals, the party needed new defining issues. Polls showed that Reform's only hope of increasing its support was to try to shift the electoral agenda away from the Liberal government's successful fight against the deficit and towards two issues on which Reform's policy stance was distinct: national unity and the accountability of politicians. The party ran a highly controversial ad campaign featuring a spot complaining that Quebecers dominated the prime minister's office. The ad was effective in shifting the campaign agenda, making national unity a central issue, but it did little to win support in Ontario. In the final week of the campaign, Reform stopped running the controversial ads in favour of softer commercials focusing on the issue of accountability, and featuring Manning as a warm family man. The turnaround in tone late in the campaign was not enough to create a breakthrough for the party in Ontario. As Ellis and Archer have observed, "accountability is often used as a code word in Western Canada to encapsulate many issues related to Western alienation and a mistrust of Ottawa ... This message ... is less relevant in Ontario."[35] In short, the return to Reform's agenda for institutional change in Ottawa did little to bolster the party's fortunes in Ontario. Although the party was able to win a slight increase in support in the West, it failed to expand in Ontario.

Even without a single seat east of Manitoba, Reform won enough seats to become the Official Opposition. Despite this apparent success, the party's leadership is well aware that, without expansion, it is likely to meet the same fate as other Western protest parties. As a result, the party's strategy is now focused on the objective of finding a way to form, or participate in the formation of, a government. This, of course, is no easy task for a party with no seats east of Manitoba, and virtually no support in Quebec or the Atlantic provinces. Reform's approach to this problem has been two-pronged.

The first part of the strategy involves reshaping the party's image to appear like a more traditional opposition party to voters outside the party's Western base. Towards this end, the party's parliamentary caucus has adapted to the traditional expectations for the opposition. Symbolic of this shift is Preston Manning's reneging on a public commitment and moving into Stornaway, the official residence of the Leader of the Opposition. In its efforts to embarrass the Liberal government, the party has championed a range of issues, not all of which are in keeping with its conservative roots. In short, the party has undertaken a concerted effort to win support outside its traditional base by taking on many of the outward trappings of a traditional, ideologically flexible, Canadian party.

The second element of Reform's expansion plan is its United Alternative (UA) campaign. This is not a simple effort to "unite the right," as it is clear that the continued vitality of the federal Progressive Conservative party and the strong antipathy between many Conservative activists and Reformers serve as profound constraints on the likelihood of a merger or takeover. Rather, Manning has chosen to champion a strategy that he calls the "united alternative." Implicit in this approach is the prospect of creating a wholly new party that is less ideologically coherent than Reform, while continuing to emphasize populist approaches to politics as well as Manning's "New Canada" constitutional vision. When he formally launched this campaign at the party's 1998 assembly, Manning told delegates that the time was right for a realignment of Canadian politics analogous to the one that had taken place prior to Confederation. This proposed political realignment, according to Manning, "meant that people who had been on different political sides ... had to work together for a while ... [It] meant that they had to find some common principles on which they could found a new federation, and set aside some issues on which they disagreed until another day."[36] The basic principles that Manning identified as the foundations for this United Alternative do not stray far from previous Reform Party policy. They include: fiscal responsibility (balanced budgets, debt reduction, tax relief), social responsibility (strengthening the family, and protecting the life and property of citizens), democratic accountability (reforming national institutions), and reformed federalism (based on the equality of citizens and provincial governments). Although these four founding principles were undoubtedly designed to reassure Reform delegates worried that the party was losing its ideological moorings, they offer little to attract new supporters to the party.

Rather than looking to take over the moribund federal Conservative party, Manning's strategy is "to attract supporters and activists from other political groups, particularly at the provincial level, who are also committed to these principles."[37] In his address to the assembly, Manning identified several specific groups to target, some of which appear more promising than others:

- supporters of the Filmon Conservatives in Manitoba, the Klein Conservatives in Alberta, and the Harris Conservatives in Ontario
- supporters of the Saskatchewan Party (a provincial alliance of Reformers, Liberals, and Conservatives)
- supporters of the provincial Reform and Liberal parties in British Columbia
- supporters of various political groups in Quebec, including those in the Liberal party and Action Démocratique du Québec (ADQ) who want reform of the federation
- supporters of various political groups in Atlantic Canada.

As the most numerous group located in the province where the party must expand, the Harris Conservatives in Ontario are clearly the most important of these groups for strategic reasons. There are already links between prominent provincial Conservatives and the Reform Party in Ontario and Alberta that might foster a cooperative arrangement or merger of some sort. Nonetheless, Premier Harris himself has steadfastly refused to endorse the United Alternative.

How great is the potential for such a strategy at the electoral level? Table 3.1 offers at least a preliminary answer to this question. It identifies respondents to the 1997 Canadian Election Study in terms of their most recent provincial vote, and reports their first and second choice in the 1997 federal election, as well as indicating what party the voter thought "too extreme" and presumably would not vote for. It reveals two distinct barriers to implementing the United Alternative strategy. The first difficulty with the strategy is the limited potential for growth. Some of the groups Manning identifies are already strong Reform supporters, including British Columbia provincial Reform supporters, Saskatchewan Conservatives, and Alberta Conservatives. In all three cases, a majority of the group voted Reform in 1997. As a result, these groups do not offer a great deal of potential for Reform growth, as only a relatively small proportion (8-16 percent) of those voters who did not cast a ballot for Reform in 1997 would have selected Reform as their second choice.

The second, and more significant, difficulty with this strategy lies in the voting preferences of the groups who do not already support Reform in large numbers. Voters who supported the Harris Conservatives in 1995 were not flocking to Reform in the 1997 election. Only 27 percent of them supported Reform, and only 15 percent identified Reform as their second choice. In addition, 27 percent of the Harris Conservatives responded that Reform was "too extreme" for them. The situation is similar for Filmon Conservatives in Manitoba, except that they are slightly less likely to consider Reform "too extreme." Reform was even

Table 3.1

Support for Reform among United Alternative target groups

	Reform as 1st choice %	Reform as 2nd choice %	Reform "too extreme" %
BC Reform	95	8	2
Saskatchewan PC	72	16	14
Alberta PC	59	13	9
BC Liberals	45	8	26
Ontario PC	27	15	27
Manitoba PC	26	12	16
Saskatchewan Liberals	18	12	30
Atlantic PC	8	5	9
Quebec Liberals	0	1	48

Note: The figures for first and second federal preferences among British Columbia Reform voters add up to more than 100 percent, due to an error in the original survey data.
Source: Calculated from 1997 Canadian Election Study.

less popular among Saskatchewan Liberals, and was virtually invisible among Atlantic Conservatives and Quebec Liberals. In short, the ground does not appear fertile for Manning to expand in any significant way east of the Saskatchewan/Manitoba border in the near future unless the party's efforts to normalize its image are highly successful or Manning is able to shift the terms of political debate.

The United Alternative proposal soon exposed significant divisions within the Reform Party. At the founding UA meeting held in February 1999, delegates passed several resolutions, setting out the policy themes for the proposed party. Although these themes differed little from the decentralist, small-government policy stances of the Reform Party, it was clear that organizers sought to jettison some positions that would not play well in Ontario. Most notable was a clear effort to move away from Reform's commitment to a triple-E (equal, elected, effective) Senate. The resolution adopted at the conference announced "an unwavering commitment to an elected Senate" but was silent on the question of equal representation for all provinces in the elected body. Clearly, this was an attempt to soften Reform policy in the hope of appealing to Ontario voters, who have little reason to support a Senate in which Ontario's representation would be on a par with that of Saskatchewan or Prince Edward Island.

A substantial proportion of Reform Party members opposed the United Alternative initiative. In the party's referendum on the question, 39.5 percent of the 32,099 Reform Party members who voted opposed the United Alternative.[38] In the weeks leading up to this vote, fifteen of the party's sixty members of Parliament were reported to oppose the UA, and some were very vocal critics.[39] A group of party members and MPs went so far as to purchase an ad in the magazine *Alberta Report* criticizing the initiative and urging party members to vote against the proposal. Opponents of the UA tended to be among the more conservative Reformers, concerned that the initiative would soften the party's position on social issues, recall of elected officials, and the triple-E Senate.

Despite this opposition, the United Alternative initiative was approved by a majority of Reform Party members in all of the provinces except Saskatchewan and the Territories (see Table 3.2). In Saskatchewan, only 37 percent of Reformers voting in the referendum approved the initiative. Although the initiative passed in all the other provinces, support was not overwhelming, and it is particularly noteworthy that the initiative was no more popular in Ontario than in the Reform heartland of Alberta

Table 3.2

Results of Reform Party referendum on the United Alternative

Provinces	Number voting	% of all voting	Number of "Yes" votes	"Yes" votes as % of total
BC	8,763	27.3	5,625	64.2
Alberta	10,619	33.1	6,558	61.8
Saskatchewan	1,836	5.7	681	37.1
Manitoba	1,560	4.9	788	50.5
Ontario	8,075	25.2	5,008	62.0
Quebec	122	0.4	78	63.9
New Brunswick	439	1.4	299	68.1
Nova Scotia	498	1.6	283	56.8
Prince Edward Island	none	—	—	—
Newfoundland	60	0.2	43	71.7
Territories	88	0.3	30	34.1

and British Columbia. The United Alternative initiative was explicitly designed to improve the party's fortunes in Ontario, but only 62 percent of voting members in that province were in favour of it, hardly a positive sign for the UA party-builders.

The considerable opposition to the United Alternative initiative within the party creates significant constraints on the pace and scope of change that Manning can pursue. It is possible that the idea of forming a new party may be set aside, at least in the short term, in favour of pursuing cooperation with Conservatives in the next election. Under this variant of the UA proposal, Reform and Conservative constituency associations would coordinate in the next election to ensure that only one of the two parties would field a candidate in each constituency. Under Joe Clark's leadership, the Conservative party has rejected this option.

These internal and external constraints on the United Alternative initiative suggest that both the Conservative and Reform parties will remain part of the Canadian political system in the foreseeable future. A devastating defeat for the Conservatives might allow Reform to achieve its objective of becoming a national party capable of unseating the Liberals, but without it Reform appears poised to remain a signifi-cant, regionally based party in a more complex and regionalized party system.

Challenging the Consensus

Although their futures remain uncertain, both the Bloc and Reform have played crucial roles in establishing several key characteristics of the emerging party system. When they burst onto the national scene with their extraordinary success in the 1993 election, both parties were unabashedly regional in their basis of support and their political vision. They disrupted the pan-Canadian character of party competition that dominated during the third party system. A consequence of this has been the greater regionalization of Canadian election campaigns. In addition, Reform's populism has had profound effects on how other parties organize their internal democratic life. The populist impulses that fuelled Reform's entry into the system have prompted all the parties to change their methods of leadership selection. Finally, the Bloc and Reform have deviated from the traditional parties' mould. Neither is a party in which ideological flexibility is employed as a way to create broad-based national coalitions. As a result, there is now much greater diversity among parties in the new system in terms of their representational approach. In short, the emergence of these two new parties on the Canadian political scene has created a stimulus to which the old parties have been forced to respond.

4

Struggling to Survive:
Three Old Parties

New parties arise and prosper by wreaking havoc on old ones. This has certainly been true during earlier Canadian party-system transformations: in the 1920s, the Progressives pushed the Conservatives out of the West; in the 1960s, the Créditistes challenged the Liberals' easy hegemony in Quebec. In both those cases, the old parties responded by reinventing themselves. They redefined leader-follower relationships, rebuilt their organizations on new principles, reforged communication channels to the electorate, and reformed their electoral financing practices.[1]

By the end of the 1980s, the old parties, with the New Democrats now joining the Conservatives and Liberals in that category, sensed that a frontal attack on the party system and their comfortable ways of managing political competition was under way. The continuing increase in the number of candidates and parties, the birth of Reform in the historically volatile West, and the unprecedented involvement of interest groups running expensive campaigns in the 1988 free-trade election all signalled growing discontent with politics as usual. The political elites responded in that most Canadian of fashions – they appointed a royal commission, which took as one of its "fundamental objectives" the need to "strengthen political parties as primary political organizations."[2]

Eager to assure their grip, the parties stocked the Royal Commission on Electoral Reform and Party Financing with their own: under the leadership of a non-partisan chair, the membership comprised prominent members of the political class: two Conservatives, a Liberal, and a New Democrat. The commissioners soon realized what the parties had only vaguely intuited: that the party system was facing serious strains, requiring major changes to both the parties and the rules governing electoral competition. They responded by quickly producing a report containing seventy pages of carefully worked-out recommendations for reform on all the issues parties traditionally had to cope with in earlier periods of transition. But before the parliamentary caucuses could bring themselves to take up much of that reform agenda, the parties were swept into the debacle of the Charlottetown referendum, and then the electoral explosion of 1993.[3]

Over the three general elections of the 1980s, the established parties had easily dominated party competition. Together, the three of them commanded more than 95 percent of the vote. Then, in 1993, their combined share suddenly plummeted by thirty percentage points, leaving them with less than two-thirds of the vote. But this collapse was not spread evenly across the three parties. The Liberals actually saw their vote rise by nine percentage points, though, given that the previous two elections had seen them at a historic low, this left them with little more than 40 percent of the vote. Still, with a comfortable majority in the House of Commons, they were able to form a government for the first time in a decade. The Conservatives took the largest electoral drubbing: their vote-share fell by twenty-seven points, to just 16 percent of the vote. The Conservatives had experienced electoral crashes of this sort of magnitude before (they dropped thirty percentage points in 1921,[4] and nineteen percentage points in 1935), but never had the electoral system left them with just two MPs, as it did in 1993. So, despite the party winning the third-largest vote-share, their weakened parliamentary standing left them reduced to a distant fifth place in a system where only the top two or three are considered serious players. The New Democrats won a few more seats than the Conservatives, but, like them, not enough to be recognized as a party under Commons rules. Their vote-share had fallen by more than thirteen percentage points, and, for the first time in its history, the party won the support of less than 10 percent of the electorate. Overrun by the Liberals, and overshadowed by the new opposition parties in the West and Quebec, both the New Democrats and the Conservatives were suddenly relegated to the margins of Canadian political life and their very future as players in the newly emerging party system called into question.

The New Democrats and the Challenges of Transition

The New Democratic Party's whole existence has been bound up with the shape and practice of the third party system and its politics of pan-Canadianism. It was established as the system was first emerging; it defined itself by its place in the system; and, as one of three parties, the

NDP played its own role in defining the period's patterns of electoral competition. It now faces the challenge of trying to adapt to the transformations that are reshaping party politics in Canada. Unlike its two older opponents, the NDP has yet to survive a remaking of Canadian party politics, so, for it, the end of the third party system represents a major crisis that will test the very existence of the party.

The NDP was deliberately created in the early 1960s as a political successor to the Cooperative Commonwealth Federation. The CCF had emerged in Western Canada at the height of the Great Depression of the 1930s as a socialist, federated, party-movement but had been condemned by the workings of the electoral system to the role of a Western protest party. The party never managed to escape that casting. Despite the rapid growth and urbanization of the population, its support regularly declined, election after election, in the postwar period. John Diefenbaker's sweep of the West in 1958 was the final straw, and for the first time the CCF vote-share dropped below 10 percent, and its seat-share below five.

Struggling to find a place in the politics of the new party system, CCF politicians decided to throw their lot in with organized labour, which had itself only recently come together to form the Canadian Labour Congress. The New Democratic Party, which was produced by this marriage with the trade unions, quickly assumed the interests of organized labour as its principal representative focus. While that gave the NDP a distinct perspective from which to assess issues and mobilize support in the pan-Canadian politics of the system, it led to internal conflict when other interests on the left tried to claim a place for themselves in the party. In the most serious case, it led to a purge of the so-called Waffle group of nationalists, who were challenging the place of the big international unions. It also limited the party's ability to engage the electorate, for labour had no distinctive position on the regional and constitutional claims that dominated much of the period's political debate.

Ideologically, the creation of the NDP represented a major shift in the orientation and approach of the country's political left. It marked a move from socialism to social democracy, and increasingly to a preoccupation with the tactical games of electoral politics. There is no doubt that this shift paid immediate electoral benefits: the NDP's vote grew every decade and, by the 1980s, was more than 60 percent larger than the CCF's average postwar support (see Figure 4.1). But it also meant that the NDP would increasingly be seen as little different from its larger opponents, and so just another part of the political establishment.

Figure 4.1

CCF–NDP vote- and seat-shares, 1945-97

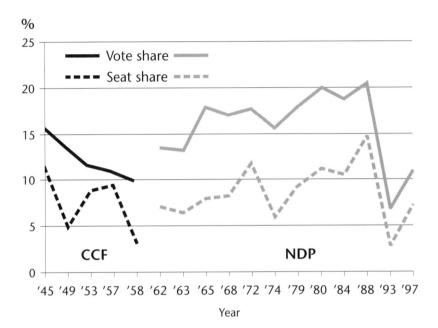

Together, the commitment to labour and the focus on winning votes in the new competitive political realities of the third party system contributed to an increased concentration on Ontario. Such a shift was natural. After all, that is where the large battalions of organized labour were located, and the province had emerged as the linchpin of the third system's competitive dynamic. Unfortunately for this new strategy, the continuing strength of several of the Western provincial NDP organizations inevitably worked at cross purposes with the national party's attempt to move its energies towards the interests of the centre.

On balance all three of these new orientations – to labour, to pragmatic electoral politics, and to the centre – made the NDP quite a different party from what the CCF had been. Advocating expansive national social policies and Keynesian economic management, the party was a natural and dynamic element in a party system driven by pan-Canadian political orientations. However, two other dimensions of the NDP reflected its organizational roots in the old CCF. First, the NDP remained a federation of provincial units, with its real organizational power left in the provincial parties. This limited its capacity to act as an independent national organization in the manner of its Conservative and Liberal opponents. And it left the NDP open to internal disputes on the many issues that divided the governments, including some of its own at the provincial level, trying to work the decision-making processes of executive federalism. Second, the party never managed to cross the Ottawa River and build a significant organizational presence in the five Eastern provinces.[5] That meant that, for all its ambition, the NDP never became a genuinely national party, and certainly never one that was relevant in French-speaking Canada.

By the 1980s, the party had become trapped by the contradictions of trying to build a left-wing politics, reconcile the growing cultural and constitutional tensions of Canadian federalism, and accommodate and represent its powerful trade union constituency. The result was that the party, ambivalent about its position but committed to maximizing its vote, adopted what Neil Bradford and Jane Jenson describe, in a withering phrase, as "contentless populism."[6] In 1979 the party adopted all the trappings and media campaign practices of the other two parties; in 1984 their campaign appealed to "ordinary Canadians"; and then, in 1988, they switched their language, but not their target, in seeking fairness for "average Canadians."

Contentless populism hardly constituted a serious left-wing alternative to the politics of the other parties, but it had its moments. In the great debate over free trade with the United States that animated the 1988 election, the New Democrats sought to avoid discussing the issue, because its US pollsters (whose very existence was a measure of how far the NDP had moved from CCF politics) pointed out that was an economic issue and that the party did poorly on such issues.[7] When it became clear that the NDP could not avoid the issue, and then found that they were unable to distance themselves from the Liberals, the party was content to retreat to a populist appeal, stressing the virtues of the party's relatively popular leader. For the first time in its history, the NDP won over 20 percent of the vote, and the party captured the largest number of seats ever. Almost half of those seats were won in British Columbia, long the country's populist heaven. The province had gone overwhelmingly for Brian Mulroney's Conservatives only four years earlier, and that should have been a warning to the party. The next election (1993) would prove the fickleness of the province's easy-come, easy-go populist voters, when Reform's sweep left the NDP with only two of British Columbia's thirty-two seats.

Despite the electoral success, labour's response to the party's inability to present a credible and distinctive alternative in the first election in over a decade to divide Canadians on economic issues was real and public anger. As a result of fiery letters from the leaders of both the Autoworkers' and the Steelworkers' unions, long the backbone of the NDP, a number of searching reviews of where the party stood and where it ought to be going were held. Little was resolved before Ed Broadbent resigned as national leader after fourteen years in office and the party was distracted by the most competitive leadership race in its history.

Previous NDP leadership contests had been coloured by a sharp left-right division, but by the end of the 1980s the party had succumbed to the imperatives of the third party system and reflected its norms and practices. The result was a contest in which ideology played little part, with most delegates simply preoccupied with finding a leader who could win. The growing strength of the women's movement, and a commitment to lead on issues of gender equity, prompted many in the party to push for a strong female candidate. When none of the party's more established figures stepped forward, Audrey McLaughlin, a rookie MP, was persuaded to run. Though labour appeared to prefer Dave Barrett, the former premier of British Columbia, more of the federal constituency delegates believed that McLaughlin would be successful at keeping the party together and leading it to victory, so she ultimately prevailed on the convention's fourth ballot.[8] In choosing a social worker from the Yukon who was hardly representative of their core constituencies, the party made its peace with contentless populism and abandoned the interest-based politics that had given it life. Ironically, the party chose the wrong leader for the politics it was embracing. Barrett was the genuine populist of the two, and it was he who was the more committed to building pragmatically on the party's existing provincial electoral strongholds.

By chance, the early 1990s beguiled many New Democrats into believing that they had made a sensible trade in giving up principle for populism. The party quite unexpectedly won office in Ontario (with 38 percent of the vote) and returned to office in both Saskatchewan and British Columbia, with the result that members could claim they governed half the population of the country. This performance, coupled with the record number of parliamentary seats that they had won in 1988, led New Democrats to believe it was the best of times. It wasn't, and it didn't last. In Ontario the government soon ran into economic trouble, for which its policies provided no ready solutions. Its subsequent budget-slashing response profoundly alienated labour, leading a number of union locals to disaffiliate from the party. In British Columbia the party slowly sank in a financial scandal that stripped it of any claims to the moral high road. In Ottawa the party lined up on the side of the political establishment to defend the Meech Lake and Charlottetown constitutional accords. The party had lost touch with the country's populist impulses, allowing Reform to paint it as just another old-line party.

Having alienated many in the labour organizations whose political interests had been its raison d'être, abandoned the distinctive policy positions that gave it direction, and then surrendered its chosen populist position to Reform, the NDP was ill prepared for the 1993 attack on the third party system. For the first time since the last campaign of the CCF, the party received less than 10 percent of the vote, and its seat-share in Parliament fell below five (Figure 4.1). The only saving grace, if there was one, was that the Conservatives actually got fewer seats, even though they had a million and a quarter more votes.

The magnitude of the party's defeat in 1993 left it in a dilemma. It recognized that some fundamental rethinking of its policies and structures was required, but organizing it was difficult, given that the party was nearly broke and had been forced to lay off most of the staff of its national headquarters. A national renewal conference was held in 1994, but the critical tone of many of the participants led the party, preoccupied with its very survival, to modify and stage-manage several subsequent regional meetings. It soon became clear that the party's principal priority was not rethinking its policy, and the full set of regional conferences originally planned was never held. Attention in the party was focused on organizational questions, and none was more vexatious than the leadership.

The party recognized that the changing norms of party democracy in Canada were demanding a new approach to leadership selection, and one that, as a would-be populist party, it could not afford to ignore. The difficulty was that, with a nominally large affiliated labour membership, the NDP was structured in a way that inhibited it from moving to an every-member leadership vote, as other parties were doing. When finally confronted with the problem by McLaughlin's resignation, the party opted for a complex primary system in which members and affiliated unionists could vote for candidates, but then left it to an old-style convention to choose among them. It was an unhappy compromise – members resisted the obvious parallels to US primaries while unionists resented the obvious attack on their privileged place in the party. Yet the party felt forced to adopt it in an attempt to bridge the growing distance between its structure and the country's shifting party culture.

The contradictory results exposed the internal tensions of the party. Lorne Nystrom, the candidate who captured by far the most votes in the series of primaries, finished last at the convention and was quickly eliminated from contention after the first ballot. Then, Svend Robinson, the candidate who had recruited the most new young members, offered the most radical alternative, and finished first on the convention's opening ballot, suddenly withdrew, leaving the leadership to the little-known Alexa McDonough by default.[9] This left the party with a new leader it hadn't quite chosen, and a leadership that hadn't been won, neither of which served the interests of populist politics. A social worker from Nova Scotia, McDonough was representative of neither labour nor the Western cadres that together constituted the muscle of the party. With no direction, the New Democrats drifted.

The 1997 election provided the first test of the party and its new leader after the shocks that had cracked the third party system. Still locked into its old strategies, the party managed to improve its vote-share, but not to its pre-1993 levels. More ominously, the NDP failed to win a single seat in Ontario, the country's industrial heartland, suggesting that its partnership with labour may have been irretrievably damaged. At the same time, Reform's more aggressively populist message kept the NDP from reclaiming much of its traditional Western base. The party's recovery was led by a wave of support in Atlantic Canada, the new leader's home region, but one long hostile to the party and in which it had few roots. This result saw almost 40 percent of the NDP caucus, and 20 percent of its total vote, drawn from the four Eastern provinces.[10] In considerable part this was the result of a revolt of the marginal and welfare dependent against the cost-cutting of the Liberal government, but it threatens to leave the New Democrats a marginal party, representing the margins of Canadian society.

Faced with that prospect, McDonough and many in her caucus began to try to accommodate themselves to the new economic environment by positioning the NDP closer to the centre of the Canadian political spectrum. But that spectrum has been pulled sharply to the right by Reform, while much of the labour movement, resisting neo-conservative impulses, has moved to the left and opposes any accommodation with business, large or small, home-grown or global.[11] The result is to again leave the party stretched between two poles, but with the populist option now effectively denied it. The NDP's future depends on how it comes to grips with its defining relationship with organized labour, and then on its capacity to find a distinctive place in the emerging party system.

The Conservatives and the Death of the Third Party System

Throughout the second party system, the Conservative party languished as an opposition party, unable to challenge the easy dominance of the Liberals. They had dealt themselves out of serious competition in Quebec in 1917 over the conscription issue and had been squeezed out of the Prairies by the Liberals' skilful accommodation of the Progressives' populist protest vote. Indeed, for most of the period the party was weaker on the Prairies than in Quebec. John Diefenbaker's populist appeal ended that when his great 1958 victory launched a major realignment of the electorate and ushered in the third party system. By 1965 the Prairies had been transformed into a Conservative bastion, leaving Quebec as the party's principal black hole.[12]

Diefenbaker's leadership ended badly: first, his government expired after a cabinet revolt; then, the party invented the leadership-review process to remove him. That new mechanism asserted the rights of party members to control their leadership, and, while it was a significant advance for internal party democracy, it strengthened the long-standing propensity of Canadian parties to translate policy disputes into leadership conflicts. From the early 1960s to the early 1980s, Conservative leaders were bounced between the expectations of the party membership and the demands of their caucus. In the process the party membership deposed Diefenbaker against the will of the caucus, and then the caucus deposed Joe Clark against the will of the membership, despite the fact that these were the only two leaders to have led the Conservatives to power since 1930.[13] This continuing cycle of instability, which George Perlin called the "Tory Syndrome," kept the national party divided and defeated.[14]

At the provincial level, Conservatives did better and, by the early 1980s, they controlled the governments in a majority of the provinces. Though the party's federal and provincial organizations were being separated, those successes did provide encouragement and, more important, a cadre of skilled organization builders and election managers. Those Conservative partisans were the first to take advantage of the passage of the first comprehensive party and election finance law in the mid-1970s. Taking their cues from the Republican party in the United States, the Conservatives quickly built a modern direct-mail program, and, by 1978, had an income greater than the governing Liberals.[15] With these resources the Conservatives were able to finance a sophisticated national campaign apparatus exploiting new polling and communication technologies. However troubled the leaderships of Stanfield and Clark, they did leave Mulroney the best modern political organization in the country, one hardened by provincial contests and supported by all the necessary resources.

Brian Mulroney's victory over Joe Clark in the Conservative leadership wars of 1983 reflected the party's determination to find a leader who could win.[16] Mulroney promised them Quebec and, with it, almost sure electoral success. And he delivered in 1984, with what proved to be one of the greatest electoral victories in Canadian history, winning, for the first time since Confederation, a majority of seats in every province. He had married Quebec to Diefenbaker's Prairies,[17] and many Conservatives believed that their new national base meant that they were about to become the country's natural governing party.

The Conservative government undid the Liberal's National Energy Policy, began the free-trade negotiations with the Americans, and revisited the constitutional issues that divided Quebec from much of English-speaking Canada. By the end of their first mandate, the Conservatives had begun to alienate some of their old, as well as their new, supporters, and the Reform Party had appeared in the West. Despite this ominous sign, the party fought the 1988 election on the Canada-U.S. Free Trade Agreement and won with the help of a division in the anti-free trade camp between the Liberals and New Democrats.[18] Unlike 1984, however, they managed to win a majority of seats in just two provinces – Alberta and Quebec – and, in the latter, had relied on the help of the province's federalist Liberal government to do so. Given that they had exploited the nationalist side of the Quebec electorate just four years earlier, it was clear that the Conservatives had not established their own roots in the province. Still, the party's profile after the 1988 election indicated that they had found a way to fill the hole Diefenbaker had left and suggested that they had become a broadly supported national party (Figure 4.2).

The Mulroney Conservatives' second government quickly exposed the contradictions that the free-trade election had managed to obscure,

Figure 4.2

Voter support for the Conservative party of Diefenbaker and Mulroney

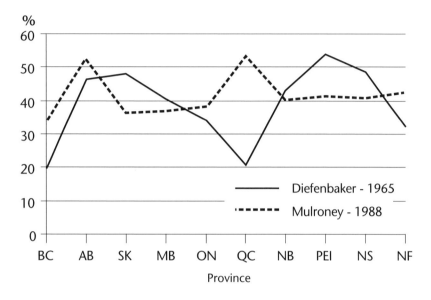

but which threatened its two bases of support. Western supporters drifted to Reform, while Quebec nationalists abandoned the Conservatives for the new Bloc Québécois. The Conservatives responded by engineering the Charlottetown Accord, which they hoped would put the constitutional issue to bed for a generation or more, and allow them to knit the party back together. By enlisting virtually the entire Canadian political elite behind the agreement, it appeared as if the Conservatives had saved themselves. But opposition to the accord was led by the core elements of their own coalition – new Reformers and Quebec nationalists – and so the defeat of the referendum sealed the party's fate. More generally, the referendum stimulated a populist uprising against the country's political parties and provided a clear signal that a new world of organized interests was demanding a fuller part in the country's political decision making and that the norms governing party activity were changing. The defeat of the accord was a popular rejection of the politics of executive federalism that had characterized Canadian government since the Diefenbaker interlude.

For 100 years, Canadian parties had defined themselves and their programs by their leader and so, in an attempt to save the party, Mulroney resigned and left the Conservatives to choose a new leader.[19] Desperate to persuade Canadians that the party had changed, the Conservatives crowned Kim Campbell their new leader in a selection process that was so rushed by pressure from the party's constituency association grass roots that no senior cabinet minister was able to mobilize enough support to run against her.[20] In the end, Jean Charest, a junior minister from Quebec, appeared to make a race of it by assembling all the doubters under his banner, but he never really had a chance. Campbell's attraction to a party eager for a quick, dramatic make-over was just too great, for she was an outsider twice over: once as a woman, and once as a resident of British Columbia, the country's least Conservative province. But with the Western and Quebec cores of Mulroney's Conservative coalition having dissolved, Campbell had little to work with and, after an inept campaign, she led the party to its worst defeat in history in the 1993 earthquake election. Despite the party winning almost as many votes as Reform and more than the Bloc, its support was spread so thinly across the country that it held only 2 of the 169 seats it had won five years earlier: Saint John in New Brunswick, and Charest's Sherbrooke in Quebec.

In the aftermath, it appeared that more than half a century's Conservative party-building had been erased. Diefenbaker's Prairies had deserted the party, and Reform had captured the two large westernmost provinces. Mulroney's Conservative Quebec had disappeared as quickly as it had arrived, and was in the grip of the Bloc. The post-election profile of the party looked like neither that of 1965 nor that of 1988. It resembled far more the party of 1935: Campbell had led the Conservatives back to where R.B. Bennett had left them in the midst of the Great Depression – indeed, they were now considerably weaker than they had been then (Figure 4.3). It took the Conservatives almost a quarter-century to rebuild and return to office after that defeat.

The crisis the Conservatives faced was not simply the desertion of their electoral constituency. The party had a large debt from the disastrous campaign and was forced to severely reduce the staff of its national office, laying off most of its employees. Many of its local associations were also in financial trouble as half the party's candidates had failed to win the minimum number of votes required to obtain their election-expense reimbursements. On the policy front, the party's room to manoeuvre was now severely reduced, as it found itself squeezed between the Liberals and Reform. No longer recognized as a party by the rules of Parliament, the Conservatives found themselves being ignored or patronized by the media.

Figure 4.3

Voter support for the Conservative party of Bennett and Campbell

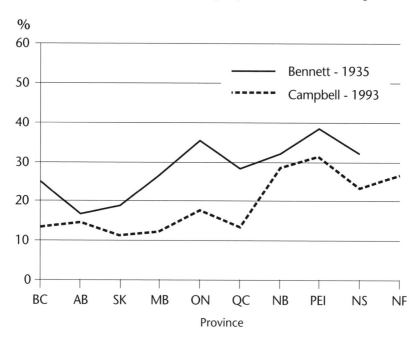

The party quickly anointed Charest as its new leader and set about a major rebuilding exercise, led by a National Restructuring Committee charged with considering all aspects of the party's operation. Unlike the similar exercise launched by the New Democrats, the Conservatives managed to make theirs work, and by the spring of 1995 a surprisingly enthusiastic national convention adopted a series of fundamental changes to the party structure. These included the creation of a National Council dominated by local association presidents that assumed control of party activity (and its budget), and a National Membership Program that provided members, for the first time, with a direct tie to the national party, as opposed to a second-hand connection via a local association. Here the Conservatives were following the lead of the Reform Party and laying the base for greater direct membership participation in party decision making. They also put in place a program of policy development and followed it up with a major policy conference in the summer of 1996.[21]

In all this the Conservatives had some marked successes. Members were being involved in policy making; new structures were in place and, after a hesitant start, were working; and, by the end of 1996, most of the party's debt had been cleared as the Tories continued to be more successful at tapping the financial resources of the country's business community than Reform. But as the 1997 election drew closer, it was clear that the party still had a long way to go. The articulation of the election platform, and the organization and direction of the national campaign team, came to be controlled, as it always had in the party, by the leader. The unsurpassed local election machinery that had served Mulroney was gone: in Ontario, a third of the riding organizations were empty shells, and another third had little more than a handful of activists with few resources, while in Quebec many ridings had no organization at all.[22] The party remained awkwardly positioned between the Liberals and Reform, without a distinctive support base that might deliver parliamentary seats in the election.

Ultimately the party's campaign was a fairly traditional one, focusing on the personality of Charest and holding itself up as the only national alternative to the Liberals. However, once Reform played the national-unity card in the campaign, the party found itself being squeezed by the polarization between the Liberals and the Bloc in Quebec. As a result it became less credible as a genuinely national party in other parts of the country. On election day the Conservatives did better than they had in 1993, but not that much better. Their vote-share rose by only three percentage points, and they continued to trail Reform. What they believed to be their party's strength, its nationwide character, again proved to be its electoral downfall, for, with a modest voter base spread across the country, the party won only twenty seats, the majority of them in Atlantic Canada, where neither of the two new parties had any presence. The Conservatives were back on the parliamentary map, but still in fifth place.

The years of pan-Canadian politics had seen the separation of federal and provincial party organizations, and nowhere was this truer than in Quebec, where a federalist-separatist division structured provincial party politics. Thus, when the provincial Liberal party's leader, Daniel Johnson, resigned in 1998, few thought it strange that it was Jean Charest, the federalist leader of the national Conservative party, who quickly emerged as the overwhelming choice to replace him. Overcoming his reluctance to leave federal politics, Charest allowed the Liberal Party of Quebec to draft him, but in so doing he left the Conservatives without the leader who had driven their restructuring and rebuilding since 1993. One of the decisions of that restructuring process had been to adopt a more populist-style leadership-selection process. Thus, Charest's departure also set in motion a contest for the leadership in which every party member would have a direct vote. It was not clear what the consequence of this would be, as, other than the Bloc, no other national party had chosen its leader this way before.

Party membership in the large Canadian parties has always been driven by electoral contests as candidates, for nominations or leadership, mobilize new and old supporters to rejoin the party in order to participate in the contest.[23] The Conservatives hoped that in giving members a new direct vote for the leader, as opposed to the old indirect vote of the delegate-convention process, they would be effectively responding to the populist impulses of the changing political culture, and that this would encourage many supporters and sympathizers to join the party. But the difficulty with the new process was that it, like the old, required a set of candidates who were attractive enough to make individuals want to join the party to vote for them. The Conservatives' real problem was that the party leadership was no longer the prize it had once been, and none of the five candidates captured the imagination of the party or the public. It was not a leadership contest fought over significant policy differences, for the leading contenders knew that the party was still struggling just to survive. Still, the campaigns did their job, mobilizing old and new members, and between June and September the party's membership roll mushroomed from 18,000 to 90,000.[24] With a proportional allocation of constituency votes replacing the old winner-take-all mechanisms of delegate selection, the outcome wasn't decided until the second ballot, when former leader and (briefly) prime minister Joe Clark defeated the anti-free trade interloper, David Orchard.

Clark's victory changed little. The party is still facing a very uncertain future. Though it has a significant number of voters, it is indebted, has little policy space in which to define itself, suffers from a much-reduced organizational capacity, and boasts few effective parliamentarians. Between Diefenbaker and Mulroney, it had its position as a competitive national party restored and was no longer simply the parliamentary opposition to the Liberals' government party that it had been for the long Mackenzie King-St. Laurent era. But, with the new patterns of regionalization that emerged in 1993, it risks falling back into the position it occupied throughout that second party system, or perhaps even falling out of Parliament, and ultimately the new Canadian party system. To avoid that, it must either push Reform back or beat the Liberals at their own game. Without a parliamentary base or the spoils of power, neither is going to be easy.

The Return of the Liberals

The Liberals were the most successful of the three parties over the life of the third party system, with Pierre Trudeau becoming the third-longest-serving prime minister in the country's history. At the heart of their success was a pragmatic marriage between a re-established Quebec base and urban Ontario, which led to the triumph of the centre in Canadian political life. It was this predominance of the centre, in the media and in business as well as politics, that fostered a pan-Canadian approach and defined the Liberals as an electoral machine.[25] Ultimately it was this same pan-Canadianism that proved the Trudeau government's downfall. Westerners came to oppose the party's economic and natural-resource policies, which they perceived as dictated by the interests of the centre; Quebec nationalists were led to oppose the party for its linguistic policies and its constitutional agenda, which they perceived as dictated by the interests of the English-speaking provinces.

The 1984 departure of Pierre Trudeau, English Canada's favourite French Canadian politician, left the Liberals vulnerable. Their instinct was to find a leader who could hold them together and whose popular appeal would return them to office. In the end they got neither. John Turner's defeat of Jean Chrétien was both a vote for an electorally marketable face, and an attempt to reposition the party more to the right and to make it less centralist. But the new highly competitive leadership convention process that had instigated a set of winner-take-all constituency battles only stimulated personal faction-building and divisiveness within the party.[26] Thus, when Chrétien's supporters, guardians of the Trudeau legacy, lost, they found themselves shut out of positions of influence in the party and forced into internal opposition. The party could not convincingly leapfrog the Conservatives on the policy issues, so Brian Mulroney easily collected the Conservatives' Western support and swept through his native Quebec to give the Liberals their worst electoral beating in history.

In defeat, the Liberals fell victim to the opposition-party syndrome wherein internal factionalism blossoms into conflict over policy and leadership within the party.[27] The disaffected Chrétien faction unsuccessfully challenged Turner's leadership at a regular biennial party convention in 1986, and in the process both reinforced the party's internal divisions and asserted their own sense of grievance and alienation. In doing so, they once again conjured up the old alchemy of Canadian parties, which have long found ways to transform policy divisions into personalized leadership conflicts.

Overwhelmed by the Conservative landslide in 1984, the Liberals slowly began a revival in 1988, when the party campaigned against the Free Trade Agreement and doubled its seats in the Commons. Several features of the party's performance in that election were harbingers of things to come. First, the party did not manage to convince many of the Canadians who had long supported it to return to the fold. They managed to win less than a third of the vote, and, while that was an improvement over the 1984 thrashing, it was the second lowest vote-share the party had received in 120 years. Second, Liberal gains in the election came in urban Canada, with seats won in Halifax, Montreal, Toronto, Ottawa, London, and Winnipeg. The party made few gains on the rural peripheries of the country. Third, and perhaps most significant, the Liberals actually lost ground (both seats and votes) in their traditional heartland of Quebec. The party won over two-fifths of its votes in Ontario, and for the first time in history over half of its caucus represented Ontario ridings (see Figure 4.4). So, even before the appearance of the Bloc and Reform, the Liberals were looking rather anemic for a national party. In a virtual caricature of their third-party-system formula for success, the Liberals were taking the shape of a party of prosperous Ontario, and in doing so were becoming less attractive to the disaffected voters of Quebec and the West.

The defeat of the party in 1988 inevitably led to John Turner's resignation as its leader, and the largest leadership-selection convention ever assembled in Canada. While the leadership had every appearance of being contested, with delegate-selection battles in the constituencies and an elaborate cross-Canada campaign by the candidates, in reality Jean Chrétien sailed to a ready victory. His network of supporters had been kept together since 1984, and had been hardened in the challenges to Turner between 1984 and 1988. They easily captured the party in the few months before the convention, and so obvious was his mastery that about 500 delegates did not bother to show up in Calgary for the vote. Chrétien claimed his leadership with a first-ballot victory, the first time that had happened in the life of the third party system. But the very ease of the convention victory was evidence that delegates themselves were no

Figure 4.4

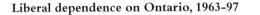

Liberal dependence on Ontario, 1963–97

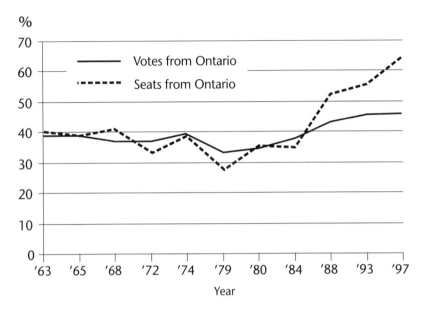

longer really choosing the leader; that battle was being won in the constituency trenches.[28] That being the case, the manipulated local delegate-
selection contests and the high cost of the process, which had driven
senior Liberal Lloyd Axworthy from the race, could no longer be tolerated as mere blemishes on the democratic face of the party's organization.
This undermining of the legitimacy of delegate leadership conventions
increased the demands for a populist reform of the process.[29] Provincial
parties were experimenting with every-member leadership votes, and the
national party realized it, too, would have to reform its processes to keep
pace with the changing norms of party democracy.

Chrétien may have seemed the obvious choice to the Liberals in 1990,
but his selection posed some risks to the party. As a long-serving cabinet
minister in Liberal governments, he did represent the very politics, and
stand for the very kind of parties, from which increasing numbers of
Canadians were becoming disaffected. At the same time, he was identified
in Quebec as having played a crucial role in the patriation of the Constitution and the adoption of the Charter of Rights and Freedoms over the

objections of that province's National Assembly, and much of its political and intellectual elite. This hardly made him the obvious man to restore Liberal pre-eminence in the province that had been a Liberal party heartland for most of the century. A sharp warning of this came on the very weekend of the leadership convention, a highly charged few days when the Meech Lake constitutional agreement was being finally overthrown by the Liberal premier and government of Newfoundland.[30] Standing on the convention floor of the Calgary Saddledome only moments after Chrétien's victory was announced, two nationalistically minded Quebec Liberal MPs declared that they could not support him and therefore would leave the caucus to sit as independents.

As they planned their return, the Liberals realized that they needed to both renew their party organization and rethink their policies. A reform commission of senior Liberals toured the country, hearing proposals for organizational modernization and change. Their report provided the agenda for a reform convention in Hull in February 1992. The reformers got only part of what they wanted – a proposed national membership system and a smaller, more focused national executive lost, but changes to candidate- and leadership-selection processes both passed. Ironically, the two major changes adopted altered the role of party members in contradictory ways. The first, designed to enable the party to respond to demands for a more representative and balanced slate of candidates, increased the power of the leadership at the expense of the local constituency associations. Not only were the rules for holding local nomination meetings and identifying acceptable candidates altered to give regional campaign officials greater control, but the leader was also given the power to simply designate a particular local candidate.[31] This second reform sought to respond to changing norms by committing the party to choosing its next leader with a process that would give every member a direct vote. Unsure how to do this, the party opted for a hybrid mechanism in which the votes of members would govern the first ballot, but not any necessary subsequent ones, of a leadership convention, largely because they had seen the Ontario Liberals successfully use such a process less than a month earlier.[32]

The policy-review process started with a thinkers' convention of the sort held early in the Pearson and Trudeau leaderships, and then moved through the party's more traditional policy-making routines aimed at providing the party with an elaborate manifesto it could present to the public during the campaign.[33] Eventually this manifesto was packaged and skilfully marketed as the "Red Book," allowing the party leader to offer voters a checklist – a kind of political guarantee – for which, he promised, a Liberal government could be held accountable. In doing so, the party was signalling that it understood growing voter mistrust and that Liberals could offer a real response to meet it. Along with their newly restructured organization, this permitted the party to go into the 1993 election claiming that they had both the team and the program the country needed.

The result was not the routine victory the Liberals expected over the Conservatives and New Democrats: it was the earthquake. Alberta and British Columbia, disillusioned by the Conservatives and disaffected by politics-as-usual, each gave the Liberals only about one-quarter of their vote and a handful of seats.[34] Quebec was slightly more forthcoming, but with only a third of the vote the Liberals could manage to win only nineteen seats, three-quarters of them in the Montreal region, where they obviously drew heavily on the anglophone and allophone vote. Jean Chrétien became the first Liberal leader in history to form a majority government without a majority of Quebec's seats behind him. With the West and Quebec providing Reform and the Bloc with their entrée into the party system, the Liberals were more than ever the party of the centre, with 55 percent of its caucus coming from Ontario (see Figure 4.4).

The first government of this new era turned out very differently than most Liberals had expected. The prime minister ran a comparatively scandal-free administration, as he had promised, and, sensing that Canadians were tired of the aggressive agenda politics of the third system, adopted a low-key approach to governing. However, the party was forced to back off several of its major policy commitments. Despite promises to force a renegotiation of the North American Free Trade Agreement (NAFTA) with Mexico and the United States, the Liberals quickly signed on. They then reneged on their high-profile promise to repeal the Conservative's much-hated Goods and Services Tax (GST). Most difficult of all was the decision to abandon an expansionary fiscal policy and institute deep public spending cuts in order to bring the budget into balance.[35] Much of that was ultimately accomplished by off-loading the cuts onto the provinces, which administer the expensive health, welfare, and education services of modern government. Like the electoral rejection of the Charlottetown Accord, this was another major attack on the cosy practices of executive federalism that had prevailed throughout the third party system. For the Liberals, this was politically easier than it would have been a generation earlier, for the national party was now free of its organizational ties to the provincial Liberal parties in all but the smallest provinces. Still, these cuts hurt, and the Liberals paid a large electoral price for them in Atlantic Canada in the 1997 general election.

The 1997 election confirmed that the return of the Liberals foreshadowed the emergence of a new party system. For it was not the old familiar Liberal party that had returned. The party's post-1997 House of Commons caucus was more Ontario-based than ever. For the third election in a row, Ontario's share had grown, and it now constituted two-thirds of the total, a major change from the third party system, during which the province constituted no more than its proportionate share of the governing party. The country had a majority government, but only because the plurality electoral system delivered all but 2 of Ontario's 103 seats to the Liberals.[36] In doing so, it undermined the Liberals' credibility as a national party. This too obvious triumph of the centre may well prove to be the national party's, and the party system's, Achilles heel.

Struggling to Survive

As a new party system is struggling to be born, none of the three old parties has been unscathed. As the Liberals wrestle with the problem of finding a way to reposition the party as the core of a new national party system, their old opponents, the New Democrats and Conservatives, face major challenges to their very survival. Badly damaged by the earthquake election of 1993, they have yet to demonstrate that they will re-emerge as major national players in the party competition of the twenty-first century.

Though Parliament has not taken up the challenges of the Royal Commission on Electoral Reform and Party Financing, all three of the old parties have worked at reforming themselves. The Liberals did it before they came back to power, but their relatively easy dominance over the fragmented opposition since 1993 has meant their changes have yet to face a significant test. That will probably first come when the party has to choose a new leader by a direct membership-vote process, without a national membership roll. Its growing dependence on Ontario threatens the Liberal party's capacity to act as a genuine national organization and government, so it must struggle to find a way back to its historic Quebec homeland if it is to re-emerge as the party Canadians have known for most of this century.

In the aftermath of their defeats, the Conservatives' and New Democrats' experiences with party reform have been quite different. The Conservatives successfully engaged in a wholesale structural overhaul of their organization; the New Democrats approached the subject, but quickly backed off in the face of sharp internal differences between the various interests in their constituency. Neither result has yet rescued the parties from their post-1993 predicaments. The Conservatives' modest support is too broadly based for them to have a significant parliamentary role in the life of the country; the New Democrats' electoral support is too divorced from their labour constituency for them to represent its interests. To survive, both must either find a way to bridge these political chasms or completely rethink what kind of political party they can and want to be.

The big questions facing the new party system is whether these old parties will remain imprisoned by the regional alignments mobilized in 1993, or whether they will find ways to overcome them, and, if they do, what kinds of organizations will be needed. For their part, the Liberals' two new opponents seem unlikely to become Canada-wide parties: Reform's call for a United Alternative is an admission it cannot escape its Western base, while the Bloc has no intention of even trying. The looming prospect for the fourth party system is that it may not develop a system of genuine national competition. Without it, a national political community will not thrive.

5

Representing Interests

In a democratic system, political parties play an important role as intermediaries between society and the state. This role is complex; intermediation requires that parties be responsive to the views of the electorate, that the full range of societal interests be given a voice in the political arena, and that salient political identities be represented. In a country with a population as diverse as Canada's, this is no easy task. Compounding these difficulties, the pattern that has emerged in Canada requires that much of the accommodation between competing interests or clashing identities take place within parties rather than between them.

Situated, as they are, at the heart of the electoral process, political parties face a challenging array of representational demands. Canadians increasingly expect their members of Parliament to act as representatives of the views of their constituents on policy questions. (This notion of delegatory representation is discussed in detail in Chapter 6.) In addition to representing constituents, members of the parliamentary parties often find themselves under pressure to represent the views of grass-roots party members on the ground. By virtue of the role they play in elite recruitment and accommodating societal differences, political parties are also the primary focus of demands for inclusion and representation by identity-based groups in political decision making. This latter representative function, as well as the competition between interest groups and parties to act as intermediaries between society and the state, form the focus of this chapter.

Each period of transition in the Canadian party system has been preceded by a multiplication of cleavages, as new interests have emerged (through Western expansion and immigration, for example) and existing groups (such as farmers or women) have become politicized. Existing parties have tried to accommodate these new groups or identities, but have, for the most part, failed to fully achieve this ambitious objective. This failure has contributed to the breakdown of coalitions within parties, usually resulting in the formation of new parties that, in turn, spark transitions from one party system to the next.

During the later years of the third party system, the parties increasingly appeared unable to accommodate the proliferation of cleavages in Canadian society. The emergence of an apparent crisis of representation within the party system in the late 1980s and early 1990s does not, however, entirely fit the pattern of earlier transitions. Just as was the case in earlier transitions, new groups and identities were mobilized, and to some degree accommodated, within the existing party system. Failure to accommodate these newly mobilized groups did not directly prompt the formation of new parties, however. Rather, formation of new parties was fuelled primarily by a breakdown of the Western and Quebec elements of the Mulroney coalition. The formation of the Reform Party can also be understood, at least in part, as a negative reaction to the Conservative party's efforts to accommodate newly mobilized groups into its coalition, leaving segments of its former electorate alienated from their partisan home. Another difference from earlier periods of transition is the emergence and growth of interest groups as a significant challenge to the primacy of parties within the political arena.

In the emerging fourth party system, the representational task facing parties remains complex as a variety of groups are calling for representation within the party system, while others continue to press their claims outside the partisan arena. Some of the tensions that constituted the crisis of representation in the later days of the third system have been resolved. Certainly, the House of Commons has become far more representative of the ethnic and gender diversity of the Canadian electorate than were previous parliaments.

A distinctive characteristic of the emerging party system is the variation in the representational practices and orientations of the parties. Although some of the parties continue to organize themselves as catch-all parties, Reform and, to a lesser extent, the Bloc and the Conservatives have taken different approaches to internal representational questions, eschewing the special measures that were characteristic of parties in the third system. The Liberal party has remained firmly in the accommodative tradition, trying to encompass as diverse a coalition as possible. At the same time as the Conservatives have jettisoned all representational quotas in favour of a system of undifferentiated membership, the Liberals have created party commissions representing Aboriginals, visible minorities, and seniors.

Parties and Representation Prior to 1963

In the party system that emerged after Confederation, the predominant social cleavage was religious and linguistic, dividing Protestant English speakers and Roman Catholic francophones. As parties formed to structure political competition in the new country, this potentially destructive cleavage was accommodated by including French-speaking Catholics and English-speaking Protestants in the governing Conservative coalition. To cement this coalition, the government relied heavily on patronage appointments, which rewarded loyal party workers in both communities.[1] This type of coalition established Canada's unusual pattern in which parties try to take both sides of fundamental cleavages, rather than taking opposing sides.[2] The first party system started to break down when tensions mounted between Protestants in Ontario and Catholics in Quebec over a series of controversies. The emergence of new interests, notably Western farmers, demanding representation placed further strain on the party system.

The party system that emerged after the First World War was better equipped to represent these interests. Several Western-based protest parties emerged to speak for some of the excluded interests. In the 1920s, the Progressives emerged as representatives of Western agrarian interests and expressed the populism that was taking root on the Prairies. After the demise of the Progressives, the Cooperative Commonwealth Federation (CCF) was formed. Although it shared its origins as a Western protest party with the Progressives, the CCF also articulated a socialist critique of Canadian capitalism, seeking to represent the emerging urban working class. Between 1935 and 1963, the conservative strain of Prairie populism was represented in Parliament by the Social Credit Party, which won substantial numbers of seats, particularly in Alberta. The Liberals, who governed for much of this era, relied on brokerage within the cabinet, where ministers acted as regional representatives. The politics of compromise were employed "to include rather than exclude interests within the Liberal party."[3] As a result, the Liberals retained a firm grasp on power throughout much of the period.

As did earlier transitions, the transition in the party system that began in 1957 reflected changes in the Canadian electorate that were not being accommodated by existing partisan arrangements. Although regional, linguistic, and, to a lesser degree, religious cleavages remained salient, other political identities were also emerging. The electorate was rapidly growing more ethnically diverse. In particular, immigration from Northern and Eastern Europe to Western Canada, and from Southern Europe to Ontario (particularly Metropolitan Toronto), was changing the shape of politics. Social change was also afoot in Quebec, where the Quiet Revolution was breaking down the role of traditional political elites and the Catholic Church, and introducing a newly confident and assertive francophone elite into Canadian politics. The Quiet Revolution sparked a transformation in the identity of francophone Québécois, and associated with this was a rejection of old forms of elite accommodation in favour of the transformation of the Canadian government into a genuinely bilingual and bicultural institution. When the CCF was disbanded and the NDP formed in 1961, the relationship between unions and the party was formalized, allowing union locals to affiliate with the party and giving unions a significant voice in internal party affairs. In establishing this formal relationship, the NDP effectively incorporated significant segments of Canadian organized labour into its electoral coalition. In so doing, the NDP created a permanent organizational presence for trade unions within the party, which limited its subsequent flexibility but gave it a reliable financial and organizational base.

From Pan-Canadianism to the Crisis of Representation

Party politics during the period from 1958 to 1993 were, above all else, national politics, and the three parties that composed the system strived to be national in scope and outlook. A rapid expansion of the Canadian state took place during this era of national initiatives and in the years just preceding it. This expansion of state activity contributed to the proliferation and increasing influence of interest groups. While interest associations of some sort have lobbied the Canadian government since Confederation, it was not until the third party system that these groups became as numerous and as important to the policy process as they are today. As a consequence of the increased scope of government, power was devolved away from the cabinet and down into the bureaucracy, which was charged with developing and implementing public policy. This increased the potential for interest-group intervention in public policy and focused those groups' activities on the bureaucracy rather than the political executive.[4] In addition, the development of television at this time created the opportunity for interest groups to engage in a very different kind of activism – creating pressure on government by capturing and mobilizing public attention through the electronic media.

Interest groups grew in number and influence at roughly the same time that public confidence in political parties was in decline. This was manifest in large part by a shift away from participation in parties towards involvement in interest groups. At the same time that Canadians have become less likely to vote, a substantial segment of the population became amenable to the idea of engaging in various unconventional forms of political action such as demonstrations, strikes, sit-ins, and boycotts.[5] It is these unconventional forms of political participation that interest groups and social movements introduced into the political lexicon during the 1960s and 1970s.

The crisis of representation experienced in the late 1980s and early 1990s stemmed from the pan-Canadianism of the parties and the rising influence of interest groups. Faced with Quebec nationalism, an increasingly diverse and assertive electorate, and criticism of their representative capacities, all three parties responded in remarkably similar ways. This left significant segments of the Canadian public without a political voice. Quebec nationalists lost the federal Conservative party when Meech Lake failed; alienated Westerners, opponents of official bilingualism and special status for Quebec, and those who espoused socially conservative family values were marginalized in the Conservative party, which was determined to maintain and project a more modern, progressive image. Ironically enough, the parties were unable to satisfy the groups calling for inclusion in the political sphere: ethnic activists and feminist organizations criticized the parties' slow progress and politics of limited inclusion. This set the stage for the explosion of discontent during the Charlottetown referendum campaign, during which alienated Westerners (represented by Preston Manning's newly formed Reform Party) joined forces with feminist groups and others on the left to reject the elite-driven constitutional agreement.

The Politics of Inclusion

Until the 1970s, Canadian political parties were relatively diverse in their regional and linguistic composition, but homogeneous in terms of ethnicity and gender. As the Canadian electorate has become more ethnically diverse, and as women have come to insist on a voice in the government of the country, political parties – like many other organizations and institutions – have had to come to terms with a new politics of inclusion. As David Elkins has argued, the tradition of brokerage politics in Canada meant that the parties were inclined to accept the claims of newly mobilized groups for inclusion: "Without any intention to do so, traditional brokerage politics in Canada ... laid the foundation for the successful demands of new groups seeking representation. People who are not 'insiders' in the newly active groups believe that certain of those groups must be represented by their own 'insiders.'"[6] As a result, an additional dimension of societal cleavage was added to the parties' representational task.

Compounding this was a gradual change in social attitudes favouring individualism and egalitarianism. The institutional manifestation of this value change was the Charter of Rights and Freedoms, entrenched in the Constitution in 1982. The charter opened the door for expansion of the franchise (for instance, to include votes for judges and prisoners) and challenges to traditional ways of drawing boundaries for electoral districts. Canadian electoral practice had long allowed remarkably large deviations in the size of constituencies within provinces. The legality of these deviations was challenged in the 1980s on the grounds that the charter's guarantee of a right to vote implied that all votes should carry roughly equal weight. The Supreme Court, ruling in 1991, rejected a strict version of this argument, but stated that the right to vote entailed the right to "effective representation." Determining whether representation is effective requires that factors such as geography, community history, community interests, and minority interests also be taken into account. Although this ruling has not yet had sweeping effects on districting practices at the federal level, it points to the changing understanding of representation and the salience of a politics of inclusion in the 1980s. Moreover, the ruling opens the door to future challenges such as the one before the courts in New Brunswick arguing that boundaries should respect the representation of Acadians.

Throughout the duration of the third party system, a relatively open immigration policy made the Canadian electorate increasingly diverse in its ethnic composition. During the period after the Second World War, Canadian society grew ever more diverse in ethnic terms as immigration from Southern Europe, Asia, and the Caribbean increased. All three parties in the third system responded to these waves of immigration through a uniform support for the principle of multiculturalism, and with efforts to win the loyalty of various ethnic groups. Although the Liberals have generally been associated with such efforts, they were not the only party to try to appeal to blocs of ethnic voters. In the late 1950s and early 1960s, all three parties were trying to win support from ethnic communities in southern Ontario, and particularly Metropolitan Toronto. The electoral imperative leading them to incorporate new Canadians into their internal coalitions forced the parties' leadership to reconsider their assumptions and behaviour. None of the parties was entirely confident in its approach to new Canadians. Organizers charged with drumming up the ethnic vote found themselves repeatedly chiding others in the party not to condescend to ethnic voters, not to ignore ethnic groups until election time rolled around, and not to assume that ethnic voters could be won over en masse by appealing to their clergy or newspaper editors.

While the Conservatives were consistently able to win the support of immigrants from Northern Europe who settled in the West, and even enjoyed some short-lived success in ethnic Toronto, it was the Liberal party that really came to be the party of recent immigrants. The Liberals' multicultural recruitment manual warned that "the party is often seen to be remote, unapproachable and closed to new members. Instead it is necessary to get across the message of an active, vigorous and open party." The manual advocated ongoing involvement with ethnic groups, attendance at cultural events, and sponsoring citizenship programs for recent immigrants. According to the manual, this latter initiative "serves the double purpose of encouraging Canadian citizenship and bringing potential members of the Liberal party into contact with established associations ... A meeting or reception should be held with these new citizens shortly after having received their citizenship. From there on they should be contacted on a regular basis and encouraged to become active in their associations."[7] In the 1950s and early 1960s, the party's organizational success in these communities was apparently attributable in large part to the work of Andrew Thompson. In the words of a Conservative organizer, Thompson "has managed to be of help to a great number of New Canadians. He knows a fantastic number of people and is seen at all important ethnic events."[8] In government, the Liberals maintained a number of programs that helped them maintain their support from "ethnic" communities. These efforts, although exploiting the state to build party machinery, were apparently effective in winning the loyalty of most new Canadian ethnic groups. However, as Stasuilis and Abu-Laban have noted, the party garnered this vote "without reflecting ethnic diversity internally, especially within the upper levels of their own organization."[9]

Throughout the 1960s and 1970s, the three major parties competed for the ethnic vote from communities that were relatively unassertive in their relations with parties. By the late 1980s this dynamic changed as members of the urban ethnic communities aggressively began to demand inclusion in the political elite. Prior to the 1988 election, four Toronto Liberals of Italian, Portuguese, and Sikh backgrounds formed a group determined to push for a more prominent role for ethnic minority groups within the party. Two of the four won Liberal nominations in 1988 in hard-fought battles. They were joined by several other ethnic-minority Liberal candidates in the Toronto area and in other major cities. The Conservatives and NDP also nominated several ethnic-minority candidates in major urban centres. For example, the Conservatives nominated Alex Franco, an active member of the Toronto Portuguese-language media, in the Toronto riding of Davenport, and Bermuda-born Joe Pimentel in Trinity-Spadina. In another Toronto constituency, the NDP nominated Raymond Cho for Scarborough-Rouge River.[10]

As these groups became more assertive and demanded entry into the partisan political arena, the major parties took steps to practise a politics of limited inclusion. The NDP adopted an affirmative action program for candidates intended to increase the number of visible-minority, Aboriginal, and female candidates, and guaranteed representation for visible minorities and Aboriginals on its federal council. The Liberals and Conservatives both tried to recruit ethnic candidates through various informal efforts. Even though they have sought ethnic candidates, both parties have on occasion faced a dilemma when candidates from minority groups have contested nominations. These candidates have often been able to draw on tight-knit networks of support from their communities, allowing them to organize highly effective nomination campaigns. Long-time party activists and organizers sometimes perceive these mobilizations as threatening, as they may overwhelm local party organizations and displace established party workers. In major centres such as Toronto and Vancouver, it has not been uncommon for candidates from two different ethnic groups, or even from the same group, to contest a nomination. This was illustrated very clearly in the 1997 Liberal nomination battle in British Columbia's Surrey Centre. In this constituency, which has a large Sikh population, all three candidates for the Liberal nomination were Sikhs, as were most of those mobilized to vote in the nomination contest.

Another significant development during the later years of the third party system was the political mobilization of women, which began in the late 1960s and early 1970s. Prior to the emergence of the feminist movement, women's participation in Canadian party politics tended to take the form of political housekeeping, channelled, for the most part, into ladies' auxiliaries that provided important support to party organizations, but had little influence on policy or in other areas. The NDP responded to the emergence of the women's movement most rapidly, owing, in large part, to a significant feminist mobilization within the party in the early 1970s. Subsequently, women have been an important and influential internal constituency within the party, managing, among other things, to elect the first female leader of a major federal party in 1989. The Liberals responded somewhat more slowly and less enthusiastically, but nonetheless took steps to try to appeal to what appeared to be an emerging women's vote. In government, the Liberals provided considerable funding to feminist organizations, and perceived these groups as supporters of the government until 1980, when feminist organizations refused to lend their support to the government's proposed Charter of Rights and Freedoms unless it included more comprehensive equality rights for women. In the early 1990s, the party made a conscious effort to increase the number of women in its caucus. The Progressive Conservatives were far slower to respond to the mobilization of feminism. In 1981, humbled by losing office after only nine months in government, the party was hoping to appeal to younger urban voters by jettisoning its image as a party dominated by elderly rural activists. As part of this effort, the party's Women's Bureau organized women's caucuses in major Canadian cities that emphasized networking and access to power for women. In 1983, newly elected party leader Brian Mulroney appointed the first woman to serve as national director of the party, and, once in government, he delegated a woman to coordinate government appointments. This latter position was part of a broader strategy to pursue something approaching gender parity in government appointments, in essence, a return to the traditional use of patronage for mediating cleavages in the Canadian electorate.[11]

Although they varied in their methods and enthusiasm for embracing some version of liberal feminism, all three parties in the old party system adopted feminist policy stances of some sort, and instituted measures to try to involve women in partisan elites during the third party system. This was remarkably similar to their response to greater ethnic diversity. In essence, all three parties had precisely the response to the emergence of newly salient cleavages that one would expect of parties trying to straddle fundamental cleavages: they tried to appeal to new groups of voters without alienating any traditional supporters of the party.

This accommodative strategy was ultimately unsuccessful. Neither feminist nor minority groups were fully satisfied with the representative gains, as increases in numeric representation were slow, and progress on substantive representation even slower. As a consequence, many activists chose to try to influence the political system from outside, working through advocacy groups rather than the parties. Ironically, even though the measures the parties took to try to accommodate these groups were not enough to satisfy them, they nonetheless served to alienate others from the party system. Canadians who opposed the idea of representational quotas, liberal feminist policy stances, and government promotion of multiculturalism were left without a partisan home by the late 1980s. In this sense, the three parties' efforts to accommodate significant internal cleavages effectively drove activists at either end of the political spectrum out of the partisan arena.

Interest-Group Politics

The proliferation and increasing influence of interest groups was threatening to parties in the third system. It represented a further erosion of their role in policy making, as well as competition for the allegiance of the Canadian public. Most significant, perhaps, was the light this phenomenon cast on the parties' ability to broker interests. Many observers of Canadian politics, both inside and outside the parties, regret the role that interest groups have played in contributing to the apparent decline of party. In their view, parties offer a preferable route for citizen engagement in the political process because the parties' brokerage functions force activists to accommodate competing interests and beliefs. This may well overstate the normative case against interest groups. Certainly, many citizen groups encompass a range of interests and opinions, and the politics of compromise and accommodation must be practised within these organizations. That said, there is no question that the changing political values of the Canadian electorate favour a politics of direct, issue-oriented involvement over the old-style politics of party brokerage. In this sense, the forces that encouraged the growth of interest groups also contributed to the demise of the party system.

Ultimately, there is little that parties could do to oppose these trends as long as they were committed to acting as omnibus parties representing a panoply of interests, and to remaining flexible on issues. In fact, parties in the third system were periodically forced to fight off incursions from interest groups determined to use the party to further their causes. The most notable case of this was the influx of anti-abortion activists into the Liberal party in the early 1990s. Calling themselves Liberals for Life (LFL), the group organized to support Tom Wappel's leadership bid in 1990. Even though Wappel's candidacy received little support, it worried party insiders. Prior to the 1993 election, Liberal leader Jean Chrétien used his new power to appoint candidates to forestall the LFL's efforts to nominate their activists as Liberal candidates in several ridings. This defensive effort did not reflect a deep commitment to reproductive freedom on the part of the Liberal party; rather, it was motivated by the party's need to retain its ability not to take a stand on this potentially divisive issue.

The NDP has been somewhat more open to cooperation with interest groups than have the two more traditional brokerage parties. The party's social-democratic ideology and self-appointed role as the party of the socially marginalized make it a natural ally for many progressive social-movement organizations. Even so, the NDP's experience in the early 1990s provides a clear illustration of the inherent limits to cooperation between groups and parties. Many New Democrats are highly suspicious of activists for whom causes or issues are of greater importance than loyalty to the party. Because of the high value placed on internal harmony, the party's ability to reach out to social movements is limited.[12] In addition, many in the party's upper echelons believe that movement organizations draw activists into single-issue groups and protest campaigns that drain activist energy and resources and do not translate into support at election time.[13] According to one NDP insider's account, many in the party believe that social-movement organizations are "full of Liberals."[14] Tensions between the NDP and social-movement organizations increased in the early 1990s, fuelled by the experience of the Ontario NDP in power, and the Action Canada Network's perceived betrayal of the party. (The Action Canada Network was an anti-free trade group that endorsed Liberals in some constituencies in 1988 for strategic reasons.) After the party's devastating loss in the 1993 election, a senior Ontario party official wrote a memo condemning the "single-issue focus" of social-movement organizations, arguing that "their agenda is not our agenda," and former MP Joy Langan lashed out at the feminist organization National Action Committee on the Status of Women (NAC) for failing to support the party during a crucial election campaign, even though the party had long been an advocate of NAC's policy agenda.[15]

The parties in the third system all agreed that interest-group involvement in elections should be restricted. Proponents of regulation argue that unrestricted spending can allow interest groups to drown out parties (whose spending is regulated), creates the potential for wealthy individuals or groups to distort the electoral agenda by monopolizing the media, and creates serious loopholes to the spending limits for candidates and parties. Opponents of regulation argue that such restrictions infringe on the constitutionally protected right to freedom of expression and give parties a virtual monopoly on political speech during elections.[16]

The first effort to limit independent expenditures came in 1974, with legislation prohibiting groups and individuals from spending during elections to promote or oppose candidates unless the expenditures were intended to gain support for a policy stance or to advocate the aims of a non-partisan organization. The wording of this legislation was so broad as to permit almost any sort of intervention, so, in 1983, the government took the Chief Electoral Officer's advice that the loophole be closed, and amended the Canada Elections Act to prohibit anyone other than parties and candidates from spending money to support or oppose candidates or parties. The next year, the National Citizens' Coalition (NCC) successfully challenged the constitutionality of the law. The Alberta Court of Queen's Bench ruled that the government had not demonstrated a clear need for the spending regulations, so the legislation could not be justified under section 1 of the charter. The government did not appeal the ruling to the Supreme Court of Canada, so there were no restrictions on interest-group spending in the 1984 and 1988 federal elections.

The 1988 election saw an explosion of interest-group activity, most of it centred on the issue dominating the national campaign – free trade between Canada and the United States. This prompted public controversy, because proponents were able to outspend opponents of the Free Trade Agreement (FTA) by a considerable margin. Of the estimated independent expenditures of over $4.7 million on the free-trade issue in 1988, approximately $3.6 million, or over 75 percent, was spent advocating the FTA.[17] In the campaign's aftermath, the government charged its newly appointed Royal Commission on Electoral Reform and Party Financing with considering the question of independent expenditures. The five members of the royal commission, four of whom had strong partisan affiliations to the three old parties, took an approach that advocated recognizing parties as "primary political organizations" and therefore defending their interests. Arguing that "any greater ability to incur independent expenditures would irreparably weaken the effectiveness of the spending limits for candidates and parties," the commission recommended that election expenses (including issue advocacy) not exceed $1,000 per group or individual, and that groups or individuals be prevented from pooling their limits. All that would remain unrestricted would be the ability of groups, associations, unions, and employers to communicate directly and exclusively with their members, employees, or shareholders on election issues.[18] The House of Commons subsequently adopted legislation virtually identical to the recommendations of the royal commission, except that the limit applied only to a group's advertising expenses during an election, and the $1,000 limit applied only to expenses directly promoting or opposing a party or candidate.

The NCC immediately launched a challenge to the constitutionality of the law, and once again the Alberta courts struck it down as an unjustifiable restriction on freedom of speech and the right to an informed vote. After a 1996 ruling from the Alberta Court of Appeal upholding the lower court's ruling to this effect, then Justice minister Allan Rock announced that the government would not appeal the ruling as the legislation was essentially indefensible under the charter. As a consequence, it was clear well in advance of the 1997 election that there would be absolutely no restriction on the amount that groups could spend, or on their ability to directly support or oppose parties or candidates in their advertising and other materials. In short, there was no legal barrier preventing an interest group or individual from spending an unlimited amount of money directly advocating a candidate or party.[19]

Representation in the Fourth Party System
In the emerging party system, the representational task facing parties remains complex, as a variety of groups are calling for representation within the party system, and others continue to press their claims outside the partisan arena. Some of the tensions that constituted the crisis of representation in the later days of the third system have been resolved. Certainly, the current House of Commons is far more representative of the diversity of the Canadian electorate than were previous parliaments. Although women remain numerically underrepresented, a Parliament with 20 percent women in 1997 is a considerable improvement over 1980's 5 percent. Similarly, the ethnic diversity of the Canadian electorate is beginning to be reflected in Parliament, and there are signs that

parties are becoming more accepting of minority groups' participation in party affairs.

One distinctive characteristic of the emerging party system is the variation in the representational practices and orientations of the parties. Although some of the parties continue to organize themselves as catch-all parties, the Reform Party and, to a lesser extent, the Bloc and the reorganized Conservatives, have taken different approaches to internal representational questions, eschewing the special measures that were characteristic of parties in the third party system.

The Liberal party has remained firmly in the accommodative tradition, trying to accommodate as diverse a coalition as possible within it. The composition of the Liberal party's national executive reveals a great deal about the cleavages it is trying to encompass. The party has two vice-presidents, one designated English and the other French, in addition to its six regional vice-presidents. There are five standing committees of the national executive, including policy development, organization, and multiculturalism. The party's three commissions – youth, women, and Aboriginals – all have representatives on the national executive.

At the other end of the spectrum, the Reform Party prides itself on not having any special measures guaranteeing representation to any group. Moreover, the party has resolutely refused to take positions on women's issues on the grounds that there are no problems specific to women, but simply social issues or family issues. It is telling that this stance was recommended by a party task force led by Preston Manning's wife, Sandra Manning. The Reform Party's antipathy to feminism is rooted in a belief that feminists, like other "special interest groups," including environmentalists and homosexuals, have come to wield a disproportionate influence in Canadian politics.[20] The party has no special measures encouraging women's participation, and vociferously criticized the Liberal party's appointment of female candidates in the 1997 election on the grounds that this was both undemocratic and insulting to women. It is perhaps no accident that women made up just 7 percent of the Reform Party's post-1997 caucus, as compared with 24 percent in the Liberal ranks.

That said, the Reform Party is not above making targeted appeals to ethnic voters. Prior to the 1997 election, the party organized half a dozen meetings with leaders of ethnic communities, and among the new Reform candidates nominated in winnable ridings were several members of visible-minority groups. Four of these candidates were elected. But the story of Rahim Jaffir's nomination contest in an Edmonton riding illustrates the continuing tensions within the party over these matters. Jaffir was a twenty-five-year old candidate of Indian descent whose family emigrated from Uganda when he was a child. His opponents alleged that Jaffir was the national office's favourite for the nomination. In contrast, Jaffir's closest competitor for the nomination personified the old Reform Party: he was an expatriate English policeman whose nomination speech "all but threatened the lives of [then Justice minister] Allan Rock and Sheila Copps." The campaign manager for another candidate called Jaffir "a boy with off-colour skin" and suggested he be screened for "exotic foreign diseases."[21] Jaffir won the nomination, was elected, and became the party's high-profile National Unity critic. In this case, at least, it appears that Reform's desire to shed its image as an extremist party won out over strict adherence to the principle of local autonomy.

Interest Groups

As in the third party system, interest groups remain important players in the emerging system. One subtle difference is that several prominent groups have come to ally themselves more clearly with specific parties rather than taking the non-partisan stances they had in the past. This new approach to alliances is attributable in large part to the polarization of the new party system around several sets of issues. A number of groups that in the past took predominantly oppositional stances vis-à-vis the party system have come to ally themselves with the Reform Party. These include the National Citizens' Coalition, the National Taxpayers' Federation, and the National Firearms Association. To a lesser degree, some groups at the opposite end of the political spectrum (such as NAC) have become vociferously anti-Reform and have developed closer ties with the NDP or Liberals.

During the 1997 election, interest groups were active on a variety of issues and in pursuing a diverse range of objectives. Some directly supported parties, while others engaged in issue advocacy and others targeted individual MPs for defeat. An examination of several groups' intervention in the campaign illustrates the extensive array of possible relationships between groups and parties during an election.

The most immediate way for a group to involve itself in an election campaign is to work on behalf of one party, regardless of whether the party wants this support. There are some clear incentives for groups to do this: if they believe their cause will be furthered when one particular party is elected or gains seats in the election, then it is reasonable to work on behalf of that party. Certainly, when the Canadian Labour Congress contributed $600,913 to the NDP in 1997, its objective was to increase the number of seats the NDP held in the House of Commons (and to maintain its influence within the party). Endorsing or supporting a party in an election also offers the potential for the group to hold some influence if the party is elected. If the party does not form the government, the group may well be left out in the cold. In this sense, the incentive for groups to endorse a party is greater if they are confident of the outcome, or if they have already despaired of gaining influence with the competing party. Endorsing a party can also entail significant internal costs for groups. If a substantial number of group members belong to another party, or reject party politics altogether, then an endorsement can mean that the group loses activists, supporters, and financial contributors. Consequently, direct support for a party is really an option only for a group whose membership is reasonably homogeneous in its partisan leanings. Given these disincentives, it is not surprising that only a small number of groups directly support one party during election campaigns.

During the 1997 election, signs bearing the somewhat ambiguous message "Remember Bill C-68 When You Vote" were a common sight in rural areas where gun ownership is concentrated. Part of the National Firearms Association's (NFA) extensive and ambitious campaign to defeat the Liberal government and the gun-control legislation it had supported, these signs signalled widespread discontent over firearms legislation in parts of the country. Long an active and vocal opponent of the federal government's effort to regulate and restrict firearms' use, the NFA's literature claims that its political education programs are "designed to increase awareness and encourage direct participation in the partisan political process by Canadian firearms community members, but the NFA supports no particular political party."[22] Despite this disclaimer, the NFA was actively and vocally pro-Reform throughout the 1997 federal election campaign.

During the campaign, the NFA's political clout was put at the disposal of the Reform Party. In a memo to supporters, NFA president David Tomlinson noted that the only party offering a "trustworthy promise of an immediate turn toward dumping the Liberal game plan, revoking Bill C-68 and bringing in a completely revised firearms control system that will attack criminals and favor our firearms community is the Reform Party." Using images of war and battle, Tomlinson exhorted any member who was not a political activist to "get off your butt and become one now." He called on NFA supporters to "work for, donate money, goods and services to, and promote the Reform Party."[23] Tomlinson himself was president of a Reform Party constituency association in Edmonton. NFA activists apparently heeded Tomlinson's call. Messages posted on the organization's listserv throughout the election reflected considerable involvement in Reform campaigns. Activists compared notes about the travails of keeping Reform signs in place, boasted about their campaign activity and contributions, and called for volunteers to help at local Reform offices.

Although presumably content to have the NFA's support, Reform was probably less enthusiastic about the Alliance for the Preservation of English in Canada's (APEC) efforts to support the party during the 1997 campaign. APEC is a vocal opponent of official bilingualism and, more recently, distinct-society status for Quebec. Ongoing opposition to official bilingualism has left APEC with a reputation for political extremism. According to its president, the group decided to get involved in the 1997 election campaign out of frustration with the Liberal and Conservative party's ongoing support of distinct-society status for Quebec, as well as a host of complaints about the Liberal government's performance in office. Convinced that giving distinct-society status to Quebec would lead to the eventual break-up of Canada, the organization's leadership believed they could not stay on the sidelines during the imminent election campaign. Their objective was to use the election to get their message about distinct society and official languages out to the public. To do this, APEC called on members to distribute thousands of pamphlets setting out the group's position on these two issues. By the end of the campaign, they had distributed 72,000 pamphlets dealing with distinct society, and 66,000 on the subject of official bilingualism. The group had also distributed about 5,000 lawn signs with the messages "Oppose Distinct Society" and "No More Prime Ministers from Quebec" as well as some 10,000 bumper stickers bearing the latter message. In addition, the group published a large newspaper advertisement in twenty-six newspapers across the country (some in small towns, but others in major daily papers such as the *Winnipeg Free Press* and *Toronto Sun*).[24] Finally, the group purchased radio spots on several stations across the country, running six times daily. The total cost of this campaign was some $140,000, all of which was raised from members' contributions.

The newspaper advertisement told readers that "the Liberals, Conservatives and New Democrats all favor Distinct Society status for Quebec.

Do not vote for them." Although not clearly stated, the message was to vote for the Reform Party. When asked why the group did not come right out and endorse Reform, the group's president indicated that the Elections Act prevented the group from doing this, as any advertising directly promoting the group would have to be counted as part of Reform's election expenses. (In fact, this was not a correct interpretation of the current legal situation, in which there are no restrictions on direct endorsements.) In this case, at least, it appears that frequent changes to the law regulating interest-group advertising have created uncertainty among some interest-group leaders.

Even though APEC's "No More Prime Ministers from Quebec" message was not too far removed from the central theme of Reform's advertising campaign, at least one grass-roots Reform worker in Ontario complained that APEC activists were making the party's task more difficult by putting their signs near Reform's, creating the impression of an association between the two. This case illustrates a problem for parties: they are unable to control which organizations support and endorse them. The only tools available to parties in this regard are public statements distancing the party from the group or asking the group leader not to endorse the party. APEC's leadership was clearly aware of the potential harm they could do to Reform, and refrained from endorsing Reform more directly, in part for that reason.

More common than direct support for a party during an election is issue advocacy, whereby a group uses the opportunity presented by an election campaign to try to force parties (in particular, the governing party) to adopt its stand on an issue. This tactic involves raising the profile of the issue and mobilizing a network of supporters to place pressure directly on candidates. Election campaigns are one time when parties have little choice but to respond to the issues raised by interest groups. During the 1997 campaign, there were numerous instances of interest-group actions eliciting prompt reactions from parties. After a coalition of environment groups placed a full-page advertisement in the *Globe and Mail* concerning the government's failure to pass legislation protecting endangered species (using the heading, "The Liberal Dead Book?"), the Liberal party promptly posted a policy statement on its Web page outlining the party's position on protecting endangered species. Under pressure from AIDS activists throughout the first half of the campaign, the Liberal government renewed funding for AIDS research on 29 April.

The most notable example of issue advocacy in the 1997 campaign was the Friends of Canadian Broadcasting's (FOCB) "Save the CBC" campaign. A national organization with some 45,000 households supporting it, FOCB is an advocacy group with the purpose of defending both the quantity and quality of public broadcasting in Canada. The group's strategy has been to place pressure on Liberal MPs in the hope that this will cause them to work for increased funding to the Canadian Broadcasting Corporation. Because its method of exerting pressure requires it to threaten the electoral chances of Liberal incumbents, a group like this faces a dilemma. If it actually defeats a Liberal MP, it might do so by delivering a seat into the hands of the Reform Party – an even less enthusiastic proponent of its cause than the governing Liberals.

Like most interest groups, the FOCB is careful to maintain a nonpartisan stance. While it was attacking the Liberal government's record, it did not endorse any other party or individual candidates. (It did encourage candidates to "take the pledge" to work for restored CBC funding.) The overarching purpose of the FOCB's activity was not to elect a different party, but to change the current Liberal government's action on this issue. The means for doing this was through a demonstration of grassroots clout. The purpose of targeting sitting MPs, then, is not so much to punish incumbents for past action as to gain their attention, impressing upon them the salience of this issue to a significant proportion of the voting public.[25]

Prior to the election call, the FOCB selected forty ridings to target during the election. The ridings were selected through a combination of objective and subjective criteria. The objective criterion was the 1993 election result in the riding – if the Liberal candidate had won or lost by a margin of less than 10 percent, then the riding was eligible to be targeted. From this pool, the group tried to select ridings where Liberal incumbents appeared vulnerable. FOCB supporters in the forty targeted ridings were asked to put up lawn or window signs with the message: "The CBC Promise: Keep It." After the election was called, the group distributed no more signs, as they did not want to compete with the parties during the campaign. Despite this, CBC signs were a common sight throughout the duration of the campaign in some parts of the country. In addition to the lawn signs, the organization distributed 60,000 of its election kits and 80,000 bumper stickers during the campaign period, focusing their distribution on the forty targeted ridings. In an interview, Ian Morrison estimated that the group spent approximately $500,000 during the pre-election and election period, which represented approximately

$250,000 more than the group would have spent during the same period had the federal election not been called.

Another technique groups frequently use is to target individual MPs to punish them for their action or inaction on the group's issue. The line between this and issue advocacy is blurry. The key distinction is that targeting incumbents tends to be a technique employed not so much to demonstrate grass-roots clout as to punish incumbents for previous action or inaction. Several organizations targeted incumbents in the 1997 election. In Quebec, the nationalist Société Saint-Jean-Baptiste published in *Le Devoir* a list of all the names and constituencies of Liberal Quebec MPs under the heading "Voici le parti qui accepte qu'on charcute le Quebec" (This is the party that believes you can butcher Quebec). Although the Liberals were the primary target of the advertisement, the Conservatives did not escape unscathed – in smaller print the advertisement asserted that "Jean Charest n'est pas moins dangereux" (Jean Charest is no less dangerous).[26] In English Canada, the campaign that received the most publicity was that of the Canadian Police Association (CPA).

The Canadian Police Association's election involvement was directed against nine Liberal incumbents who had voted against a private member's bill proposed by John Nunziata to repeal the section of the Criminal Code allowing murderers sentenced to twenty-five years in prison to appeal for early release after fifteen years (the "faint hope" clause). In the most controversial interest-group advertising campaign of the election, the CPA erected billboards in targeted ridings featuring photos of the Liberal incumbent beside photos of convicted serial killers and murderers. The text of the billboard read: "[incumbent's name] voted to give these killers a chance at early parole. On June 2 it's your turn to vote." The advertisement sparked considerable controversy in the press, and the targeted MPs counter-attacked by saying that the advertisements served only to feed convicted serial killer Clifford Olson's thirst for publicity. One of the MPs, Dianne Brushett from Truro-Cumberland-Colchester, responded by filing a libel suit against the CPA; the suit was subsequently withdrawn.

Considerable effort and money went into interest-group involvement in the 1997 election campaign. This raises an important question: how effective is such activity? The answer to this question varies, depending on how we define effectiveness. If the group's objective is to influence the outcome of the election, then effectiveness would involve changing how people vote. There is not a great deal of evidence available regarding the extent to which interest-group involvement affects electoral outcomes. When a group claims to have influenced an election because the candidates they targeted were defeated, there is no way of being certain that it was the group's activity that influenced voter's choices. One way to measure group influence is through survey research. Because of the extensive advertising over the free-trade issue during the 1988 campaign, the Canadian Election Study tried to determine what effect, if any, this advertising had on voting behaviour. Their findings were inconclusive: they could find no reliable indicators showing consistent effects from third-party advertising.[27] To measure the effect of interest-group activity on electoral outcomes in the 1997 election, Brian Tanguay and Barry Kay examined the percentage change in support for incumbents targeted by the National Citizens' Coalition and candidates endorsed by Campaign Life and Catholic Insight, both pro-life groups. They compared the change in support for these candidates to the average change in support for their parties' candidates in the same province. Tanguay and Kay conclude that these groups' efforts "have had very little success despite the bold claims made by group leaders."[28] In fact, of the thirty-nine candidates targeted by the NCC, thirty-six actually improved their performances over 1993.[29]

Of course, groups have objectives other than affecting the outcome of the election contest itself. A common objective, noted above, is generating publicity and support for an issue. For example, by running its provocative billboards, the Canadian Police Association was able to gain considerable media coverage for both the organization and its target issue. Aside from these external objectives, groups sometimes engage in electoral activity to achieve certain objectives within the group. Because elections are highly visible occasions, group involvement can rally the troops by creating the appearance of political activity. Elections also serve as a time for raising money from supporters and recruiting new activists. When asked whether their electoral involvement was successful, several group leaders noted that the recruitment of new activists during the campaign was a welcome, and sometimes unexpected, additional benefit of their electoral activity. In this sense, electoral involvement strengthens not only the group's public image, but also its internal viability.

Interest groups have every reason to continue to involve themselves in election campaigns. To a degree, this means that they compete with parties as political organizations and for the attention of the public. Groups also cooperate with parties, explicitly or implicitly, to pursue common objectives. The increased ideological coherence of some of the parties in the new system has encouraged this cooperation, which would have been far more difficult in the era of brokerage parties. If, however, parties seek to decrease their ideological coherence and become more flexible on policy issues in order to expand their appeal, the potential for this cooperation may wane.

Although interest groups are certainly active during campaigns, their spending does not nearly approach the total amounts spent by parties. In the 1988 election, when interest-group spending reached unprecedented highs, the total cost for their national campaigns was about $4.7 million at a time when the three major parties were spending $36.7 million, almost eight times as much.[30] Although there is no similar estimate available for the 1997 election, the most expensive interest-group activity was undertaken by the Public Service Alliance of Canada (a union representing federal government employees), which spent some $750,000.[31] The second-largest outlay was made by the FOCB, which spent between $250,000 and $500,000. Again, these expenditures did not begin to approach the $34 million spent by the five major parties during the 1997 campaign.

Despite this record of comparatively modest election spending, there is renewed pressure for regulation of interest-group spending. The Supreme Court may have opened the door for the federal government to introduce new legislation limiting independent expenditures. In its ruling on the constitutionality of provisions of Quebec's Referendum Act, the Court included a rebuttal of the Alberta Court of Appeal's 1996 ruling that the restrictions on independent expenditures were an unconstitutional intrusion on freedom of speech. By including this in its judgment, the Supreme Court was essentially inviting the federal government to introduce new legislation.

Some of the parties, including the governing Liberals, have been quick to pick up on this. When the House of Commons Committee on Procedure and House Affairs held hearings regarding the Canada Elections Act in June 1998, representatives of both the Liberal party and the Bloc Québécois advocated restricting interest-group spending. The national director of the Liberal party told the committee that the party is "opposed to any third party intervention. We need to tighten the rules ... If you have something to say, put your name on the ballot."[32] The Reform Party, in contrast, strongly opposed the idea of placing restrictions on interest-group spending, arguing that groups should be given the opportunity to draw attention to issues. What this points to is the considerable variation in parties' understanding of their representative functions in the emerging party system.

In June 1999, the federal government introduced legislation calling for a $150,000 limit on spending by groups or individuals, and requiring disclosure of such expenditures. If the legislation is adopted, its constitutionality will no doubt be tested in the courts. The disclosure provision is entirely new, but is in keeping with recommendations made by the Chief Electoral Officer in recent years.

Representing Interests

As the new party system takes shape, one of its defining characteristics is the considerable variation among parties in how they approach their representative tasks. The Liberal party, and to a degree the NDP and even the Conservatives, have maintained the representative orientations of the third party system. They seek to be national parties, straddling significant cleavages and being as inclusive as possible. In the case of the Liberals, this policy also includes a continued commitment to ensuring that parties maintain a monopoly on representation and articulation of citizens' interests during election campaigns. The new parties do not share the old parties' approach to representation. They do not strive to straddle cleavages, and are content to speak for relatively limited segments of the population. The Reform Party, in particular, makes few efforts to ensure that its caucus is socially inclusive in the terms defined by the old parties. Moreover, Reform rejects the notion that parties should enjoy representational monopolies during elections. The implications of these variations among parties are profound. Parties in the new system offer voters meaningful choices among different representational visions at the cost of heightened interregional conflict, as parties, aside from the Liberals, no longer try to broker regional and linguistic cleavages.

As was the case in the later years of the third party system, interest groups continue to play a significant role in electoral politics. Although they appear to have only the most limited effect on the outcomes of elections, such groups do provide some competition to the parties' ability to monopolize political discussion during the elections. Some of the parties welcome this, while others contest it. Given the difficulties inherent in creating strict limits on interest-group involvement in election campaigns, it is likely that the existing tension between parties and groups as representative institutions will remain a feature of the party system that will organize democratic political competition in the first decades of the twenty-first century.

6

Remaking Party Democracy

While some citizens are dropping out of the party system to participate in Canadian politics through interest groups and social movements, others are pressuring the parties to reform themselves by offering greater grass-roots participatory opportunities. It is because the parties play such a central role in Canadian government – nominating candidates, selecting leaders, setting the policy agenda – that many grass-roots activists are unwilling to move outside the party system but prefer to seek avenues for participation within the parties. Party elites, not wanting to share power, have often resisted these efforts. However, during periods of transition in the party system, when demands for participatory reforms have been strongest, the parties have responded to these expectations by reforming their internal practices and trying to conform to democratic ideals in the hope of retaining their activists and attracting voters. The tension between activists wanting a more direct say in the governance and platform of their party, and elites clinging to their power to control the party's direction, is an ongoing story. In periods of transition between party systems, however, the tension becomes greater and reforms are more likely to be adopted.

A defining characteristic of Canadian politics in the 1990s has been the significant change in public attitudes towards political leaders and institutions. Canadians were once content to defer to the decisions of political elites, thereby allowing parties to broker compromises in the "national interest." This deferential attitude has eroded over the past twenty years, as has Canadians' confidence in their political institutions and parties.[1] This change in attitudes happened gradually, but its effects were becoming apparent by the late 1980s. Canadians' confidence in most political institutions declined substantially over this period, and no group or institution fared worse than political parties. In 1979, 30 percent of Canadians polled by Gallup had a great deal or quite a lot of respect for and confidence in parties; by 1989, the figure was 18 percent; by 1993 it had plummeted to a mere 9 percent.[2]

Changing attitudes and rising public discontent played a significant role in sparking the transition to a new party system in the early 1990s. In this sense, there are clear parallels to the transition periods between earlier party systems. Growing public discontent and unrest early in the twentieth century sparked the formation of new parties as well as changes in the internal practices of the existing parties. During the transition of the 1960s, the impulse for greater popular participation was contained within the existing parties, but resulted in significant changes in the parties' internal practices. Similarly, in the current transition, public discontent has sparked the creation of new parties as well as changes in the internal decision-making practices of the existing parties.

The sources of this change are complex: the first source is a gradual shift in the electorate's political values and attitudes. A second, and related, source is the changing attitudes of partisan activists, who are, after all, part of the electorate. A third source of change is the disruption in patterns of electoral support. The entry of new parties introduces innovation into the political system and sets new standards for party organization and conduct. Moreover, serious electoral losses tend to make parties more open to internal reform; a clear pattern exists of democratizing reforms following on the heels of major electoral defeats.

To understand how and why changing attitudes have brought about changes in the parties' internal practices, it is important to understand what underlies this discontent and the directions in which party reform is being pushed. The most important element of this attitude change is anti-elite sentiment. This encompasses not only a resentment of political elites per se, but also a sense that the elites are incapable of solving political problems. A 1990 survey of Canadians found that 74 percent agreed with the statement that "we would probably solve most of our big national problems if decisions could be brought back to the people at the grassroots."[3] This anti-elite sentiment is closely related to a pervasive sense that political elites are unresponsive to the needs and opinions of the electorate. The same survey found that 79 percent of respondents agreed that "those elected to Parliament seem to lose touch with the people" and 70 percent agreed that governments did not "care much what people like me think."[4] Both of these results reflect mounting discontent. A survey

taken in 1979 had asked the same questions, and found that only 65 percent agreed that MPs lose touch, and 53 percent thought government
didn't care.[5] Taken as a whole, these changing attitudes have created
pressure for more direct citizen influence on decision making, and for a
political leadership that is more responsive to the views of the electorate.
The Mulroney government's decision to hold a national referendum on
the 1992 Charlottetown Constitutional Accord was but one example
of the impact that these changing attitudes have worked on Canadian
politics.

Pressures for meaningful grass-roots participation and responsive leadership have affected both the shape of the new party system (in the form
of the Reform Party) and the internal practices of parties within the system. These internal reforms have included efforts to consult more broadly
with constituents on policy questions, and more inclusive decision-
making processes for activists within the party – especially in the case of
leadership selection. This chapter examines these reforms in some detail,
after noting how similar tensions and changes marked the two earlier
party-system transitions.

Party Democracy in Earlier Transition Periods

Public pressure for increased participation in party affairs is strongest during periods of transition in the party system. One of the important events
marking the transition from the first to the second party system was the
emergence of populist farmers' parties (and governments) in Western
Canada and Ontario. Supporters of these parties – Progressives at the
federal level, with provincial variations such as the United Farmers of
Alberta or of Ontario (the UFA and the UFO) – argued that the traditional parties were elite-driven and unresponsive to the views of ordinary
voters. According to David Laycock, the farmers' populism was distinguished by "a principled rejection of party politics and an insistence on
functionally co-ordinated delegate democracy."[6] Accordingly, the new
activists initially sought to avoid a party-like structure that they believed
would inevitably lead to elite domination. The central tool for accom-
plishing this goal was delegate democracy. Rather than imposing party
discipline on their elected representatives, the UFA and Progressives
encouraged elected members to represent the will of their constituents.
As the 1921 UFA election platform stated, "each elected representative is
answerable directly to the organization in the constituency that elected
him."[7] In the course of this election campaign, many local associations

adopted their own platforms in addition to the provincial platform, and these local platforms "were held to be binding on the representative."[8]

Responding to similar pressures, the Liberal party forever changed leadership selection in Canada by convening the first-ever federal leadership convention in 1919. Prior to this, party leaders were selected by their parliamentary caucuses. While the Liberals' action resulted from a number of concerns, including a regionally unbalanced caucus, they were also responding to local activists' demands for greater participation in party affairs. As John Courtney has written, the parties made the change "to fashion a more 'representative' and 'democratic' leadership selection process."[9] While the new process was still elite-driven, it did provide a voice for the broader party membership.

The next significant change in leadership-selection politics occurred as the second party system was being replaced by the third. Leadership conventions of the 1960s and thereafter hardly resemble the earlier variety. The parties amended their leadership-convention rules to give the party grass roots more power by increasing the number of constituency delegates, decreasing the number of ex officio delegates, and ensuring representation for previously underrepresented groups such as women and youth. A result of this expanded role for grass-roots party activists was greater competition for party leaderships.[10]

At the outset of the third party system, the extra-parliamentary membership claimed for itself the right not only to choose the party leader, but also to oust a sitting leader at its sole discretion – a power previously vested in the parliamentary caucus. The famous case is that of the Conservative party in the 1960s. Party president Dalton Camp ran for re-election in 1966 on a platform that included a promise to call a leadership convention. Camp was re-elected and subsequently called a leadership convention, even though the leadership was not vacant and the party constitution made no provision for such action. At this 1967 convention, incumbent leader John Diefenbaker was soundly defeated. The Liberal party made a similar change at nearly the same time, formally amending its constitution in 1966 to provide for a leadership review vote at the first party assembly following each general election.

At the same time, grass-roots activists in the parties were challenging party elites and demanding greater participation in other aspects of party life, most notably within the New Democratic and the Liberal parties. For the NDP, this took the form of the Waffle movement. The Waffle members were radical activists, many of whom were students or academics, who wanted the party to "waffle to the left."[11] The 1969 Waffle Manifesto espoused a strong economic nationalism, driven by concerns about US domination of the Canadian economy and by a critique of US society as militaristic and racist. Members of the Waffle also sought to increase the role of the NDP's grass-roots activists in setting party policy and to lessen the power of organized labour and the party's parliamentary caucus. In 1972, only three years after the publication of the Waffle Manifesto, the movement came to an end when it was purged from the Ontario provincial party. The Waffle was unsuccessful in its efforts to change the NDP, and its primary legacy is an ongoing distrust of dissenting groups within the party.

Within the Liberal party, grass-roots activists were also calling for greater participation and democracy. A Toronto-based group called Cell 13 was formed in the aftermath of the party's devastating electoral defeat in 1958, and was associated with an effort to keep the party left of centre and to replace the party's old guard with fresh faces. This was not so much a grass-roots effort as a new elite group seeking to replace the old party elite, but their ideals did include greater grass-roots participation. According to Christina McCall-Newman, what the Cell 13 activists "wanted was to make the party truly democratic, to free it from the influence that big business had on St. Laurent and that old-fashioned small-time party bosses had on party organization, and to make it respond to an uncorrupted grassroots."[12] This vision was the blueprint for a decade of reforms to the party, and transformed the radicals into the new party elite. The reforms that took place during the 1960s included a revitalization of riding associations to make them more open and responsive to local concerns, reactivation and strengthening of the party's standing committees, non-scripted national policy meetings in 1966 and 1970, policy-oriented local groups, and the creation of youth and women's commissions. As well, ministers were required to report at every national party convention on the policies adopted by their departments that differed from existing party policies. Party members were then asked to adopt the government policy as party policy.[13] The party also initiated something called the "political cabinet." This expanded cabinet included representatives from the party's non-parliamentary wing. Its purpose was to ensure that political and policy concerns of the wider party membership were considered in government decision making. As David Smith has written, "the belief that policy should be the product of exchange of opinion and not a balancing of interests ... were all new ideas to the party of King and St. Laurent."[14]

Just as the parties experienced pressures to reform their leadership and decision-making procedures during those earlier periods of transition, parties once again are undertaking reforms to accommodate the demands of activists and to present a more inclusive and democratic face to voters. Though all parties have responded to voter demands for more effective participation in some fashion, some have been more receptive than others. One of the characteristics of the new system may be that the parties will substantially differ from each other in the quantity and quality of grass-roots participation within their organizations, whereas in the third party system the major parties largely mirrored each other in this regard. At the outset of the new system, highly participatory partisan organizations are most evident in one of the new parties (Reform), and in the Conservative party, which is attempting to revitalize itself after its 1993 election debacle. The New Democrats launched a renewal process in the wake of the 1993 election, and adopted a few reforms as a result. Before they returned to office in 1993, the Liberals had begun an organizational reform process, but once they returned to their customary role as the government party, they became somewhat more cautious and deliberate.[15]

Party Democracy in a New Participatory Era

Representing Constituents
One of the primary functions of the political party is representation of public opinion in Parliament. Debates concerning how legislators should approach the task of representing constituents are as old as representative democracy itself. Much has been written regarding whether the legislators' primary responsibility is to reflect the views of their constituents (the delegate model of representation) or their own personal views (the trustee model), or to always support their party's policy positions (the party-discipline model).[16] The delegate model is currently in vogue among Canadian voters. In their study of Canadians' views of their political institutions, André Blais and Elisabeth Gidengil discovered not only that Canadians believe their MPs to be unresponsive, but also that they strongly support a revised form of parliamentary representation – three-quarters expressed support for the proposition that MPs should vote free from party discipline, and two-thirds agreed that MPs should follow the views of people in their ridings.[17]

This voter sentiment has not, however, led to substantial change in the role of the MP in Parliament. Despite some 1993 campaign rhetoric that they would provide individual MPs with more freedom in the House of Commons, the Chrétien Liberals have enforced party discipline and punished those who dare break party ranks on important issues. For example, in 1995, long-time MP and former cabinet minister Warren Allmand was removed from his position as chair of the Commons' Justice Committee for voting against the government's budget. For their part, neither the Conservatives nor the NDP show any evidence of changing their disciplinary practices. This said, while party discipline in the House of Commons remains strong, there are signs that an increasing number of MPs are willing to ignore their party whips on occasion. In a 1998 study of party voting, Joseph Wearing found that "the last three parliaments have witnessed the largest number of dissenting votes since 1945 and the number grows with each successive parliament."[18]

It has been the Reform Party that has capitalized on voter discontent and been in the forefront in pushing for a more strictly delegate-style role for its parliamentarians. As part of its political-accountability package, Reform's platform supports the use of referendum and recall. Reform argues that the threat of recall would provide a strong incentive for MPs to vote in the House of Commons in a manner that reflects their constituents' wishes. (Though experience in British Columbia, the only province that currently has recall legislation, provides no support for that claim.)

Consistent with its support for recall and referendum, the party's constitution calls for individual MPs to give their first loyalty to their constituents and not to their political party.[19] Reform MPs are expected to vote in a manner that is consistent with the views of their constituents on policy issues, even when those views are inconsistent with party policy as adopted by party members at an assembly. This provision does not provide MPs the freedom to deviate from their party's position whenever they wish. Reform MPs are required to establish to their leader's satisfaction that their constituents hold a particular view on a policy question and that this view differs from the party's official position. Only then is the member permitted to deviate from the party line with impunity.

Use of this provision requires that Reform MPs be able to determine, with a fair amount of precision, their constituents' views on specific policy questions. It is not the views of local party members or Reform activists that are of interest, but the views of all constituents. Whereas the Progressives of the 1920s sought to represent the views of local party activists, Reform MPs' first responsibility is to their constituents. This creates a real hurdle for MPs wanting to deviate from the party line. A hundred responses to a survey included in an MP's regular householder mailing, a few dozen phone calls from concerned constituents, or the opinions of the few dozen constituents the MP talks with during a trip home are not sufficient evidence of the views of constituents to permit divergence from the official party position. At best, these efforts result in MPs having partial and impressionistic information concerning constituents' views on specific policy questions. No MPs are able to communicate personally with anything approaching a majority of their constituents, and there is no reason to believe that those they do communicate with are representative of their constituents as a whole.

What separates Reform's delegate model from earlier approaches is the party's attempts to use modern communication technologies to facilitate the participation of many more voters than was ever before imagined possible. By availing themselves of new technology, the parties – in particular, Reform – are attempting to communicate directly with voters, not simply with activist party members. Serious efforts in this regard have involved Reform MPs using various means to inform their constituents about a policy question, and then utilizing telephone and computer automation to record the constituents' views.

In 1994, a group of Calgary-area Reform MPs used cable television in conjunction with telephone automation in an attempt to determine constituents' views regarding physician-assisted suicide. The Reform MPs first organized a cable television program that presented a full and balanced debate of the issue, and then invited viewers to telephone a 1-900 number and express their opinion. Reform MP Ted White engaged in a similar exercise with his North Vancouver constituents on the issue of reforming the Young Offenders Act. White communicated with his constituents on the issue through mailings and newspaper advertisements and also encouraged them to record their views by telephoning a 1-900 number.[20]

In these cases the MPs were genuinely interested in learning and reflecting the views of their constituents on these particular issues, and they expended great effort and expense in attempting to determine these views. After his constituents voiced strong support for legislation allowing physician-assisted suicide, Preston Manning reversed his earlier opposition to such legislation and announced that, "if a government bill was presented to Parliament tomorrow permitting physician-assisted suicide ... the participating MPs would vote for it in accordance with the expression of those constituents."[21]

Several MPs and political parties have used the Internet to communicate with their constituents and to gather their opinions on policy matters. Manitoba Liberal MP Reg Alcock has been in the forefront of this activity. Alcock has a home page on the World Wide Web that provides voters with access to information such as the Liberals' campaign "Red Book," and that asks voters for their opinions on policy-related questions. For example, Alcock has asked constituents to send him by electronic mail their responses to a series of questions concerning social-policy reform.

Voters have not participated in these projects with much enthusiasm. Reform's efforts in Calgary and North Vancouver have stimulated the greatest participation rates: slightly more than 1,500 voters phoned in their views on physician-assisted suicide, while 4,600 (less than 7 percent of eligible voters) participated in White's televote on the Young Offenders Act. Nevertheless, the numbers participating certainly provide the sponsors with the opinions of more constituents than can be contacted through more traditional communication channels. However, considering that all participants in the projects are self-selected, there is no guarantee that the higher number of voters makes the results any more representative of the opinion of all constituents. The Calgary-area Reform MPs acknowledged this when they coupled their physician-assisted suicide telephone poll with a scientific survey of their constituents on the question before deciding what position to take.

Some users of the technology, however, have not understood that the responses they have generated may not be representative of the broader community view. For example, White stated that "voter participation was lower than we predicted it would be when we announced the referendum about seven weeks ago ... Even so the total was many times greater than any opinion poll conducted in the area. People with polling experience will tell you that voting patterns are established within a few hundred calls so referendum '94 [White's teledemocracy project] represents a very significant result."[22] But this is not true. The results of White's project reveal nothing more than the views of the 4,600 constituents who participated in the project. In the absence of a rigorous sampling process, there is no reason to believe that those who responded hold views that are similar to the more than 90 percent of constituents whose views were never ascertained. The low level of participation, and the concomitant diminished usefulness of the information gathered, are probably an important reason why White's project has not been duplicated by other

Reform MPs. The party and its MPs have yet to find a way to successfully use these technologies to determine their constituents' views on matters of public policy.

At first glance there appears to be a contradiction between the voters' apparent eagerness to have a more direct say in public decision making and their low response levels when Reform has offered them the opportunity to participate. This pattern probably derives from the public's realistic perception of the effectiveness of these exercises. As even White has acknowledged, voting in an opposition MP's telephone referendum is not the same thing as having a direct say on the outcome of a policy question. In a list of factors explaining why the participation rate was considerably lower than expected, White suggested that voters believed the Justice minister's proposals would be pushed through Parliament with little or no input, and thus felt that their participation in this project would ultimately have no influence over the government's decision.[23] This is a reflection of our political tradition rather than an inherent shortcoming of the technology. It does, however, present something of a catch-22 for the Reform MPs: they are willing to reflect the views of their constituents if they can determine them, yet voters are reluctant to participate in these projects since they believe their views will not have an impact on the final policy decisions. Thus it is difficult to assess the success of these new technologies in facilitating communication between voters and parties when the principal efforts in this regard have been made by an opposition party with limited opportunity to substantively influence public policy. It remains to be seen if the expansion in availability of the technology and its use by Reform result in voter pressure being placed on the old-line parties to adopt more of these techniques.

US political scientists Christopher Arterton and Benjamin Barber have suggested that advances in communication technology offer the possibility of true plebiscitary democracy.[24] The lessons of the Reform Party's experiments suggest that this is not yet true in Canada. While at present there is a problem insofar as the technology is not universally available, the more fundamental issue of the nature of parliamentary parties and their relationship with voters needs to be resolved before this technology can even be considered for use in this way. Many students of Canadian politics would not agree that plebiscitary democracy, even if practicable, would be a good thing for Canada. Practitioners of brokerage politics have often resisted effective grass-roots participation in policy making on the grounds that it would complicate the processes of consensus building and accommodation on difficult issues touching region and language. Of course, an electoral victory by the Reform Party could significantly fast-track the implementation of these changes, and could highlight the tensions between Reform's populist stance and the Canadian practice of responsible government.

While the old-line parties, and, in particular, the governing Liberals, have not moved nearly as far as Reform on this question, there has been some movement. For example, some parties and individual MPs now routinely run Internet polls through their Web sites. As well, the increasingly common practice of parties publishing detailed policy plans during election campaigns – and referring to these as a contract with voters – reflects the parties' desire to be seen as more responsive. In the 1997 campaign, this desire led to the Liberals' "Securing Our Future Together"; the Conservatives' "Let the Future Begin" document; and Reform's early publishing of "A Fresh Start for Canadians." It now seems unlikely that any major party leader would suggest that election campaigns are a poor time for substantive policy debate, as Conservative leader and prime minister Kim Campbell did in 1993.

Party Decision Making

Parties have long struggled with the question of how best to involve their grass-roots activists in their internal decision-making processes. This can include everything from setting election strategy to the selection of a party leader, to the determination of party policy. Significant attention was paid to this issue in the earlier transitions, and the emergence of Reform as a populist party and the electoral setbacks of two of the three traditional parties have prompted new attempts to empower party activists.

Survey data collected after the 1993 election illustrate the high degree of discontent felt by party activists in the old-line parties over their (limited) role in party decision making. For example, a majority of Conservative riding association presidents and more than a quarter of Liberals believed that insufficient means existed for local associations to report their views on matters of public policy to their national party. Similarly, only one in twenty Conservatives and half of Liberal riding presidents believed that their national party carefully considered the views of local associations in drafting its 1993 election platform.[25] The Reform Party has capitalized on this grass-roots discontent by adopting a comprehensive and wide-ranging approach to internal democracy.

One of the most basic ways of acknowledging the importance of local constituency activists in a national party is by providing meaningful recognition of them as members of the party. Reform was the first federal party to have its members join the national party directly, thus creating an unmediated relationship between the grass roots and the party's national office.[26] Reform's unique relationship with its membership was illustrated in the run-up to the 1997 election. On the weekend the election was called, Reform held a convention in Toronto to which all party members were invited. The party's senior campaign strategists (including pollsters and media experts) laid out Reform's election plan and strategy in substantial detail. While the plan was not up for substantive debate and revision, the exercise demonstrated significant transparency in the party, and a covenant between the party's leadership and its membership not seen in the third party system. The party leadership believes that grassroots activists are significant stakeholders in their election efforts and that success can be achieved only if they understand and agree with the national strategy. This view reflects Reform's explicit commitment to maintaining strong ties between its national office and its grass roots. The party's constitution establishes an "Executive Council-Party Caucus Liaison Committee." This committee's mandate is to "ensure a close and harmonious working relationship between the Reform Party grassroots membership and the caucus of Reformers elected to Parliament."[27]

At the heart of the Reform efforts to be a bottom-up party is a policy process that is dominated by constituency activists. The party's "Blue Book" is the official policy "bible" of the Reform Party. The party's election platform consists only of policies found in the "Blue Book," and the only way a policy position can be included in the "Blue Book" is for it to be adopted by the membership at a party convention. In contrast, the Liberals and Conservatives do not have a party-policy book from which their election platforms are drawn. While the Liberals made much of their 1993 and 1997 campaign "Red Books," the party's membership played no direct role in deciding what would be included in them.

There is some elite scepticism concerning just how democratic the Reform Party is. Some observers point to a pattern of the party leader consistently getting his way on important matters.[28] This results from Manning's position as the charismatic founding leader of the party, his strong control over the party's national office, and an absence of plausible alternative leadership. That Manning has to this point been consistently able to win widespread party support on key issues does not detract from the nature of grass-roots democracy in the party; instead, it illustrates Manning's nurturing of the membership, and their resulting confidence in him. The party's turning to its membership to decide by a referendum whether to pursue the United Alternative strategy, and the fact that 40 percent of the membership voted against the leader's position, illustrate the party's commitment to letting its membership make crucial decisions even when the outcome is far from certain.

That grass-roots Reformers believe their voices are listened to is illustrated in the results of the 1993 constituency association survey referred to above. A staggering 98 percent of riding association presidents believe that their participation in Reform assemblies is worthwhile and that their views on policy are given careful consideration by the national party, compared with only three-quarters of Liberals, and fewer than half of Conservatives.[29] Unlike his success in winning support from the party membership, Manning has, however, not always been able to win the full support of his caucus colleagues. On these occasions the Reform leader has often responded harshly, both suspending and expelling dissenting MPs from the caucus.

Of the three traditional parties, the Conservatives have been the most proactive in responding to these efforts by Reform. In the wake of their 1993 electoral devastation, and loss of significant voter support to Reform, the Conservatives took steps in this direction as part of their reorganization process. To a considerable extent, the Tories' efforts are a consequence of the rise of the Reform Party, whose leadership early on identified dissatisfaction among Conservative voters and made a conscious effort to present themselves to disaffected Tories as being more responsive. In an attempt to rebuild the party and to recapture lost voters, the Conservatives embarked on a rebuilding process that concentrated on finding ways to increase the role of the grass roots in party decision making. Following the 1993 election, the party hierarchy consistently heard that one of the causes of the party's downfall was that the national office was too isolated from its constituency associations. Party members complained that there was little place for meaningful membership participation in important party decision making. In response, the Conservatives have taken several steps to increase their members' role (both real and symbolic), including creation of a national membership program, changing the party's decision-making structure, and developing plans to create a permanent policy foundation. Pierre Fortier, who was president of the Conservative party during the reorganization, summarized the party's blueprint for reform in three words: transparency, accountability, and communication.

One of the first steps taken by the party was the introduction of a national membership program patterned after Reform's. In return for a ten-dollar annual membership fee, the party issues a membership card from its Ottawa office. The party's National Membership Program Coordinator explains that the program has been quite successful as it gives individual supporters a sense of belonging to and ownership in the party.

The party also responded by creating a new decision-making body: the "National Council." The council is primarily made up of the local association presidents from all 301 ridings. This new body is vested with the "management and control of the activities of the party" between national conventions.[30] The council appears to have genuinely elevated the status of the riding associations in party decision making, and is proving an effective mechanism for increasing the flow of communication between local party members and the national office (in both directions). An example is that details of the party's campaign budget were presented to the council for their review and approval prior to the 1997 campaign, a significant change from earlier practices that kept such information restricted to a small number of central campaign planners.

In the Conservatives' restructuring process, special emphasis has been placed on the role of the party membership in policy development. The party's leadership found substantial dissatisfaction among its membership over a perceived lack of accountability by the parliamentary party to the grass roots. For example, members complained that many of the policy resolutions adopted at the party's 1991 convention were ignored, and that "there are few mechanisms within the Party to provide for follow-up to ensure accountability."[31]

In response to these sentiments, the party's restructuring task force suggested the creation of a permanent policy foundation within the party to act as "a mechanism for Party member and riding level involvement in, and input to, the policy process."[32] The policy foundation "could be designed to forge some new and important linkages between rank and file Party members and the policy process," and it could "report regularly to the Party membership on the progress made in implementing the resolutions from the previous national policy conference."[33] This suggestion was adopted by the party and included in its new constitution, which commits the party to "a continuous policy process and a permanent policy resource which respects and encourages the participation of

Members."[34] The party's National Council is given responsibility to "facilitate the full and continuing involvement of all Members ... in the formulation, discussion and dissemination of policy proposals and resolutions," and to "facilitate and promote on a regular and timely basis responses from the leadership to Members, constituency associations ... on policy proposals and resolutions put forward by them."[35] While the party has made these commitments to its members, it has not yet succeeded in putting in place a permanent policy foundation or completely abandoning its traditional election-time centralization.

Grass-roots involvement in party policy making is meaningful only if there is some connection between the policy positions of the party and the positions taken by its parliamentary caucus. This is a tension that is as old as organized political parties. It was one of the leading concerns in the formation of the farmers' parties in the 1920s, and in the internal reforms to the Liberal party in the 1960s. Parties in the third system made little progress in striking an effective balance in this regard, and so the predictable cycle of caucus domination followed by a period of upheaval, with the extra-parliamentary party members demanding a more effective role in policy making, has continued. Even Reform struggles with this question. It has established a "Democratic Populism Taskforce," with a mandate to grapple with the issue of how best to ensure an effective role for the party's grass-roots membership in a future Reform government. If Reform is successful in striking a new balance, it may well set in motion a series of meaningful and lasting reforms in the old-line parties as they, too, struggle to keep up with public demands for more direct, unmediated participation, and their local activists' desire for a more meaningful role in party decision making. But considering past experience, it is likely that any such rebalancing will only be temporary and will itself be challenged by party activists in future reform cycles during periods of party-system transformation.

Leadership Selection
There has been a steady progression towards increased public participation in party-leadership selection. In the first system, leaders were chosen by the parliamentary caucuses; in the second, by elite-dominated conventions; and, in the third, by conventions comprising mainly delegates representing constituency associations and, in the case of the NDP, labour unions. In the new party system, leaders are being chosen through a direct vote of the parties' grass-roots membership. The Bloc was the first

federal party to use direct election, having selected Gilles Duceppe by a mail ballot of their membership in March 1997.[36] The Conservatives subsequently selected Joe Clark by a direct vote of their membership, and both the Reform and the Liberal party have amended their party constitution to allow for future direct votes.[37] In their most recent leadership convention, the New Democrats used a combination of direct vote and delegate convention. To understand the parties' adoption of direct elections, it is necessary to examine their experience with the leadership conventions and their motivation for changing selection methods.

Leadership conventions in the third party system substantially increased grass-roots participation in the parties. These leadership contests centred on organizational efforts to mobilize new party members in support of a favoured candidate. Party-membership rules were liberally written, allowing the supporters of leadership candidates to enrol hundreds of new members in each riding. Parties routinely experienced a dramatic increase in their membership rolls during the delegate-selection process – more so than during any other period of party life. The reason is simple: leadership politics touches more party activists and generates more local organizational activity than even a general election. In an election there will inevitably be a number of local associations that, because they have either no fear of losing or no hope of winning, will mobilize few new members and run a low-intensity campaign. In a leadership campaign, there are no such constituencies. All riding associations send voting delegates to the convention, and so their delegate-selection meetings are all potential campaign arenas for the candidates.

The local associations benefit from this member mobilization principally through an infusion of funds in the form of membership dues. Potentially, the scores of new members may also form an organizational foundation for an association's efforts in the next election campaign. In practice, however, many of these new members are transient partisans with little connection to the local association. Unlike nomination and general election campaigns, constituency-level activity in leadership contests is typically managed by outsiders who sweep into a constituency to direct a campaign designed to capture the local delegates, and then move on. These activists are concerned solely with the selection of delegates favouring their candidate, and not with the long-term interests of the riding association. Having a slate of committed delegates virtually imposed on a constituency association by a national leadership campaign team often causes distress for long-time local party supporters, who see their association flooded at this critical juncture by instant members, many of whom will never again attend a party meeting. That the mobilization is normally orchestrated by forces from outside the riding and, in urban centres, often includes the recruitment of large numbers of visible minorities and members of ethnic communities not previously active in the party, only sharpens the tensions.

In those ridings managing to escape large-scale mobilization of new members and slate voting, the process is often not a deliberative one in which members cast meaningful ballots on the leadership question. Members choose delegates, who are then free to vote (secretly) as they wish at the convention. Delegate candidates often do not declare which leadership candidate they prefer (two-fifths of 1993 Conservative delegates made no such declaration to their riding associations) and, accordingly, the selection of delegates in these ridings has little to do with the leadership choice.[38] Data from the most recent leadership contests in the federal Liberal and Conservative parties indicate that a substantial majority of convention delegates are chosen for reasons other than their preferred leadership candidate. Party members report that the most important factor is "how active the delegate candidate has been in party affairs."[39]

Conventions have also been criticized for not being representative of either the broader party membership or the electorate. Leadership-convention delegates have typically been disproportionately male, well educated, financially well-off, and young. For example, the most recent traditional leadership conventions of the federal New Democrats (1989), Liberals (1990), and Conservatives (1993) had female representation of 37, 44, and 34 percent, respectively; four-fifths of delegates at all three conventions had some postsecondary education; and a majority of Liberals and Conservatives had family incomes in excess of $60,000.[40]

In recent years, a growing awareness of the shortcomings in the delegate-selection process, the skewed demographics of convention delegates, and changing norms of democratic participation have undermined the legitimacy of the delegate-convention process. As a result, Canadian parties are rushing to abandon it for systems in which all local members will have a direct vote for the party's leader.

The parties' principal motivations in adopting direct election have been the need to rebuild flagging memberships, and a desire not to appear less democratic than their opponents. Initially it was the provincial parties that led in the adoption of direct election processes, particularly those seeking a way to revitalize their membership after electoral defeat or from a low standing in public-opinion polls. Within a short period, however, direct election came to be seen by most partisans as a more legitimate and democratic selection method, and the pressures were great for all parties to adopt the new process. The federal parties were not immune to these pressures. The early success of the Reform Party gave increased credibility to the message of direct and universal participation in political decision making. Coupled with the decimation of two of the older parties in 1993, and their need to revitalize a dispirited membership, this served as a catalyst, making direct election the standard mechanism for selecting federal party leaders in the new system.

This is very clear in the case of the NDP, which would not have changed its mechanism of leadership selection had it not been for the results of the 1993 election. The idea of electing party leaders directly was not entirely new to the party: the 1989 leadership convention had adopted a resolution allowing the party to explore the feasibility of a new selection method and to report back to the convention. The report that resulted did not endorse the idea of direct election, and in 1991 both the federal council and delegates to the federal convention voted not to alter the process. As Keith Archer and Alan Whitehorn observed, "the party might well have continued for several years along the same course had it not been for the 1993 electoral fiasco. The status quo no longer appeared adequate."[41] In the aftermath of the 1993 election, the NDP launched into an extensive renewal process that brought together party activists to discuss policy and internal party organization. In the course of the renewal process, activists and party leaders once again discussed the possibility of implementing a new method of choosing a leader. The idea of directly electing a leader gained support in some segments of the party, which saw it as a promising way to revitalize the party's sagging electoral fortunes. As it happened, however, Audrey McLaughlin's resignation as party leader meant that the 1995 convention, intended to be the culmination of a reform process, was turned into a leadership convention. Designing a new process for choosing their leader on the fly, the party adopted a curious hybrid of primary elections and a delegate convention.

Several variations in the conduct of direct elections have been tried at the provincial level.[42] Some parties have held telephone votes, others have used mail-in ballots, and still others have invited all party members to vote either in their ridings or at convention sites. Indeed, some parties have used combinations of these different practices. While each process has had somewhat different results, important generalizations can be made regarding the impact on party democracy.

Direct election processes allow a far greater number of party members to cast an unmediated vote on the leadership question than conventions ever could. A typical convention in the third system would have any-where from several hundred delegates in the smaller provincial parties to several thousand in the federal parties. These were the only party members who cast ballots directly on the leadership question. Tens of thousands of other party members participated in the delegate-selection meetings, but, as noted above, these decisions were often made on bases other than the leadership question (it is estimated that between 70,000 and 100,000 members participated in the delegate-selection meetings for the federal Conservatives and Liberals in the 1980s and 1990s).[43]

Rates of participation in direct elections have varied, depending on the political circumstances of the party and the type of electoral process used.[44] Provincial parties replacing an incumbent premier through direct election have enjoyed very high participation rates: the Alberta Conservatives and the Parti Québécois had more than 78,000 and 97,000 voters, respectively. Smaller parties selecting leaders during periods of internal turmoil and weakened popular support have enjoyed less-favourable participation rates. For example, the Manitoba Liberals, Saskatchewan Conservatives, British Columbia Reform, and British Columbia Social Credit each had between 2,000 and 3,000 members participate. Federal parties' initial experiences with direct election have also varied. In the primaries held the months before the NDP 1995 leadership convention, fewer than 23,000 votes were cast, representing 28 percent of eligible members. More than 50,000 participated in the Bloc's vote in 1997, representing about 45 percent of party members. In 1998, 48,000 Conservative party members participated in the process that selected Joe Clark as the new leader, a turnout rate of 52 percent.[45] While we can conclude from these early experiments that more party members cast ballots in direct elections than in conventions, it is not clear that more routinely participate in direct elections than in delegate-selection meetings. What is clear, though, is that more party members are now casting a direct, unmediated vote on the leadership question.

Participation in direct elections is also accessible to a broader range of party members as it requires far less in terms of time and money than does attendance at an out-of-town convention. Depending on the type of process used, one can vote in a matter of minutes without ever leaving home.[46] As a result, direct-election voters have been more representative of the broader electorate than have convention delegates. Studies of direct-election voters in the Alberta Conservative, and British Columbia, Alberta, and Nova Scotia Liberal, contests all measure slightly different voter characteristics but generally show that direct elections have more representative electorates than do conventions.[47] In these direct elections, the proportion of women and senior citizens increased, while the number of very young voters declined. In the case of the British Columbia Liberals, the percentage of voters with a university education decreased, from nearly two-thirds in the convention to half in the direct vote. On all of these indicators, the direct-election voters were more representative of their provincial electorates than were delegates at the parties' preceding conventions.

While direct election facilitates the meaningful participation of the rank-and-file party membership, there is concern that it does not provide for sufficient communication, both between the leadership candidates and the party members, and among the members. Because there are normally far fewer voters in conventions than in direct elections, convention delegates are far more likely to have personal communication with the leadership hopefuls than are direct-election voters. For example, less than one-third of the electorate in the 1992 Alberta Conservative direct election had met any of the candidates, while a large majority of delegates to the party's 1985 convention had met at least one candidate, and almost two-thirds had met the winning candidate. Similarly, only one in five direct-election voters attended an all-candidates forum, compared with a strong majority of convention voters.[48]

In direct elections, voters' information sources are more like those available in general elections. Thus direct-election voters are more dependent on the media for information about the candidates. The traditional lines of internal party communication, so very important in leadership conventions, are replaced by general appeals through the mass media. Gone are the opportunities that convention delegates have to observe the candidates in person during bear-pit sessions, candidate speeches, and various social functions hosted by the candidates.

Convention delegates also benefit from the opportunity to communicate with one another at the leadership convention. Delegates spend several days at the convention site, visiting with their fellow party members and discussing the leadership choice with voters from different socioeconomic backgrounds and different geographic regions. When voting day arrives, all delegates are assembled in one hall and therefore can develop a sense of collective decision making. Direct elections, on the other hand, are often very atomistic affairs. Voters in contests using the telephone or mail can participate from their homes without ever meeting another party member.

This lack of opportunity for collective decision making poses particular problems for those traditional parties concerned with the brokering of interests. In parties with deep regional, linguistic, or rural/urban cleavages, the convention offers the possibility of consensus-building after an often long and divisive leadership contest. Though convention participation is limited to party elites and local activists, these are precisely the individuals most preoccupied with the long-term interests of the party, and thus with the greatest incentive to try to leave the convention united. John Courtney reports that "the responsiveness of candidates to regional concerns was clearly a factor for some, though not a majority, of the delegates attending the 1983 and 1984 conventions. A candidate's perceived responsiveness to regional interests was 'very influential' in the first ballot vote decisions of 40 percent of the Liberal delegates and 45 percent of the Conservative delegates."[49]

In ensuring that regional voices continue to be heard in leadership-selection contests, federal parties have adopted rules aimed at maintaining equitable regional representation. For example, concerned about their status as a national party, the Conservatives are concerned that candidates not limit their efforts to those regions where they are able to sign up the greatest number of members, thereby ignoring other parts of the country. This dilemma was addressed in the traditional leadership convention by allocating an equal number of delegates to each riding – regardless of the degree of party strength in the riding.[50] In moving to a direct vote, the Conservatives determined to replicate that feature of the old process and allocated all ridings the same number of votes (100): actual riding vote totals were reported in percentage terms so that the official vote count totalled 30,100 (301 ridings × 100). As before, this system encourages candidates to campaign and organize in areas where the party is weak. A few dozen members signed up in a moribund riding association can have more impact on the final outcome than will the same number of recruits in a vibrant association that already has several hundred members.

The type of leadership-selection process adopted not only has meaning for questions of party democracy, but also influences the leadership choice itself. The NDP's use of a mixture of direct election and delegate convention illustrates how the two processes can produce very different outcomes. All party members were eligible to vote in regional primary elections or in a series of union primaries held a month before the party's 1995 leadership convention. In order to compete at the convention, a candidate needed either to win one of the primaries or to take more than 15 percent of the combined total vote. One of the four candidates did not meet this minimum and so was forced to withdraw after the primaries. However, the results of the membership vote were not binding on the convention and appeared to have little influence on the delegates. Lorne Nystrom, who had far outdistanced his rivals, having earned 45 percent of the members' votes, compared with only 19 percent for Alexa McDonough, was quickly eliminated after a third-place finish on the first ballot, while McDonough went on to be acclaimed the new leader.

While the parties generally agree that direct election is a more democratic process, they are concerned with the potential loss of publicity generated by the leadership convention. The *Montreal Gazette* captured this sentiment when it said of the Bloc contest, "It's a highly democratic process and will leave the new leader with a strong mandate from the party rank-and-file but it doesn't create the suspense a traditional campaign does."[51] The Bloc responded to this concern by staging an elaborate party convention in Montreal for the announcement of the mail-in results. More than 2,000 party members attended the well-orchestrated, made-for-TV event. While lacking the excitement of a traditional leadership convention, the event made for good television as the results (ballots were counted by party workers earlier in the day but kept secret) were released in bits and pieces during the first hour of the ninety-minute program. Party organizers orchestrated the event down to the minute, planning for the final results to be announced at 7:03 p.m. to allow the winning candidate time to make an acceptance speech before Radio-Canada turned its television cameras to "La Soirée du Hockey Molson." Veterans of leadership conventions, which often end well past the hour of television prime time, may appreciate this precise stage management.

The decline of the leadership convention in favour of direct elections is an important part of the story of the decline of the third party system. The leadership convention effectively encapsulated the idea of pan-Canadianism and accommodation, bringing together activists from across the country to form alliances and make trade-offs. Delegates to leadership conventions constituted a sort of sub-elite empowered to make decisions on behalf of the party. With direct election, the intermediaries are eliminated and grass-roots members have a direct say in choosing new party leaders without having their preferences filtered through convention delegates. Direct-election processes capture the essence of the changing norms in party democracy as they allow more members an opportunity for meaningful, unmediated participation. What remains to be seen is whether these reforms are sufficient to satisfy voter demands, or whether they are a way station en route to a system of US-style party primaries.

The move to direct election leaves unanswered the question of who the leader is ultimately responsible to. In the third party system, the leader was chosen by party convention and was responsible to the convention through the mechanism of leadership review. Parties are now beginning to grapple with the issue of leadership review in the case of leaders chosen by direct election. At least one party, the Nova Scotia Liberals, has conducted a review vote in which all party members were eligible to participate. In that case, the party became so concerned about infiltration of the process by trade unionists and civil servants unhappy with the premier that it postponed the vote for almost a year. The federal Liberals have adopted a process by which two different party bodies vote on whether to call a leadership convention following each general election. The first vote is by all party members attending delegate-selection meetings for the next national convention, and the second is by the delegates to the convention. While the party's constitution does not address how the votes are to be counted, in practice the votes of the two groups have been combined and released as one result. While party members have been overwhelmingly opposed to a leadership review following Chrétien's two majority victories, the process leaves open the possibility that in a contentious vote after an electoral defeat, a close riding-level vote could be overturned by convention delegates, a situation that may create significant questions of legitimacy.

Party Democracy

For the third time in history, a period of transition between party systems has seen Canadian parties work to democratize their internal affairs. The electorate's antipathy towards political elites, its demand for politicians who are responsive, and its demand for opportunities to participate directly in political decision making have pushed the parties to reform their internal practices and, in some cases, to rethink how their parliamentary caucuses should approach the job of representing their constituents. It remains to be seen how, or even whether, these reforms will be institutionalized, and to what extent they will be adequate to stem the tide of public dissatisfaction and discontent with political parties and leadership in Canada.

7
Paying for Parties

No matter how profoundly the Canadian party system is transformed, the parties' need for money to maintain their organizations and to contest elections remains constant. From funds spent on buying whiskey for voters in the post-Confederation era, to the millions spent on polling, advertising, and focus groups today, parties have faced a continuing imperative to raise money. That said, the sources from which this money is raised, the way it is spent, and the way it is regulated have all evolved significantly. The most notable change to party financing in Canada occurred in 1974, when Parliament enacted regulations limiting election spending, requiring disclosure of the source of contributions, offering reimbursements of parties' and candidates' election expenses, and providing a tax credit designed to encourage small contributions to parties by individuals.

By the late 1980s, this regulatory regime was under challenge from a number of sources. Several scandals gave the appearance of undue influence of large contributions, pro-free trade interest groups spent heavily in the 1988 campaign, and spending in nomination and leadership campaigns seemed out of control. All this created the impetus to reconsider, if not to reform, the regulation of campaign finance. The Mulroney government in 1989 appointed the Royal Commission on Electoral Reform and Party Financing (Lortie Commission), giving it a mandate to study and recommend reforms to all aspects of the regulation of political finance. The Lortie Commission's report recommended a number of significant changes to the regulatory regime, but few were adopted before the cataclysmic election of 1993.

As the new party system emerges, the basic elements of the regulatory regime remain in place but are being called into question by the two new parties and are facing a series of challenges on the basis of the Charter of Rights and Freedoms. Once the question of political finance regulation is again on the table for discussion, there will be little of the cosy consensus among parties that marked such discussions in the old party system. Rather, both the Bloc and Reform will be advocating approaches to the question that are vastly different from those of the old parties.

Party Finance from 1867 to 1974

During the first century after Confederation, there was little effective regulation of campaign finance. Legislation adopted in 1874 required candidates to disclose how and where campaign funds were spent. The law applied only to candidates, as political parties were not recognized in law. No body was responsible for enforcing the legislation, and no sanction could be made against losing candidates who did not comply. Legislation adopted in 1908 and 1920 prohibited candidates from accepting contributions from corporations or trade unions. The 1920 legislation also required that candidates disclose the names of all contributors. The law ignored the existence of political parties, so there was no restriction or requirement for disclosure of contributions to parties. The ban on contributions by corporations and labour unions was repealed in 1930.[1]

These laws were ineffective, largely because they ignored the important role that the national political parties played in raising money. Prior to the First World War, party leaders were personally charged with the task of raising enough money for their party to contest elections. Distribution of campaign funds from the leader was an important means of fostering the loyalty of MPs, so fund-raising was a useful tool for party leaders as they sought to control their parties. The bulk of the money came from corporate contributions, mainly the railways, banks, and other major business undertakings, but in some cases party leaders went into personal debt in order to obtain the necessary campaign funds.[2] These funds were transferred to the party's candidates and spent in local contests. Because party finances were entirely unregulated, there was no record of the source of contributions or of the amounts transferred from the national to the local level. Once funds reached the local level, they were used to fight the election on the ground. According to André Siegfried, writing in 1907, "in each local centre the candidate chooses four or five influential men ... He hands them sums of $20, $40, or $60, which it is understood that they are to expend in the interest of the cause. Naturally a portion of this money stops en route."[3] These funds were then used to hire a campaign office and encourage voters to support the candidate.

It is therefore not surprising that party finance during this era was characterized by practices that would, in the contemporary period, be considered inappropriate or corrupt. Various scandals erupted when railway or other interests contributed significant sums to parties in return for policy concessions. Notable among these cases were the Pacific scandal of 1873 and the Beauharnois affair in the 1930s. In 1873, Prime Minister Macdonald was found taking large campaign contributions from the promoters of the Canadian Pacific Railway, and it led to the collapse of the Conservative government and its electoral defeat the following year.[4] In 1930, the Liberals under Mackenzie King accepted substantial contributions from the Beauharnois Power Company, which was seeking concessions for developing power on the St. Lawrence River. King admitted that his party was "in the valley of humiliation" as a result of this exposure, but denied the connection between governmental concessions and the contributions.[5]

The Beauharnois affair notwithstanding, the excesses of the post-Confederation period were generally avoided from the 1920s on. At the local level, alcohol was no longer a major campaign expense. As E.E. Harrill notes, "candidates admitted that in small home meetings they might hand beer around. They said, however, that such refreshments no longer are considered an expensive campaign item."[6] Rather, the major election expenses for national parties were the leader's tour, organization of party headquarters (including salaries), national radio and newspaper advertising, and contributions to candidates. In this era, the party's leader was no longer personally responsible for fund-raising as well-connected party supporters were charged with the task of soliciting contributions. For the most part, the party leaders were both uninvolved in fund-raising and deliberately kept themselves unaware of the sources of contributions.

Patterns of party finance began to change in the late 1950s and early 1960s as the era of electronic politics dawned. As television advertising became an essential element of national campaigns, parties found themselves trapped in an upward spiral of spending. In 1964, the federal government appointed an "Advisory Committee to Study Curtailment of Election Expenses." The findings of this committee, known as the Barbeau Report, were released in 1966. The report recommended spending limits, public subsidies, and disclosure laws, but did not recommend any limits on the size or source of contributions. Between 1962 and 1974, the parties had to fight six general elections because several minority governments had been formed. At the same time, the cost of mounting a competitive campaign was increasing substantially. One prominent observer of Canadian electoral finance suggested that the 1974 general election was the most expensive to that point in Canadian history.[7] These escalating costs were the primary impetus for the parties to adopt significant reforms to the regulation of electoral finance. An additional factor was public opinion favouring reform. Richard Nixon had just been ousted from the White House because of his cover-up of dirty tricks during the 1972 presidential election, heightening public concerns about political corruption. Within Canada, the government of Quebec had led the way for substantial reform of political finance by adopting a comprehensive new electoral law.

The 1974 Election Expenses Reforms
Unlike earlier electoral finance laws, the 1974 reforms recognized in law the existence and central role of political parties in the financing and conduct of election campaigns. In so doing, the reforms allowed for the first meaningful regulation of Canadian political finance. The Election Expenses Act (amending the Canada Elections Act) tackled the problem of the rising cost of elections in three ways. The first was to limit the amount of money that parties and candidates can spend during elections. The second was to provide some public funding to candidates and parties both by directly reimbursing a portion of their election expenses and by providing their contributors with a generous tax credit. The third was to guarantee parties' access to radio and television advertising time. In addition to these measures, the Election Expenses Act established procedures for parties to register as officially recognized entities, and required candidates and parties to disclose the source and amount of all contributions over $100, and to report their election expenses. There have been only relatively minor changes to the electoral finance provisions of the Election Expenses Act since 1974.[8]

The 1974 legislation reflected the pan-Canadian ethos of the three major parties at the time. It required that, in order to be considered a registered party eligible for public funding, a party had to be national in scope. In practice, this meant that a party had to run candidates in at least 50 of the almost 300 ridings. For the first time in Canadian law, it formally recognized the existence of national parties, putting their names on ballots beside those of their candidates. The legislation also recognized and, arguably, added to the power of the party leaders by giving them an effective veto over candidate nominations.

The most immediate effects of the 1974 reforms were, first, to alleviate the financial pressures parties were experiencing as a result of escalating advertising costs and the upward competitive spiral of spending; and, second, to increase substantially the importance of individual contributions relative to corporate contributions because of the incentives offered through the political-contribution tax credit.[9] These two effects combined to allow national parties to develop more permanent and professionalized organizations than they had in the past because more funds were made available to them and they were better able to raise money between elections.

Taken as a whole, the regulatory regime put in place in 1974 served the interests of the three major parties at the time. Formulas for public funding, registration requirements, and limits on independent expenditures acted as barriers to new parties seeking to enter the system. Spending limits, public funding, and guarantees of broadcast time reduced the financial pressures parties were facing, yet were made flexible enough that parties could later circumvent them.[10] The tax credit encouraged individual contributions. Following the framework set out in the Barbeau report, no limits were placed on corporate or union contributions, which remained the steadiest source of election cash for the parties.

Spending Limits
When they adopted spending limits for parties and candidates in 1974, the established parties essentially entered into an agreement to put an end to the upward spiral of election spending. Enshrining this arrangement in law prevented any one of the parties from breaking the agreement and outspending the others. However, the spending limits are not just self-serving conspiracies among the existing parties to keep their costs under control. They also reflect one of the fundamental principles guiding electoral regulation: fairness. In 1991, the Royal Commission on Electoral Reform and Party Financing concluded that spending limits "constitute a significant instrument for promoting fairness in the electoral process. They reduce the potential advantage of those with access to significant financial resources and thus help foster a reasonable balance in debate during elections. They also encourage access to the election process."[11]

The spending limit for a party is calculated in terms of the number of candidates it is running in an election. The limit for a party running candidates in all 301 ridings in 1997 was $11.4 million. The limits for candidates are set according to a formula that takes into account the number of eligible voters in the riding as well as the geographic size of the riding (in the case of large northern constituencies). All of the candidates running in a given constituency must abide by the same limit. The spending limits for candidates in the 1997 election ranged from $49,414 in the Prince Edward Island constituency of Malpeque, to a high of $78,589 in the Northern Alberta riding of Peace River. The average spending limit for constituencies across the country was $62,625.[12] When the limits for candidates are compared to those for parties, it becomes evident that the legislation reflects a preference for local over national spending. The total amount that could be spent by the 301 candidates of a party contesting every constituency in 1997 was $18.8 million, substantially more than the $11.4 million that the national party could spend.[13]

Even though they adopted these spending limits to protect themselves from escalating expenses, the parties subsequently devised ways to circumvent these constraints. The most notable instance of this is in the definition of election expenses. The Elections Act does not specify what expenditures are to be counted as election expenses, leaving this decision to the Chief Electoral Officer (CEO). The CEO acts on the advice of the Ad Hoc Committee on Election Expenses, comprising representatives of the parties in Parliament. As Leslie Seidle has pointed out, the result has been a definition of election expenses that was developed in private, never debated in Parliament, and yet is available as a shield against prosecution.[14] The definition adopted excludes polling, research and analysis relating to the party's policies, programs and strategies, and 50 percent of the costs of fund-raising. This definition allows parties to spend during the campaign on a range of items that might otherwise be considered election expenses. Because the spending limits are in place only during the campaign, there is nothing stopping a party from spending on advertising or other election-related activities before the election writs are issued. In its 1991 report, *Reforming Electoral Democracy,* the royal commission recommended that the definition of election expenses be expanded to include virtually all election-related expenditures, including polling. The commission also recommended a substantial increase in the limits, to take this broader definition into account. Although they would not have dealt with the question of pre-writ spending, these measures would have at least limited the amount of money now being spent. Parliament has taken no action on these recommendations.

Figure 7.1 shows the major parties' spending, exclusive of election expenses, over the period from 1975 to 1997, adjusted for inflation. Not all parties increased their spending in election years, but those with greater financial resources certainly did. The most notable instances of this were around the elections of 1984, 1988, and 1993, when the Conservatives' spending increased to almost double the amount spent in previous or subsequent years.[15] Conversely, parties without a great deal of ready money at their disposal try to claim as many of their costs as possible as election expenses. This is the case because parties receive a reimbursement of a portion of their election expenses from the state, and so have an incentive to report as many expenditures as election expenses as they can. The result is that, in those cases (see, for example, the NDP in 1997, or Reform in 1993 and 1997), the party's reported non-election spending may actually appear to decline in election years.[16] However, such cases continue to be the exception rather than the rule.

It is difficult to discern the precise effect of spending limits on the party

Figure 7.1

Parties' annual expenditures, 1975-97

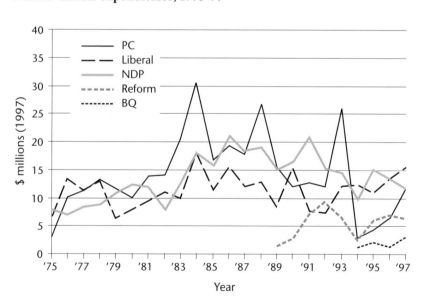

Notes: Figures do not include election expenses.
Source: Parties' annual returns to Elections Canada.

system. There is some evidence that spending limits level the playing field for political competition. This at least partially removes the advantages that might be enjoyed by a party that had access to a great deal of money. In this sense, spending limits make the party system more competitive, and reduce barriers to the entry of parties and candidates that do not have substantial financial resources available to them. There is considerable consensus in Canada that spending limits are a desirable element of the regulatory regime. The Royal Commission on Electoral Reform and Party Financing found that the vast majority of interveners in public hearings, members of the public, and parties' constituency association presidents all agreed with the principle of spending limits. Similarly, 96 percent of respondents to the 1997 Canadian Election Study agreed that there should be limits on the amount parties and candidates can spend.[17]

When evaluating the effect of spending limits, it is important to keep in mind that money cannot necessarily buy electoral success. In 1993, the Conservative party incurred $10.3 million in election expenses, as well as $24.8 million in non-election expenses, yet won only two seats in the House of Commons. The same year, the Bloc spent only $1.9 million and became the Official Opposition.[18]

If the primary purpose of spending limits was to prevent upward spirals in spending, they were not entirely successful, at least at the national level. Figure 7.1 shows that the parties' total spending increased substantially in the mid-1980s, led by massive spending by the Conservatives, and has remained at these higher levels ever since. Given that the law does not restrict spending on items that do not count as election expenses or pre-writ spending, it appears that the factor restricting spending most significantly is the availability of funds. Although less pronounced, there has also been an upward trend in candidates' expenditures, as shown in Figure 7.2. This upward trend was driven by substantial changes in Conservative candidates' spending in 1984, by increases in NDP candidates' spending in 1988, and by the growth of Reform and the Bloc Québécois in 1993. The overall trend, then, has been for consistent growth in total spending in election years. As Figure 7.3 illustrates, this total amount increased from just over $80 million (in constant 1997 dollars) in 1979 to in excess of $130 million in 1993.

Public Funding

A second important element of the regulatory regime established in 1974 was public funding for parties and candidates. There are several rationales

Figure 7.2

Candidate spending, 1979-97

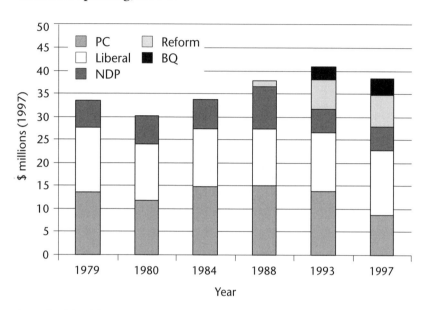

Source: Candidates' election expense returns to Elections Canada.

that justify the use of public money to support political parties during and between elections. First, the availability of public money limits parties' and candidates' reliance on large contributions from corporations, unions, or wealthy individuals, and thereby reduces the likelihood of undue influence being exercised. In this sense, it contributes to public confidence in the fairness of the electoral system. Second, public funding helps parties to cope with the costs of elections, thereby helping them to maintain their role as primary political organizations. Third, it contributes to a level playing field among political competitors in the hope that financial barriers that restrict otherwise credible candidacies will be reduced, if not eliminated. In this way, public funding contributes to the fairness of the political system.

Not everyone agrees that public funding for parties is desirable or beneficial for the integrity of the political system. Some object to the idea of offering public money to subsidize private organizations, arguing that parties ought to remain distinct from the state in a democratic system.

Figure 7.3

**Total party and candidate spending in election years
(major parties only)**

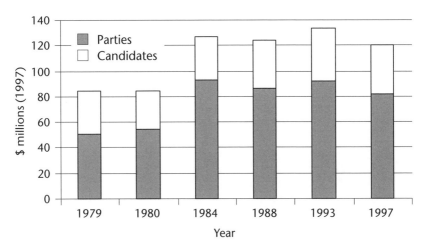

Source: Parties' and candidates' returns to Elections Canada.

Others, including the Reform Party, simply object to taxpayers' dollars going to political parties. The Christian Heritage Party, one of the party system's marginal players, objects to public funding on the grounds that such funding requires taxpayers to support parties regardless of whether they endorse the parties' policies.[19] Some academic observers have argued that, if parties rely too heavily on public money, they grow distant from the electorate, and become unable to perform their essential functions of aggregating and articulating societal interests in the public sphere.[20]

Public funding of Canadian parties takes two forms: the first is reimbursement of election campaign expenses for both parties and candidates, and the second is a tax credit for contributions to registered parties and nominated candidates. Candidates who win at least 15 percent of the votes cast in their district are eligible to have 50 percent of their election expenses reimbursed from the public treasury. In 1997, 801 (or 48 percent of all) candidates were eligible for this reimbursement. The 1974 legislation also provided for partial reimbursement to registered national parties. Between 1974 and 1983, parties were entitled to reimbursement for 50 percent of the standard media costs for radio and television advertisements during the campaign period. From 1983 on, the rule was changed to reimburse 22.5 percent of each registered party's election expenses as long as that party spent at least 10 percent of its expense limit. When compared with the approaches in other countries, the rules governing reimbursement of parties in Canada appear to be somewhat unusual, as they reward spending rather than electoral success.

In its 1991 report, the Royal Commission on Electoral Reform and Party Financing recommended significant changes to the rules governing reimbursement of campaign expenses. Its report criticized the existing rules on the grounds that the thresholds to qualify for reimbursement were too restrictive and that the formula for reimbursement rewarded spending rather than electoral success. The commission argued that the threshold of 15 percent of the popular vote for candidates, and 10 percent of the spending limit for parties, sent "a clear message to smaller parties and their candidates as well as to independent candidates: their participation is not welcome. This may also contribute to unwarranted rigidity in the Canadian party system, an effect that should not be underestimated."[21] The commission recommended that the threshold for reimbursement for both parties and candidates be set at 1 percent of the popular vote. The formula for reimbursements under this proposal would be based on electoral success. Parties would receive $0.60 for every vote they won, up to 50 percent of their total election expenses, and candidates would be reimbursed $1.00 for every vote received. The commission argued that "a reimbursement system based on electoral support, and not the ability to spend money, would lead to a fairer distribution of public funding to election participants by introducing greater equity ... [It] would be more responsive, giving emerging parties a fair opportunity to grow and lowering the obstacles many candidates now face."[22]

Parliament took no immediate action on this. It did not act until the Natural Law Party, an essentially apolitical front for a new-age religious movement whose platform relied heavily on "yogic flying," used the provisions of the Elections Act to get its quirky message across during the 1993 election campaign. The party spent more than $3.3 million in the 1993 election campaign, and received a reimbursement in excess of $700,000, even though the party garnered less than 1 percent of the popular vote. In an amendment to the Elections Act in 1996, Parliament established that parties must receive either 2 percent of the valid votes cast nationally, or at least 5 percent of the valid votes cast in the electoral districts in which it endorsed candidates, to be eligible for partial reimbursement of election expenses. The formula for reimbursement did not change. As a result of this amendment, only the five major parties received reimbursements of their election expenses after the 1997 election. Thus the cost of reimbursements to parties decreased, from $8 million in 1993 to $7.5 million in 1997.[23] The change in the law apparently discouraged the Natural Law Party, which reported only $292,253 in election expenses in 1997.

The Lortie Commission's recommendations regarding reimbursements were also intended to address the imbalance in funding between local and national levels. One effect of the 1974 reforms was to enrich local parties relative to the national party. Because they do not have the same advertising and polling costs that the national party incurs, local campaigns are not particularly expensive. And the spending limits on local campaigns are low enough that it would be difficult for a candidate to undertake extensive advertising and polling, even if that was his or her desire. The formula for reimbursement of election expenses is considerably more generous towards candidates than national parties. Candidates who qualify are reimbursed for 50 percent of their election expenses, compared with 22.5 percent for national parties. In 1993, candidates received approximately $14 million in total reimbursements, and parties received only $8 million. In 1997, the figures were $16.5 million for candidates and $7.5 million for parties.[24] As a consequence, candidates tend to operate with a surplus, while national parties run at a deficit. Stanbury reports that, in the elections between 1979 and 1985, most candidates were able to raise enough money to cover their election expenses, irrespective of any reimbursement. As a result, most campaigns posted substantial surpluses, though, because local associations are not subject to the disclosure provisions in the law, the precise amounts they have banked are not known.[25] This imbalance between local- and national-level financing has prompted the national parties to devise various ways of "taxing back" portions of the candidates' reimbursements. In 1993 the Liberal party collected $3 million by requiring candidates to hand over 50 percent of their reimbursements.[26] During the run-up to the 1997 election, some Reform candidates were in such good financial shape that they voluntarily turned over almost $1.4 million to help pay for a national television advertising campaign. The largest contribution from a riding was more than $40,000.[27]

The second way in which parties and candidates receive public funding is through the political-contribution tax credit. When individuals give a contribution to a nominated candidate or a registered party, they are eligible to claim a tax credit on their federal income tax return. This reduces an individual's actual cost of making a political contribution: someone who gives $100 to a party is able to claim $75 as a tax credit, and so is out of pocket only $25. These credits are "tax expenditures" and therefore constitute an indirect form of public funding – the federal government does not give money directly to the parties, but rather forgoes tax revenue when it offers the credit. Between 1989 and 1993, the total value of these political-contribution tax credits for individuals was $63.7 million.[28] The tax credit is based on a sliding scale that provides a less generous credit for larger contributions, and from 1974 neither the value of the tax credit nor the ceiling amount for the most generous credit was changed. Given the effects of inflation, this has meant that the real value of a $100 contribution has declined substantially, which may explain in part the downward trend in the average real size of contributions to parties depicted in Figure 7.4. In response, the Liberal government introduced legislation in 1999 that would increase the amount eligible for the most generous tax credit from $100 to $200.

According to William Stanbury, the introduction of public funding was a significant factor in the broadening of all three major parties' financial bases. This result he attributes in large part to the incentive that the political-contribution tax credit created for individuals to provide funds to the parties. The funds available to the NDP increased substantially, and the Liberals and Conservatives became less reliant on large corporate contributions.[29] The 1974 reforms also changed patterns of party organization by providing the major parties with "vastly larger sums to spend in the years between elections," thereby increasing substantially the degree of institutionalization of the national parties.[30]

Although public funds have become an important source of money for Canadian parties, they are not the primary source of financial support. A study of party financing during the 1988 federal election cycle (from 1985 to 1988) calculated the proportion of public funding to both parties and candidates to be 31.4 percent of their combined total spending. When the market value of free broadcasting time was added into this calculation, the proportion increases to 34.4 percent.[31] In short, public funds still remain less important to parties than funds from private-sector donors.

Figure 7.4

Average size of individual contributions, 1975-97

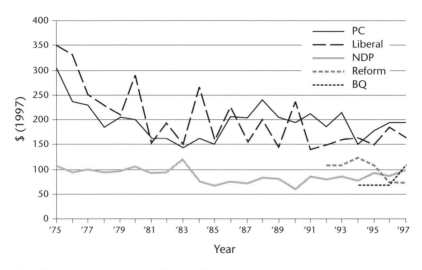

Source: Parties' and annual returns to Elections Canada.

Broadcasting
In addition to limiting spending and providing direct public subsidies to parties and candidates, the 1974 legislation required all radio and television networks to provide six and a half hours of free television time to the registered parties.[32] The six and a half hours were divided among the registered parties according to a formula established by the Broadcasting Arbitrator, a lawyer appointed through the unanimous agreement of all the political parties represented in the House of Commons. The allocation of free advertising time was based largely on each party's performance in the previous election, and therefore tended to favour the existing parties at the expense of new parties, and larger parties at the expense of smaller parties. For example, in the 1988 election, the Conservative party was allocated 195 minutes of paid time, the Liberals 89 minutes, and the NDP 67 minutes. All of the other registered parties were allocated between 3 and 7 minutes of paid time.

The 1974 legislation also required all broadcasters to make six and a half hours of air time available for purchase by political parties during election campaigns without inflating the price paid for the time. This provision was intended, at least in part, to ensure that broadcasters would make adequate time available to parties during elections, pre-empting other commercials where necessary. The act also made it illegal for broadcasters to sell additional time to parties during the campaign period, so it essentially created a limit on paid advertising that complemented the spending limit. These six and a half hours of time were allocated among the parties according to the same formula as for free time. Parties could not purchase any paid time beyond their limit.

After the 1988 election, Reform went to court to determine the constitutionality of several sections of the Canada Elections Act, arguing that the broadcasting time allocation scheme unduly violated freedom of expression and association; the right to vote; and the right to equality of smaller, emerging, and unestablished parties. In 1995, the Alberta Court of Appeal ruled that two sections of the act – those that prevented parties from purchasing more than their allocated time on any station – were unconstitutional. As a result, there were no direct restrictions on the amount of television or radio advertising time that a party could buy during the 1997 election. The only such restriction parties faced was their overall campaign expenditure limit, as campaign advertising is included in the definition of election expenses.

Compounding this change, the Broadcasting Arbitrator also revised the formula for allocating both paid and free time among parties. He concluded that the old system was "neither in the public interest nor was it fair to all the registered parties" because it "unduly fettered the ability of emerging parties to purchase time to make a meaningful case to the Canadian public."[33] Using the discretion that the Canada Elections Act gives him, the Broadcasting Arbitrator decided to allocate two-thirds of the available time using the old formula. The remaining one-third of the time was divided equally among all the registered parties. Because the allocation of free time determines the allocation of paid time, this significantly increased the amount of broadcast time made available to new and smaller parties. As a result of the court decision in the Reform Party's challenge to the constitutionality of the law, and the Broadcasting Arbitrator's subsequent decision regarding the allocation of paid time, the rules governing broadcasting are no longer as restrictive to new and smaller parties as they were in the past. In the 1997 election, new and smaller parties could buy as much paid time as they could afford, and had greater access to free time. For example, the Natural Law Party was allocated 18 minutes of free time, and the Green Party 13 minutes. This was substantially less than the 120 minutes allocated to the governing Liberals, but more than these parties would have received under the old rules.

The Parties' Finances

As the third party system gives way to a new one, substantial continuities in the parties' sources of financing persist. The Liberal and Conservative parties both continue to receive substantial portions of their funding from the corporate sector, while the NDP relies on its trade union partners. Of the new parties, the Bloc is entirely reliant on individual contributions, while Reform's reliance on individuals is decreasing, as its ability to raise corporate funds has increased. As has always been the case in Canadian politics, the governing party is able to attract corporate funds more readily and is consequently able to outspend its rivals in election years. Contributions from individuals remain a very significant source of funding for the party system, as is illustrated in Figure 7.5. Contributions from

Figure 7.5

Individual contributions as a percentage of total contributions, 1975-97

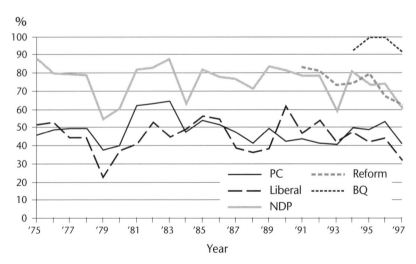

Source: Parties' annual returns to Elections Canada.

individuals account for between 40 and 60 percent of the total value of contributions to the Liberal and Conservative parties, around 70 percent of the total value of contributions to the NDP and Reform, and over 90 percent of contributions to the Bloc.

For the Liberal party, patterns of political finance have changed little in the aftermath of the 1993 election. Having regained its place as the country's "natural governing party" in 1993, the party has once again been in receipt of the generous corporate contributions that flow to the party in power. The party received more than $11 million from corporations in 1997, a substantial increase from the $8 million it received in 1988 and 1993. The party was in debt throughout the latter half of the 1980s, and even in 1993 the Liberals' total spending (including election expenses) only matched that of the NDP, and was dwarfed by the Conservatives (see Figure 7.6). By 1997, however, the Liberals were able to outspend the other parties, although certainly not by the kind of margin by which the Conservatives outspent their rivals in the elections from

Figure 7.6

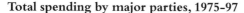

Total spending by major parties, 1975-97

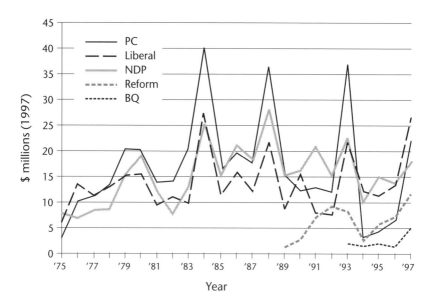

Source: Parties' annual and election returns to Elections Canada.

1984 to 1993. In the 1997 election, the Liberals spent $11.2 million, or 99 percent of the amount allowed under the spending limits.[34] The largest expenses for the party were advertising ($3 million), purchasing television time ($2.8 million), and the leader's tour ($1.7 million). The Liberal party's 301 candidates vastly outspent the other parties. Their combined spending was $13.8 million, some $5 million more than the next-highest group of spenders, the 301 Conservative candidates. This no doubt reflects the confidence of many Liberal candidates that they would qualify for a reimbursement of 50 percent of their expenses.

Having spent $10.3 million in the 1993 election to win only two seats, the Conservatives subsequently found themselves in serious financial difficulty. Like the Liberals after 1984, the Conservatives had to struggle with a substantial debt and a significant decline in contributions. As a result, the party's spending plummeted after 1993. However, the corporate sector did not abandon the Conservatives. Major corporate donors ignored the party's abysmal standings in the House and continued to contribute as though the Conservatives had formed the Official Opposition. For example, the Royal Bank of Canada in 1997 gave the Liberals $95,417, the Conservatives $94,706, and Reform $41,780. Bombardier gave those three parties $86,885, $79,054, and $0, respectively. Overall, the Conservatives received 3,235 contributions from the business community, in contrast to Reform's 1,259. This yielded some $4.5 million in corporate contributions for the Conservatives, as compared with $1.9 million for Reform. In part, this pattern of continued corporate support for the Conservatives probably reflected the presence of Conservative activists and supporters on corporate boards, but it was also an expression of the corporate sector's suspicion of Reform and conviction that the party system would return to normal after the next election. Continued support from the corporate sector allowed the Conservatives to outspend all the other parties except the Liberals in 1997. The Conservatives spent $10.2 million in 1997, or 91 percent of the legal limit. The party's largest expenses were television advertising, which cost $4.9 million, and the leader's tour, at $1.6 million.[35] Conservative candidates also outspent all their rivals except the Liberals. The party's 301 candidates spent a combined total of $8.8 million. Although a substantial sum, this represents less than 50 percent of the total amount that Conservative candidates were allowed to spend under the current spending limits.

The outcome of the 1993 election was almost as much of a blow to the NDP as to the Conservatives, and the NDP also emerged from the election with a debt burden, in their case $2 million. Like the Conservatives, however, the NDP was able to maintain the support of its most important financial backer – the trade unions. Union contributions continued to be a significant source of funds for the party in 1997, making up $2.2 million of the $16 million the party received. The integration of provincial and national party finances also cushioned the federal party to some degree. Although its level of spending did not return to pre-1993 levels, the party was able to outspend both the Bloc and Reform in the 1997 campaign. The NDP spent $6 million in 1997, which was 53 percent of its limit: $2 million went on television advertising and $1 million for its leader's tour.[36] Like the Liberals and Conservatives, the NDP ran candidates in all 301 ridings in 1997. Collectively, at $5.3 million, these candidates spent less than their Liberal or Conservative counterparts.

Between 1993 and 1997, the Reform Party was able to almost double its contributions from corporations, although it still lagged far behind the Conservatives. This is in large part a reflection of the approach that many major contributors have apparently adopted: contributing to Reform, but a substantially smaller amount than contributed to either of the two parties that traditionally received corporate contributions. Other major corporate donors, particularly those based in Quebec such as Bombardier, the Banque Nationale du Canada, or the Power Corporation, did not contribute to Reform at all. Even oil companies and others headquartered in Calgary have tended not to shift their contributions from the Conservatives to Reform. The party's leadership is clearly frustrated by their inability to raise money from corporations. Reform officials attribute this (probably correctly) to the influential presence of Liberal and Conservative loyalists on corporate boards but have nonetheless continued their efforts to raise money from large corporations, employing one full-time fund-raiser and recruiting volunteer fund-raisers from the corporate arena. Although Reform's ability to raise corporate funds has not improved as rapidly as party officials would hope, the party has nonetheless been able to mount competitive campaigns – in part, because the party is able to solicit contributions from individuals. In 1997, Reform received contributions from 75,587 individuals (considerably more than the Conservatives' 23,352). These contributions were, on average, smaller than contributions to the Conservatives (see Figure 7.4), as individual contributions totalled $5.5 million for Reform, and $4.5 million for the Conservatives. In 1997, Reform was outspent by the NDP, Liberals, and Conservatives, but not by as large a margin as in 1993. Reform spent

$4.9 million in 1997. Because the party was running candidates in only 227 ridings, its national spending limit was $8.5 million. The party's actual expenditures totalled 58 percent of its limit. As with the other parties, television ($2.8 million) and the leader's tour ($1.15 million) were the largest expenses.[37] Reform's 227 candidates spent a total of $6.7 million during the 1997 campaign. Although less in the aggregate than the Conservatives' outlay, Reform's spending per candidate slightly exceeded that of the Conservatives: Reform candidates spent $29,624 on average, while Conservative candidates spent $29,240.

The Bloc Québécois relies on individual contributions to fund its campaigns. In 1997, the party received contributions from 18,886 individuals, yielding $2.1 million. The number of contributors to the party has declined from 1994 and 1995, when it received 29,085 and 25,848 individual contributions, respectively. Compensating for this somewhat is a trend towards larger contributions. The $2.1 million the party received in individual contributions in 1997 was greater than the total amount in either 1994 ($2 million) or 1995 ($1.7 million). As a result of its limited base of fund-raising and its decision to run only in Quebec ridings, the Bloc's total spending is less than that of the other parties. But in spending $1.6 million in 1997 (54 percent of its limit), the party was financially competitive in the province. The Bloc's seventy-five candidates spent a total of $3.8 million, or $50,016 per candidate on average, which exceeded the average spending for candidates in any other party – Liberal candidates on average spent $46,059. As with the Liberals, this relatively high spending by Bloc candidates probably reflects their confidence that they would meet the 15 percent threshold, guaranteeing an election-expense reimbursement from the state.

Pressures for Change

Although the basic elements of the 1974 Election Expenses Act have remained in place, there are some significant pressures for change to the regulatory regime. First, as nomination and leadership contests become more inclusive events, with thousands of people – some of them instant party members – casting ballots, there is likely to be pressure from the public, and possibly even from within the parties, for greater state regulation. Second, challenges to electoral rules under the Charter of Rights and Freedoms will continue, and the regulation of election expenses and party financing will have to be changed to respond to these challenges. Because the parties that constitute the emerging party system have profoundly different positions on a range of potentially divisive issues relating to the regulation of electoral finance, any efforts to change the regulatory framework are likely to spark considerable public controversy.

As citizens have come to expect political parties to conduct their internal affairs in a more democratic manner, nomination and leadership contests within the parties have become more open to involvement of significant numbers of citizens who may not be long-term party members. Once these contests have expanded so that thousands are casting ballots in nomination contests, and tens of thousands are casting ballots in leadership contests, any sort of irregularity in voting or evidence of excessive spending may spark calls for public regulation of these contests. Essentially, such broad participation in nomination and leadership contests, and the blurring of the distinction between party members and non-members, make these contests more similar to US-style primaries than to the internal, private party affairs of the past. As these contests become more public, and thus more expensive, more tax dollars will be involved as parties issue tax receipts for contributions made to leadership candidates. Given the substantial amounts of public money involved, there is bound to be a call for greater state involvement in regulation.

As Table 7.1 shows, spending in leadership contests increased considerably in the course of the third party system. To win the Conservative leadership in 1967, Robert Stanfield spent $288 (in 1993 dollars) per delegate voting at the convention. In 1983 and 1993, Brian Mulroney and Kim Campbell spent $853 and $865 per delegate, respectively. A similar upward trend in Liberal leadership contests drove Lloyd Axworthy out of the Liberal party leadership race in 1990. Though a senior MP and former cabinet minister, Axworthy announced that he could not run because of the costs involved. There is no doubt that these escalating costs contributed to the disenchantment with the leadership-convention process and the parties' decisions to adopt new mechanisms for choosing their leaders. However, it remains to be seen if the membership direct-vote systems will be any cheaper or any easier to control.[38]

In light of the upward spiral of spending in leadership races, the Royal Commission on Electoral Reform and Party Financing recommended regulating leadership and nomination races and coupled this with a proposal to formally extend the use of the tax credit for these purposes. In its report, the commission argued that "the selection of national leaders is a central responsibility of our political parties ... The principle of fairness is undermined in leadership selection by the absence of credible or

Table 7.1

Costs of winning party leadership campaigns, 1967-93

Year	Party	Winning candidate	Campaign expenditure ($)	Expenditure per delegate ($)	Expenditure per first ballot vote ($)	Expenditure per winning vote ($)
1967	PC	Stanfield	642,000	288	1,237	558
1968	Liberal	Trudeau	1,240,000	524	1,649	1,031
1983	PC	Mulroney	2,550,000	853	2,918	1,610
1984	Liberal	Turner	2,077,000	605	1,304	1,115
1990	Liberal	Chrétien	2,556,000	549	964	964
1993	PC	Campbell	3,000,000	865	1,803	1,651

Note: Expenditures in 1993 dollars.
Source: Calculated from data in Courtney, *Do Conventions Matter?*, Chaps. 2 and 4.

enforceable spending limits ... These considerations lead us to conclude that ... minimum requirements should be set out in electoral law to ensure that leadership selection in all registered parties is guided by common values and principles that promote the integrity of the electoral process and that affirm the principle of fairness in electoral competition."[39] This would have represented an unprecedented intrusion into internal party affairs, and was met with considerable resistance from the parties. Since the parties are already using the tax credit for their leadership contests, they see no compelling reason to change the system.[40]

A second source of pressure for change comes from challenges to the constitutionality of various electoral rules. Court decisions have struck down restrictions on interest-group spending during elections, restrictions on the amount of advertising time parties can purchase during campaigns, and rules governing the definition of a registered party. In the two former cases, the courts ruled that the importance of freedom of expression outweighed other considerations. This raises the intriguing question of whether spending limits would be able to survive a charter challenge. In the third case, a lower court in Ontario ruled that legislation requiring that parties run fifty candidates in order to qualify as a registered party was unconstitutional. The federal government is not challenging the portion of the ruling that struck down provisions allowing the Chief Electoral Officer to seize the assets of formerly registered parties, but it is challenging the portion of the ruling that strikes down the fifty-candidate requirement.

The courts have not been entirely activist in their interpretations of electoral law. Challenges to high thresholds for candidate reimbursement and rules for allocation of free broadcast time that favour the major parties have both failed. In these cases, the courts have essentially ruled that the legislative definition of the public interest is defensible, and does not interfere unduly with the equality and democratic rights guaranteed by the charter.

The third source of challenge to the existing regulatory regime is the breakdown of the consensus among the major parties regarding electoral regulation. The entry of Reform and the Bloc into the party system has shattered the comfortable understandings that facilitated the 1974 reforms and subsequent amendments. As noted in Chapter 5, parties vary considerably in their stances on interest-group advertising during elections. The new parties diverge from the old consensus on a range of other issues. The Bloc Québécois advocates limits on the size and source of political contributions, seeking to mimic the Quebec system described as *financement populaire;* the Reform Party "opposes any assistance to political parties and political lobbies from public funds, including any refund of candidate or party expenses, government advertising during the electoral period, the 'renting' of Parliament staff for reimbursement, tax credits for contributions to federal political parties, and the transfer of tax credits to leadership or nomination campaigns."[41] The Bloc's support of contribution limits has prompted the party to refuse contributions that would not be permitted under Quebec law, but the Reform Party plays by the existing rules and accepts the same reimbursements as its opponents.

Paying for Parties

As the Canadian party system has evolved, the parties' need for substantial sums of money has remained constant. From Confederation to the present, the Liberals and Conservatives have looked to the corporate sector for a substantial portion of their income. Other elements of the system of party financing have, however, changed as the party system evolved. Introduction of spending limits, disclosure laws, and systems of public funding have all transformed election financing, encouraged greater reliance on small contributions from individuals, and strengthened national party organizations by making public funds available to the parties.

In the current transition between party systems, the regulatory regime governing political money is coming under contradictory pressures. Demands to regulate internal party affairs such as leadership and candidate-nomination contests would result in greater state intervention, while charter challenges and the breakdown of consensus among the parties on public funding may move the system in the opposite direction.

Even though the pattern of financing put in place in 1974 was designed to reinforce the pre-eminence of the existing major parties, it did not protect the Liberals, Conservatives, or New Democrats from the rise of Reform and the Bloc in 1993. Both new parties have tried to change the system of political finance: the Bloc by power of example, and Reform by challenging parts of the law in court. As a consequence of Reform's efforts, the system of party finance has become slightly more favourable to emerging parties. But as long as the parties in Parliament disagree on the fundamentals of electoral reform, it is unlikely that we will soon see major changes to the system.

8

On the Ground:
The Local Campaign

Party politics seems inherently to be national politics. Party leaders dominate the scene and the screen, overshadowing members of Parliament, their pronouncements given more weight than a weekend's set of policy resolutions adopted by a convention hall full of party members. During elections, uniform party signs overrun the landscape, giving voters from one end of the country to the other the illusion that they are participating in a common choice. But Canadian political reality is more complex, more layered, than this simple portrait implies.

Canadian parties, as Siegfried noted almost a century ago, are election machines[1] – organizations for vacuuming up votes – and, as such, their organizations and activities follow the course laid down by the electoral system. The most important feature of it is the fact that elections are fought in geographically defined, single-member districts. So, while parties in their search for attention, support, and office have every incentive to portray themselves as genuinely national organizations, the reality is they have to do this in up to (now) 301 distinct areas across the country. Each of these 301 separate elections requires that a candidate be found and a campaign mounted on his or her behalf, as well as for the party generally. Not surprisingly, then, the local constituency association has become the fundamental organizational unit of Canadian political parties, the locus of much critical activity. It is on the ground, in the constituencies, that much of the hard work of Canadian party politics takes place, for, at the end of the day, winning constituencies is more important than winning votes in the quest for power.[2] Despite all the change transforming other aspects of the party system, this very local dimension of political life goes on much as it has for over a century. And it is here that the forces of continuity show themselves strongest.

This reality of both a local and a national dimension to party life and competition is rooted in the institutional imperatives of Canada's ancient, first-past-the-post electoral process. It is sustained by the fundamental dilemma facing Canadian political parties. As the instruments of mass electoral choice, parties in all democracies serve as the primary organizational link between the society and the institutions of the state. In Canada the task of providing this linkage is particularly difficult. On the one hand, there is a new-world, American-style society: ethnically diverse, regionally diversified, with a mobile, growing population that is becoming increasingly pluralistic with every decade – a society in which geography and demography continue to overwhelm history and which has developed no settled sense of national community. Confronted with this political cacophony is a very traditional European system of government: monarchial, parliamentary, disciplined, and bureaucratic. Federalism merely replicates this pattern twice over, while the Charter of Rights and Freedoms has yet to open the patterns of closed and secretive decision making in any dramatic way.

The political impulses of the society flow up from the base; the governing mechanisms of the state attempt to reach down from the national capital. The challenge for Canadian parties is to somehow connect this American-style society to its European institutions. In practical terms, it means finding some organizational form that will allow parties to reconcile the tensions between local impulses and national needs, between politics and governing. The problem is that disciplined national parties of the sort demanded by our inherited notions of majority parliamentary government cannot for long contain the fluidity and diversity of Canadian society. European-style parties are simply not like American parties. Yet it is the unceasing pressure of trying to consummate this unnatural balancing act that explains the peculiar structure of Canadian parties and that infuses the dualism marking the country's electoral realities.

Successful Canadian parties have dealt with their problem of linking a loose society to tight institutions by adopting a basic organizational trade-off: local autonomy for national discipline. Constituency party associations are left free to run their own affairs, including choosing candidates for Parliament. National party leaders are deferred to in setting policy directions and enforcing the parliamentary discipline required by the system. It is a trade-off that has not always worked perfectly, that has often seen each side attempting to intrude on the prerogatives of the other, but one that has continually been the central reality of the country's distinctive pattern of party organization and activity.

The tension between autonomy and discipline is at once the source of both the stability and the instability that mark the Canadian party system. It is just this historic bargain that allowed two nineteenth-century parties, the Liberals and the Conservatives, to survive and triumph as dominant national political forces for more than a century in a constantly changing country. At the same time, the very organizational incongruity at the parties' core has not been lost on Canadians. As a result, voter volatility has been comparatively high as electors discover that local and party interests are often at greater-than-advertised odds, party activists move across partisan lines to meet their locally rooted needs, and regionally based parties continue to burst into the system. When the tension between society and state has become too great for the national parties to bear, the party system has broken down and has been forced to re-create itself. It did so in the 1920s, and again in the 1960s, and is now doing so again.[3] Despite these transformations in the party system, each of which saw the emergence of distinctive patterns of party politics and new forms of party governance, individual Canadian parties have continually rebalanced this basic, if precarious, local-national organizational trade-off.

Whatever set of internal structures a party may adopt, the local constituency level association remains its basic organizational unit. The national party ultimately rests on the base of these local associations in an elaborate network not unlike the franchise systems widely used by modern business organizations. Party activity, especially the organization of electoral politics, is bifurcated. The national party is ultimately responsible for producing the product, be it policy or leadership, and for creating the grand marketing plan that drives the national electoral campaign. But it is the local association that must maintain and operate the local outlet, finding a candidate and creating a campaign that will mobilize support on election day. This makes the relationship between the local associations and the central leadership team the key organizational linkage in Canadian parties.

The analogy that compares a Canadian political party to a franchise system, perhaps a fast-food chain, is not a perfect one, however. The most important difference is that the local constituency associations are populated and worked by volunteers who come and go as they please. Beyond setting a basic framework of rules governing the structure and activity of their constituency associations, national parties have only a limited capacity to manage their local activists, who always have the option to leave, perhaps even move to a competing party, if they are not happy. Thus the national parties must ultimately put themselves in the hands of whatever local volunteers they can attract and hold. This franchise-style organizational form that is the essence of most Canadian party organization is but a modern manifestation of what Maurice Duverger called a "cadre party," a group of interested activists clustered around some local political notable, primarily interested in seeing to it their candidate gets elected.[4]

For their part, most activists relate to the wider party only through their participation at the local constituency level. It is at that level that they are provided with an opportunity to be politically active and to participate in an internal party choice of candidates for elections and delegates to leadership-selection conventions. Indeed, it is just this chance to become directly involved in local party decisions that stimulates much party membership. Thus any analysis of parties on the ground needs to start with the question of party membership.

Party Membership

The parties' approach to membership is simple. They seek to be as open and inclusive as possible, and so impose few constraints. In many local associations, it is not even necessary to be either a citizen or of voting age to join and participate as a full member. Indeed, that very casualness has been one of the targets of Reform's critique of the traditional parties, and the party deliberately limits its membership to eligible voters. The separation of federal and provincial party organizations means that, with the exception of New Democrats, individuals may well be members of different parties at the two levels of political life. For Reform, this is necessarily true of all its members who are politically active provincially, for the party has consciously decided against building any provincial affiliates.

Within any party, the size of the local constituency associations' memberships varies enormously, from a handful in areas of limited party appeal and presence, to several thousand where the party is popular and has an incumbent MP concerned to maintain an electoral machine.[5] Some local associations are no more than paper organizations, inactive, with few, if any, members, and no money. They exist to allow the party to maintain the fiction that it is a national organization capable of mounting a campaign in every riding at election time: New Democrat local associations in Quebec have almost always been of this sort. At the other extreme, some local constituency party associations are active, vigorous, and rich. The difficulty with drawing a portrait of constituency party life in Canada is that it is anything but stable. Local memberships are very volatile, and an association that is strong and active one year may easily find itself depopulated and dormant the next.Virtually all Ontario's constituencies had active, well-financed Conservative associations in 1988, but less than a decade later the party was in dire straits and "only about a third of the riding associations were viable."[6]

Over the past decade, the typical local association in one of the major parties has probably had between 300 and 500 members on its books in an average non-election year. Given that there are now upwards of 100,000 people in the average riding, it appears that the parties have shallow organizational roots in most districts. Between elections these local associations are quiescent, perhaps meeting once or twice a year but otherwise leaving the routine tasks of maintaining membership lists and raising money to a small coterie of dedicated activists.Where the riding party has an incumbent MP, its local association may well be larger and more active, but in those instances it is likely to be as focused on the member him- or herself as on the wider party.

Elections are what activate the parties' grass roots. Members are mobilized to find a candidate and then to campaign for his or her election. Membership rolls grow as party supporters renew their cards in order to be able to vote at nomination meetings. It is not unusual for a local association to experience a 60 to 70 percent membership increase in an election year as individuals who take little part in party affairs between elections rejoin for the electoral battle. But local politics is not always a matter of constituency-association members finding a candidate. Sometimes it is just the reverse, with would-be candidates mobilizing new instant members to support them in a contested nomination. The very openness of constituency associations to this practice has seen average local party memberships grow by up to 300 percent in such cases during recent elections.

Thus the typical party association at the constituency level has a membership pattern that reflects the electoral cycle. It jumps in election years, only to sink once the election is over, remaining at a fairly low level until the next one is called.The individual members are of three types: the regular activists who maintain their party affiliation year-in and year-out, supporters who become active only at the peak of the election cycle, and individuals who are mobilized into the party only to support a particular candidate. Figure 8.1 illustrates this pattern of membership surge and decline by tracing changes in the Conservative party over the 1988 and 1993 electoral cycles. It reveals in rather dramatic fashion the importance

Figure 8.1

Average Conservative local association membership size, 1987-94

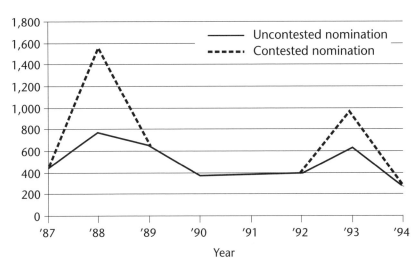

Source: Carty (1991); Cross (1996).

a contested nomination plays in mobilizing individuals into the local associations. While the same pattern holds in the Liberal and Reform parties, New Democrat riding associations have been better at both holding their partisans between elections and keeping instant members out.[7] As a result their membership profiles are comparatively flat over time, though their local activity is probably no less driven by electoral imperatives.

For Canadian parties, membership has become equated with a party franchise conferring the right to participate in party contests to choose candidates or leaders.[8] This makes membership fees a kind of poll tax. Individuals have little reason to maintain their membership in non-election years, especially since it is easy to renew their status when being a member has some value. The devaluing of party membership in this way has encouraged individuals to trade in memberships, thus facilitating, as well as legitimating, the flooding of local associations with instant members.[9] The result has been that, as these practices have flourished in recent decades, local party decision making has become less stable and less predictable. And that has stimulated the national organizations to try to impose some order and control over local activity. In doing so, they have infringed on the long-standing local-national bargain, and have unsettled party practice. This has been most obvious in the local associations' quintessential task of determining who their candidate will be.

Choosing Candidates

At the heart of local-party-association autonomy lies the right to select their own candidate for election. From the very first Canadian election, local partisans have jealously guarded this prerogative, and have insisted that even incumbent MPs return each election to face their supporters and be reconfirmed as the local choice. While it is generally assumed that an MP will get renominated without too much difficulty, it is not an automatic process, and there has hardly been an election in which some hapless MP has not removed by his or her local party as its candidate. These examples are not lost on other members, or other associations, and they serve to perpetuate this tradition of local control of party nominations.

One measure of the importance Canadians have given to the principle of local autonomy can be seen in successive election acts. Despite the fact that virtually all other aspects of the electoral process are carefully and heavily regulated, nominations have been left untouched, but for the need to collect a handful of signatures. Parliamentarians have recognized that local activists (and perhaps they themselves) do not want to be constrained when it comes to candidate selection. In the 1970s, when the imperatives of national television advertising pushed the politicians to include party labels on the ballot, the law assigned party leaders the power to endorse candidates for this purpose. Quickly the power of endorsement became a power of veto. This ability to say who would not be the candidate strengthened considerably the position of the leader and threatened local autonomy with respect to candidate selection. Party members have been ambivalent about this development: most now accept it as necessary and would oppose abolishing it, but most also think the leader should always accept the choice of the local association.[10]

In practice, local party nomination processes are remarkably accessible, allowing all party members to participate by voting at a nomination meeting.[11] Given the fluidity in the membership of local associations, this makes the candidate-selection process an open one. Individuals who want to be candidates can easily recruit new party members and urge them to come to the nomination meeting. Individuals who want a say in who a party's candidate will be can easily join and vote at a nomination meeting, even if they have never participated in any other party activity. And many local associations feel free to enlist individuals who are not even current party members to become their candidate. The new Reform Party has been particularly aggressive about this. Its local associations set up formal candidate-recruitment committees that run advertisements in local papers indicating that they are looking for a candidate and welcoming applications.[12] This openness to anyone who chooses to become a party member, even if only for the occasion, is defended in terms of local party democracy and, in turn, it has come to be one of the legitimating bulwarks of local autonomy. Thus any national party challenge to local autonomy is inevitably resisted as a challenge to one of the central features of Canadian party democracy.

Despite this openness, and a tradition of local democracy, most Canadian party nominations are not particularly competitive. In part, this can be explained by the logic of the local electoral contexts. Although some incumbents seeking re-election are challenged, most are not, as local partisans are anxious to present a united face to their opponents. In a multiparty system, many of the nominations available offer little promise of election, and so are not particularly desirable prizes. More often, they are seen as sacrifices some individuals need make so that the party can claim to be genuinely national by running candidates in all parts of the country. So, in electoral districts in which their prospect is rated hopeless, a local party is twice as likely to have an uncontested nomination as one that is considered safe.[13] Taken together, these realities have led to only about a third of the major parties' nominations being contested in recent elections.

Local party associations are most likely to have an uncontested nomination in two quite opposite situations: where they are so strong that they already hold the riding and where they are so weak that the nominee cannot possibly hope to win. The politics of these cases are obviously quite different and they produce different kinds of candidates. In his book on riding-level politics, Anthony Sayers calls incumbents, and strong candidates who have somehow managed to tie up a nomination without significant open competition, "high profile" candidates.[14] Their very profile, and prospect of success, attract individuals to join, or rejoin, the local party and work for them during an election campaign. Over time, these candidates (often as MPs) develop a considerable local following, and the local association tends to be dominated as much by personal as by party supporters. While that can make nomination challenges less likely, a preoccupation with the political fortunes of their local champion can narrow the reach or appeal of a constituency party association.

Highly personalized local party organizations often face a difficult test when their leader retires, or is defeated, and one of the classic responses has always been to nominate a son or daughter of the former MP in an attempt to hold the organization together, exploit the family's recognition in the community, and recapture the seat. In the 1997 election, as in most that had gone before, a number of the new candidates enjoyed a high profile by virtue of some family political connection. Prominent examples included Michael Savage (son of the Liberal premier) and Peter MacKay (son of a former Tory minister) in Nova Scotia, Dominic LeBlanc (son of a former Liberal minister, and then governor general) in New Brunswick, and Joe Jordan (son of a retiring MP) in Ontario.[15] The impulses that produce such candidates persist because local organizational and nomination autonomy persists.

In 1997, with at least four serious parties contesting each of the 301 ridings, it is clear that many of their more than 1,200 local candidates stood little chance of winning, and they knew it.[16] But the compulsion to present a nationwide face to the electorate, and claim the maximum television free time, drives the parties to nominate candidates in all ridings, including those where they have little support and/or no substantial local organization. The individuals that the parties put forward in such districts are best seen as "stopgap" candidates. These constituency parties rarely have a contested nomination, and they often have to get help from provincial or national party figures to find and persuade some individual to run: in 1997, half the Conservative ridings in Quebec had to have candidates parachuted in.[17] Not surprisingly, these undesirable candidacies are often filled by loyal partisans who might not otherwise get the opportunity to contest the seat. The fact that the parties are nominating more individuals from groups traditionally excluded from political office (e.g., women and minority groups) than they are electing suggests that many of these individuals are still filling stopgap roles. A good example of this can be seen in Quebec, where the uncompetitive New Democrats have nominated a disproportionate number of women in recent elections. The party then made a virtue out of necessity by trumpeting that they had more women candidates than the other large parties.[18] In Reform's case, the fear that it might lose control and have its local associations penetrated by extremists has led the party to forgo nominating stopgap candidates in areas of weakness. This meant that it ran candidates in only three-quarters of the ridings in 1997.

Although the largest number of local associations have uncontested nominations in any given election, it is those that have contests that command the most attention from the media and in the party.[19] In part this is the case because contests make news. Equally important, every local contest stimulates participation by ordinary party members, reaffirms the sanctity of local autonomy, and fortifies the norms of party democracy that legitimate the electoral process. There appear to be basically two types of contested nominations. The first takes place within local party associations that maintain tight control over their internal affairs and have quite stable memberships. These associations generally find that their nomination contest is waged between long-serving party activists who are well known to other members and who do not engage in extensive attempts to explode the local association with instant members. Sayers calls the candidates produced by these processes "party insiders." They are most commonly found in NDP associations in areas such as British Columbia or Saskatchewan, where the party has good reason to expect to do well. Often throwing up individuals who have a history of having worked for the party, or its elected politicians, as candidates, these associations nourish a self-perpetuating political class within the party.

Finally, there is the stereotypical open contest between individuals who, on their own or at the urging of friends or other partisans, decide to compete for a party's nomination. There have traditionally been few constraints, either legal or party-based, on these contests, and the person with the most supporters at the party nomination meeting has carried the day. Given the easy permeability of party membership, individuals seeking a nomination have strong incentives to recruit new members. And as they are doing so, their opponents are driven to do the same if they want to remain competitive. The result is a membership recruitment war, and associations with a desirable nomination can see their membership grow from several dozen to several thousand in a matter of weeks. In 1993, for example, over 80 percent of the contested nominations led to the recruitment of instant members, many associations having their membership double in a matter of weeks.[20]

Signing up that many individuals is no easy task if done one person at a time, so inevitably would-be candidates recruit groups of supporters. These groups may come from workplace associates (e.g., teachers recruit other teachers) or social networks accessible to party recruiters. Interest and ethnic groups are among those most regularly called upon for help. In one heavily publicized contest in 1997, two individuals from the Sikh community fought over the Liberal nomination in Surrey Centre, a suburban Vancouver riding, and both recruited heavily from competing factions in their own community. The result was that the association suddenly grew to more than 5,000 members; the riding party was divided by local Sikh temple rivalries; and the police were called in to ensure violence did not break out at the nomination vote, which was conducted far more like a primary election than a party meeting. In some ways there is nothing particularly new in this sort of nomination struggle. Similar accounts, of nomination contests featuring the members of local Orange Halls and immigrant-protective societies, can be told of elections held a century ago. The pattern persists because nominations remain the prerogative of local activists, and the candidates that emerge out of them are genuine "local notables."

Local associations are ambivalent about such unrestrained nomination battles, for it means the regular party activists who do the hard work of sustaining the association between elections lose any control over who will be their candidate. As naming the candidate is the most important decision local activists can make, this is a high cost. On the other hand, party activists know that the vast bulk of these new members are not only instant members but also short-term members, unlikely ever to darken the door of a party meeting again. The real benefit they bring to a local association is their membership fees, paid by them or the campaign organization of the candidate they support. With a local membership fee of $10, the addition of 5,000 new members can quickly swell the local coffers by $50,000, enough to pay for the local constituency association's election campaign.

Most party nomination contests do not assume the sorts of proportions reached in Surrey Centre. Rather more typical was the Conservative nomination in Vancouver Centre, a riding lost by the party in the previous election, when the incumbent, Prime Minister Kim Campbell, was defeated. Two new young candidates emerged to seek the nomination, and in a few weeks they had stimulated a 50 percent growth in the Vancouver Centre Conservative association's membership. On the night of the party nomination meeting, however, only about one-third of the members managed to turn out to vote in a basement room of the Vancouver Public Library. Victoria Mines defeated Chris Farber by seventy-five to fifty-five and became the candidate, largely because more of her supporters showed up to vote.

The most ferocious nomination battles often involve a challenge to an incumbent MP from within his or her own local party organization. While such challenges are rare in most other single-member parliamentary systems, they are not uncommon in Canadian parties, with their traditions of local autonomy and democracy. In 1988, for example, some 10 percent of the incumbent MPs had to win a contested nomination meeting in order to run again. Such challenges generally lead to large membership increases and very high turnouts at nomination meetings, as MPs use all the resources available to them to defend their seats against determined opponents.[21] Whatever the impact of the new parties on increased party competition, individual incumbents' home bases are no safer than ever. Indeed, the 1997 election appears to have been a banner year for challenges as four MPs had their bids for renomination rejected when their riding association chose another candidate at the local nomination meeting.

Two Bloc Québécois members (in Charlesbourg and Lotbinière) suffered that fate. Although one of them (Jean Landry, in Lotbinière) subsequently ran as an independent, the Bloc managed to recapture both constituencies. In Newfoundland, Liberal MP Jean Payne was challenged by Rex Gibbons, a provincial cabinet minister, and despite Prime Minister Chrétien's commitment to increasing the number of Liberal women candidates, national party officials did not interfere in the local nomination battle. Payne was handily defeated (by 2,190 to 870) at a meeting of the St. John's West riding association, at which only about one-third of the 8,600 members were present. Gibbons then went on to lose the seat to the Conservatives in the election. The fourth incumbent to lose in a renomination contest was Margaret Bridgeman, the Reform MP in British Columbia's Surrey North. Her opponent, Chuck Cadman, a community activist pushing issues related to youth crime, had no difficulty holding the constituency for the party.

It is difficult to trace any obvious common thread through these cases. They occurred in three different parties, two new and one old, spread across three provinces. One or two of the MPs were undoubtedly in local hot water before their nomination meeting, but probably no more so than some other parliamentarians. Some were issue-driven challenges; others focused on the personality of the individuals involved. What is common to all of the cases is that someone else in the community wanted the MP's seat, and the openness of the parties' nomination processes made a local challenge both possible and viable. The fact that three of the successful challengers held the constituencies only a few weeks later in the general election indicates that it was the MP, and not the party, that had lost local support. And, when that happens, local party activists feel free, and are able, to deprive MPs of their seats.

One of the striking consequences of the current volatility in Canadian party politics, and the high rates of seat turnover, is that local party associations often find themselves in sharply different situations from election to election. One election year they may have a quiescent membership, supporting a popular and unchallenged MP; the next, a bruising battle may take place that grossly (if only temporarily) inflates and divides the membership; while, by the time of the subsequent contest, the association may be little more than a corporal's guard of partisans scrambling to find a stopgap candidate. This makes it difficult for the national parties to develop an overall nomination strategy and leaves individuals considering a candidacy unsure what the politics of the local nomination process they face is likely to entail.

The enormous changes to the party system over the 1990s has forced those wanting to run for Parliament to reconsider the political landscape, both nationally and in terms of the partisan forces in their constituency. The freedom most local associations have in choosing their candidate, irrespective of any previous political involvement, has facilitated a good deal of partisan movement. Of course, to the extent that the new parties' candidates had any previous political involvement in national politics, it had to have been in some other federal party, but local associations in all parties have no compunction about nominating individuals with varied party histories. The 1997 general election was no exception and illustrates the patchwork pattern to which local choice can lead. All of the national parties had locally chosen candidates who had once played a prominent role in other parties.

Given that the Bloc had been founded by dissident Conservative and Liberal MPs, it is not surprising that some of them (e.g., Louis Plamondon, in Richelieu, and Pierette Venne, in St. Hubert) continued to be nominated under their new colours. Reform associations drew heavily from former Conservatives such as John Reynolds (in West Vancouver-Sunshine Coast), a former Conservative MP and then British Columbia Social Credit legislator and cabinet minister, but it also attracted past Liberals such as Jason Kenney (Calgary Southeast), a former vice-president of the Saskatchewan young Liberals, and Joe Peschisolido (Mississauga South), a past executive vice-president of the Young Liberals of Canada. However, despite Reform's newness, traffic was already beginning to move the other way, as the Conservatives nominated former Reform MP Jan Brown in Calgary Southeast and a former Reform regional director, Kevin Garvey, in British Columbia's Delta–South Richmond.

Constituency parties in the other established parties also embraced former opponents. The Liberals (in Edmonton Southeast) renominated David Kilgour, a former Conservative MP, while their associations in Churchill and Okanagan-Shuswap nominated prominent former NDP provincial officeholders. In Toronto's high-profile Rosedale constituency, the New Democrats nominated David MacDonald, a former Conservative MP and cabinet minister in the Clark government, while the party's association in Nova Scotia's Southshore constituency chose Willie Nickerson, a man who had left both the Liberal and the Conservative party.

Occasionally local associations will raid another party in search of a candidate. In 1997 the Conservative association in Quebec's Châteauguay recruited George Lavoie to be its candidate only weeks after he lost a close, two-way race for the Liberal nomination. Vancouver Kingsway's Reform association nominated Raymond Leung, a former Liberal candidate, when Prime Minister Chrétien thwarted his ambition to run again by declaring the party was to have a woman candidate in that constituency.[22] Given that both Lavoie and Leung finished a distant third in the general election, we can assume that both were adopted as little more than stopgap candidates by the local party associations that ultimately nominated them.

Perhaps the most politically agile of all the candidates to run in 1997 was Guy St. Julien, in Abitibi, a huge, remote northern Quebec constituency. A local born and bred, St. Julien spent the 1970s as an organizer for the federal Liberal association. Then the 1980s saw him change sides, moving to the Conservatives, who nominated and elected him to Parliament in 1984 and 1988. Defeated by the Bloc in the 1993 electoral devastation of the Conservative party, St. Julien moved back to the Liberals and won nomination, and election, as a Liberal in 1997. Now it may be that St. Julien's principal interest lies in getting elected as a government MP, but it is the local associations' freedom to choose their own candidate that opens up these kinds of political career paths.

While individual riding parties feel free to nominate individuals with checkered political pasts, they also often recruit men and women with no previous party or political experience. In the 1993 election, almost 20 percent of candidates nominated had not been active in their party before becoming a candidate, and only 27 percent (including incumbents) had ever run in a previous general election. The reason for this is that local party activists rate "political experience" at the bottom of a list of eleven qualities sought in a candidate: being a "local resident" or someone "committed to the constituency" is more important to the local members whose votes determine who the candidates will be.[23] Local activists want local representatives, and their ability to produce them is one of the key elements in keeping the Canadian Parliament full of political amateurs.[24] It is also why they remain so firmly committed to maintaining local control over candidate selection.

One of the clearest examples of the tension between local political choice and the parties' broader electoral interest can be seen in relation to the issue of nominating more women candidates. Throughout the period of the second party system, and the first decade of the third, most women found their way into Parliament as political widows.[25] This situation has now changed. With the exception of Reform, all of the parties repeatedly claim that it is important to nominate and elect more women, and their leaders have indicated that they believe it to be an important issue. Yet, as Figure 8.2 indicates, progress in increasing the number of women candidates has been slow. Even this change is deceptive, for the proportions of women being elected continues to lag behind the proportions nominated, indicating that many of the women running are still being offered up as stopgap candidates in marginal or hopeless seats. The national parties' inability to change this as quickly as they would like flows from the strength of the local autonomy norm and its importance in governing participation in riding-level associations.

As the third system lurched towards its collapse, several of the parties attempted to increase their leverage over the local nomination politics of their constituency associations. The New Democrats, particularly concerned with increasing their number of women candidates, adopted affirmative action plans based on targets set by the party for groups of local associations. Though there was considerable sympathy in the party for the goal of increasing female representation, this mechanism has been overridden by what most members view as the superior claims of local democracy. The Reform Party, more concerned with keeping extremists out than getting women in, has developed a fairly extensive prescreening process that it requires of all its local associations. Given the party's

Figure 8.2

Percentage of women candidates, 1980-97

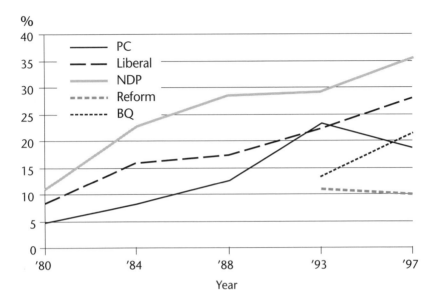

much-heralded commitment to a populist politics and the sovereignty of local voters, the guidelines start by conceding that, while the party insists on a "unified program in all ridings," the goals of the process include "maintaining constituency independence" and "maximiz[ing] the opportunity for input at the grassroots level."[26]

The Liberals have been the party most concerned with increasing control over their candidate-selection processes and they have moved most aggressively to challenge the deep-seated tradition of local autonomy. The national party has done this both indirectly and directly. The indirect methods have involved party campaign officials setting dates by which would-be candidates must register with, and get approval from, party campaign officials,[27] and controlling when local associations may hold recognized nomination meetings. With these powers, the party has developed (provincially varied) rules and practices that can allow it to announce the date for a nomination meeting after the filing deadline has passed, a process that effectively let party bosses "declare nominations closed before they were opened."[28] In 1997 Carolyn Bennett, in Toronto-St. Paul's, was one of several beneficiaries of this tactic when she won her nomination by acclamation as the only candidate to have declared her intention by the (unknown to others) cut-off date. In a variation on this theme, party organizers worked to effect the outcome of the Notre-Dame-de-Grâce-Lachine nomination contest by freezing the acceptance of new memberships and thereby effectively thwarting the recruitment efforts of individuals it did not want to see chosen.[29]

The party has also challenged local-constituency autonomy more directly by providing that the leader may intervene in any district to appoint the local candidate. In the past two general elections, Chrétien has used this power in twenty different cases, and for a number of different, though sometimes overlapping, reasons. First has been the party's concern to increase the number of women and minority candidates: twelve of the twenty appointees have been women. The second category of appointees have been individuals identified as "star" candidates that the party was anxious to have in its parliamentary caucus (and government) but was afraid might not survive the considerable uncertainties of a local nomination battle. During the 1993 election, both Marcel Masse, in Hull-Aylmer, and Art Eggleton, in York Centre, fell into this category. Such cases are not unlike opening a seat through a by-election to recruit a new member into the cabinet, something Chrétien did three times between the 1993 and 1997 elections. A third reason for the leader's direct intervention has been to defend a sitting MP from local challenges (e.g., Len Hopkins, in Renfrew-Nippising-Pembroke, in 1993) or support one caught in a redistribution squeeze (e.g., Sarkis Assourian, in Brampton Centre, in 1997). Finally, the leader has used this power to defend local associations from the threat of a takeover by single-interest groups, something that had emerged as a significant problem when Tom Wappel's pro-life supporters captured a number of constituency associations during the party's 1990 leadership contest in an attempt to push their cause on the party.[30]

Despite the fact that it was a national party convention that gave the leader the power to appoint candidates, its use provokes considerable local controversy and is widely denounced by members in the ridings as inimical to Canadian notions of party democracy.[31] In a number of instances, it has disrupted the constituency organization and driven disappointed activists and their supporters to abandon the party. Most of the Hull-Aylmer executive quit after Masse was imposed on them in 1993, while a former Vancouver-Kingsway candidate upstaged by a 1997 appointment deserted the party to run for Reform. The impact of these leaders' appointments has been mixed: after 1997, only eleven of the twenty made for the 1993 and 1997 elections were in the House of Commons. The number of appointments made in 1997 (six) was less than half that of 1993 (fourteen), so it may be that the party is responding to internal criticism and intends to rely more on indirect methods in the future. Given the importance of the local nomination process in stimulating membership, the party needs to be careful that its direct attacks on local autonomy do not imperil its capacity to recruit enough volunteers to staff the constituency electoral organizations needed to fight its local campaigns.

Local Campaigning

The dominant interpretation of Canadian electoral politics now suggests that local party activity is pretty inconsequential to the outcome of national elections. It may be that the local battles over nominations determine who will get to carry the party banner, but we are told that voters are drawn to support the party by the national campaign that focuses on leadership and party policy, all delivered by sophisticated mass-media messages.[32] Local campaigns, by this account, are simply the final organizational pieces of a centrally planned and integrated national politics. The franchise metaphor is helpful here. Just as hungry consumers flock to their local McDonald's not because it is local, but because it is McDonald's, voters are believed to vote for the party candidate not because of the local candidate's virtue, but to support the party. But surely this is an exaggeration. There is good reason to think that the local organizations parties have on the ground are more important in shaping outcomes than this portrait suggests.

Certainly the national parties make a good deal of effort to control their local campaigns. They impose common communication packages, complete with lawn signs, brochures, and so on, bearing a common party logo; provide campaign manuals and organize campaign schools for candidates and party workers; manage direct-mail and run phone banks; hire skilled organizers to manage specially targeted constituency campaigns; and, during the election period, regional coordinators bombard the candidate's organization with endless unsolicited advice by phone, fax, e-mail, and personal contact. However, they do all this not only as part of delivering a national campaign to the voters, but because they believe that local campaigns do matter, that they do make a difference.

Parties know that elections are decided by seats won and that it is the local candidate's campaign that must deliver them. Canadian election outcomes are extraordinarily variable, so that few seats can be counted on.[33] Over the decade 1987-97, at least 80 percent of the country's constituencies were represented by members from at least two different parties. In 1997, an election that narrowly returned the Liberals, the government's majority was provided by five MPs who won by less than a two-percentage-point margin. Overall, nine MPs won their seats by less than one percentage point, sixteen of them by less than a three-percentage-point margin, and five with less than a third of the vote in their electoral district. Of the 211 incumbents who ran, 35 were defeated, 5 of them by a margin of less than two percentage points, and 3 by opponents who themselves had less than a third of the local vote. On the other hand, five incumbents squeaked back in by a margin of less than two percentage points, three did so despite winning less than 34 percent of the vote in their riding, and four MPs won by fewer than 100 votes. In the face of these realities, the parties know that their parliamentary fate is intimately tied up with the success of their local campaigns.

Candidate and party election spending provides a direct measure of the balance of local and national campaign efforts. The Canada Elections Act constrains the spending of both candidates and national parties, so that these patterns are not entirely the result of free choices by the parties. Nevertheless, they are revealing about the current play of local campaigning in Canadian elections. Figure 8.3 plots the local proportion of total election spending, by party, over the past quarter-century. It indicates that close to 60 percent of all election-period spending is done by candidates in local contests. In the two new parties, the proportion spent by local candidates has so far been even higher, as their campaign efforts have especially focused on the regions and constituencies where they expected to win. The New Democrats are something of an exception, their local share having dropped below 50 percent in the 1990s, reflecting the fact that their stopgap candidates run only very nominal contests in a large number of constituencies.[34] These very large amounts are being spent by local organizations (over $39 million, as compared with $34 million for the five national party campaigns in 1997) with the expectation that they will have an impact on the election of their candidates.

Any election campaign, if it is to be successful, needs to identify and organize its supporters, communicate its message to the electorate, and then mobilize its voters to turn out at the polls. While the national campaign sets the framework for these activities, and is particularly important

Figure 8.3

Local spending as a percentage of election spending, 1974-97

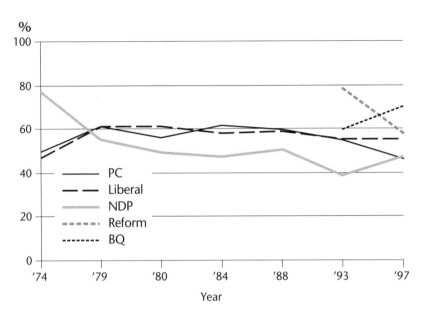

in running the mass-media advertising that dominates so much of modern electoral discourse, the local organization is crucial to targeting a local electorate and getting the parties' vote into the ballot boxes on election day. And for all of their activities, local party organizations need the two basic resources of any campaign: money and volunteer labour.

Given the importance of local campaigns, and the large amounts of money spent on them during elections, one might expect that the finances of a party's local and national campaigns would be carefully tied together. Surprisingly, they are not. A study done for the Royal Commission on Electoral Reform indicated that in only about one-quarter of the cases were local associations' electoral finances fully integrated with those of their national party, with funds flowing back and forth between them. Almost as many riding parties are taxed to support the national campaign while getting no financial support in return, a relationship that offers the national party only limited leverage over the conduct of a constituency campaign.[35]

By far the largest number of riding parties are financially autonomous; they neither support the national party campaign nor receive any money from it. This is more evidence of the local autonomy that characterizes the relationship between the national parties and their local associations at the grass-roots level.

The majority of local associations are left to their own devices to raise, and spend, their election campaign funds. The most important way of doing this is still personal contact – simply directly asking individuals or organizations (local firms, unions, or interest groups) for a donation. In the ridings, it is the local candidate who is the focus of the fund-raising campaign. The majority of local associations admit that their local candidate is "very important" to the success of their election fund-raising, a proportion that rises to two-thirds for winning organizations. Parties do not just ask for money to support this or that candidate: nearly half of all associations report that the personal effort and attention of the candidate him- or herself is crucial to successful local campaign fund-raising.[36] For parties, this makes the selection of their candidates more than merely the identification of local standard-bearers. Since local campaigns depend on local funds, the prospects for success of many constituency parties rests on the ability and willingness of their candidate to raise money.

Besides money, local party organizations need to staff a campaign team. Campaign managers are, for the most part, chosen by the local candidate, and while an increasing number now employ paid managers, and some even paid staff, the large majority must depend on local volunteers to manage their campaign.[37] Certainly volunteers continue to populate the teams of workers contacting voters, delivering party messages, and staffing the election-day organization designed to maximize supporter turnout at the polls. Many of these volunteers are just those individuals drawn back to party membership and political activity by the nomination process that starts another political cycle. They come to support a particular local candidate. If their favourite wins the nomination, they often stay to work in the election campaign; if they have supported a losing nomination bid, they are likely to drift out of the riding association as quickly as they entered. Thus, despite the importance often attributed to party loyalty, policy, or leadership, it is the local candidate who is the most important factor in attracting volunteers to work on election campaigns. Choosing a different candidate usually means ending up with a different set of volunteers. Taken with the candidate's role in fund-raising, this is why the local nomination process inevitably sets the tone for the constituency-level campaign, and often predicts the success with which the party will run it.[38] One important consequence is that there is not a great deal of continuity in the campaign organizations of riding parties: half the volunteers in the 1988 general election hadn't worked in their association's campaign only four years earlier.[39] Of course, with the arrival of two new parties in 1993, many of the volunteers working in the campaigns found themselves supporting different parties from those they had supported only a few years earlier.

Local campaigns, irrespective of how similar they are made to appear by the parties, can be quite idiosyncratic. The resources (in people and money) that they have varies enormously across the parties, from riding to riding, and even from election to election, for the same riding party. While the national media focus on leadership and big policy issues such as the economy, local campaigns are frequently preoccupied with the concerns of voters in the constituency. Sometimes these reflect local manifestations of national issues, but often they do not. In 1988, one of the most nationalized general elections in recent decades, half of the candidates of the major parties found themselves having to deal with single-interest groups that attempted to influence the local campaign. So, while the national campaign seemed preoccupied with the Free Trade Agreement, candidates in one-quarter of the ridings were trying to cope with pressures to debate the merits of abortion, while in another quarter they were dealing with two dozen other issues.

In 1997, with the Liberal government defending its economic record, Reform trying to make national unity a salient issue, the Conservatives demanding tax breaks, and the New Democrats arguing for employment targets, the candidates in Vancouver Centre soon discovered that another issue was on the minds of that riding's voters. Canvassers for all the parties reported that they were continually being asked for their position on the regulation of herbal medicines. As it happened, that issue had not made the national parties' policy manuals, but within days all the local campaigns had drafted positions and published hand-outs on the subject. None thought it would be a definitive issue, and it wasn't (Liberal candidate Hedy Fry won with just 41 percent of the vote, but a healthy eighteen-percentage-point lead), but none forgot that Kim Campbell had won the same riding in 1988 by just 269 votes, fewer than the number of spoiled ballots, and none was prepared to take the chance that it could not be that close again. So whatever the focus of the national campaigns, the candidates campaigning in Vancouver Centre were ready to talk to voters about herbal medicines.[40]

So what evidence is there that these local campaigns make a difference to the outcome in the constituencies? A recent study of constituency-level campaigning demonstrates that money and personnel do make a significant difference: the more a campaign has of both the better it can do. There are limitations to this: campaigns of the leading party garner a smaller pay-off, largely because they have less room to improve their vote-share than do opposition parties, and the country's election law ultimately constrains the impact of money by limiting just how much a constituency campaign can spend. But, that said, local campaign efforts can move local votes. Even in the highly nationalized 1988 campaign, adding an extra 100 volunteers increased a Liberal riding party's local vote share by 1.4 percent (the comparable NDP figure was 0.9 percent), and the impact of increased spending was equally significant.[41] Given the number of seats that turn over by margins no bigger than this, the parties are right to recognize that, while there is a national election battle to be fought, there are also 301 distinct local battles that can be ignored only at their peril.

The thirty-five incumbents who lost their seats in 1997 were as much losers of local battles as victims of a larger electoral war. Two were leading cabinet ministers in a government losing its lustre in Atlantic Canada, but among the others were Bloc MPs defeated by Conservatives and Liberals in Quebec, and Liberals defeated by Conservatives in Manitoba, by New Democrats in the Maritimes and Winnipeg, and by Reformers on the Prairies. But there were also Reformers defeated by New Democrats, and New Democrats defeated by Reformers, in Saskatchewan. In all of their ridings, the local battle had some impact on the outcome, and worked to change the face of Parliament and the national party system it housed.

On the Ground

Canadian parties are defined by the very practice of nominating candidates and then conducting an election campaign on their behalf. As we have seen, these activities are rooted in the individual constituencies, where long traditions of local autonomy and local democracy work to shape them. However, the electoral orientation of the parties, with open and highly permeable memberships that move with the electoral cycle, guarantees that their local organizational roots are shallow and constantly being remade.

The parties are defined by the candidates they nominate. These individuals are chosen in largely autonomous and idiosyncratic local processes, are important to the success of the local electoral campaign, and then leave politics after a comparatively short career, and the process begins again.[42] The parliamentary caucuses that define the day-to-day national party system are made up of the survivors of this volatile local politics. In years such as 1984 or 1993, when heavy partisan winds are blowing, the local political climate may count for relatively little, though even then it will be the results of local nomination contests that determine much of the character of the winning party's caucus. In less clearcut election years such as 1997, local impulses make even stronger marks on the party system.

There are some differences across the parties in terms of their nomination and campaign practices (the Conservatives practise the greatest amount of local autonomy, the Liberals and New Democrats the least), but they pale in terms of the variation within the parties from local association to local association. More important are the political, financial, and personnel resources available to local partisans and their determination to employ them. With the addition of the Bloc and Reform as serious competitors, many constituency contests have become both more complex and more marginal, factors that have increased the importance of the local campaign.

In this, Canadian parties have not changed much over the century, even as the party system has been turned on its head more than once. The new party system emerging in the 1990s is wrestling with the long-standing local autonomy for national discipline equation: the Liberals trying to strengthen national discipline, Reformers advocating more local autonomy. But the old trade-off continues to hold as a defining characteristic of our politics because it continues to be Canadian parties' organizational solution to their problem of linking a plural society to majority cabinet government.

9

In the Air:
National Campaign Communication

One of the primary activities of political parties in democratic nations is the waging of election campaigns. On the ground, Canadian federal elections are 301 unique, local contests. In the air, it is the national parties that structure the electoral competition. The previous chapter compared local party associations to franchises of a national retail chain. To carry the analogy one step further, it is the national strategists that create and execute the parties' marketing plans. The national parties use radio, television, airplanes, and cyberspace to execute their campaign strategies; thus this phase of their efforts can be called the "air campaign." While the parties' principal campaign objective has remained the same – to convince voters to support their candidates – the methods have changed over time. In the new party system, responding to the changing context of party competition, and making use of new communication technologies, the parties are increasingly targeting discrete groups of voters with campaign messages designed specifically for the targeted group.

The election efforts of the parties' national offices are in some ways an ongoing affair. Parties are constantly raising funds with an eye towards building a war chest for their next campaign, and are always watching public opinion for shifting voter attitudes. In between election campaigns, however, the parties' national staff are largely occupied with the more routine activity of providing organizational support to their riding associations and preparing for biennial conventions. About eighteen months prior to an anticipated election call, the pace of election preparation increases. These early preparations are highly centralized, involving only a small group of party strategists – most often with close ties to the party leader. Many of these individuals are the same men and women who played central roles in the party leader's winning leadership campaign and have remained part of his or her personal team.[1]

Early on, this small group, often about half a dozen in number, makes preliminary decisions about campaign personnel and begins to identify key groups of voters and to test potential campaign themes. If the group does not include a campaign pollster, one is brought in, and an advertising team is put in place. During this period, there is a perceptible shift in responsibility and authority in most parties' organizational structure from what one former party president calls the "peacetime generals" to the "wartime generals." The peacetime generals are the parties' apparatchiks; they keep the extra-parliamentary party functioning between election campaigns. The wartime generals are the campaign strategists and managers, usually steeped in election experience, but working in the private sector between election campaigns.

This core group of party strategists works with one goal in mind: maximizing the number of seats held by their party in the House of Commons. The national parties involve themselves, to some degree, with the ground campaign, for example, overseeing candidate nominations, preparing riding services packages, and organizing candidate-training sessions. However, most of the energy of the core strategy team is focused on the air campaign – developing the best message to communicate to voters, and the most effective way to package and deliver the message. Studies of Canadian national elections make it clear that, while individual riding-campaign dynamics have some influence on voters, the national air campaign has the greatest influence. Cognizant of this fact, the parties expend considerable effort and resources planning and executing their national campaigns, including the election platforms and the campaign themes that flow from them, the leaders' national tours, and the television and radio advertising strategies designed to deliver their message.

In parties' attempts to maximize their number of seats in the House of Commons, the strategic imperative is to identify the right message to convey to the right voters. Party pollsters play a crucial role in identifying the voters to be targeted and the issues that will influence their voting decision. The parties' creative teams then develop and package the campaign's messages in a manner most likely to be persuasive to these voters. It is this set of activities that are at the heart of national election campaigning in the new party system, for it is the success of a party in identifying the right ridings, targeting the right voters within these ridings, developing a persuasive message for these voters, and delivering that message to them in a convincing package that largely determines their electoral fate. The result of all these efforts is a pattern of increasingly targeted and fragmented political communication that leaves little room for a national campaign dialogue.

In the third party system, the parties used methods of mass communication to send a national message to voters from coast to coast. David Smith refers to this method of campaigning and governing as "pan-Canadianism." Smith identifies television as playing a critical role in this development as it provided the method by which parties could simultaneously communicate with all Canadians. Television had a nationalizing effect on political communication, "with a consequent sacrifice of regional perspective."[2] The national parties were able, for the first time, to set a national agenda for campaigns and to present a common front to all voters. This was accomplished through television commercials broadcast on the national networks, national leaders' tours with reporters following along to capture common footage for broadcast on both local newscasts and the national networks, and events such as leaders' debates broadcast across the country. All Canadians, regardless of their location, or the activities of their local party associations, were provided with a base of common political information. The influence of this pan-Canadian approach is evident in the public policy issues with an inherently national scope that dominated political discourse during the third party system.

After more than three decades of pan-Canadianism, which culminated in one of the country's most nationalized elections in 1988, the traditional parties were surprised to watch the 1993 federal election develop into a series of unique regional contests. A different constellation of parties was competitive in each of the country's regions, with different issues the focus of voter attention in each. While the old-line parties had often stressed different issues in different regions, there had never before been an election quite like 1993's, with the parties winning the second- and third-largest number of parliamentary seats effectively ignoring as much or more of the country than they aggressively competed in.

With the exception of the Liberals, who found some national traction for their version of the simple but venerable message of "Throw the bums out," the old-line parties experienced great difficulty in successfully implementing their national strategies in the 1993 campaign. The parties learned from their 1993 experiences and prepared very differently for the 1997 campaign. They acknowledged that there would no longer be one national campaign, but rather a number of different regional campaigns for each party. The Liberals, the only party to compete aggressively in all parts of the country in 1997, prepared different strategies and messages for each region, reflecting both the political competition in the region and the issues of concern to local voters.

Campaign communication at the outset of the fourth party system is no longer national in scope, but rather is targeted by region and a host of socio-economic factors. Just as the advent of television and public-opinion polling initially facilitated the adoption of pan-Canadian politics, new changes in the way Canadians use television and more advanced methods of public-opinion polling have now made possible centrally organized but regionally discrete communications – all occurring during the course of a "national" election campaign.

Campaign Communication in the First Three Party Systems

Political-campaign communication history in Canada falls into three periods: from Confederation until 1930, 1930 up until the late 1950s, and from then until the transforming election of 1993. The transition from one period to the next is defined by the application of new communication technologies resulting in fundamental change to the character of electoral competition. It is not surprising that the transition periods marking the adoption of new technological techniques roughly coincide with the transition periods for party systems, as changes in party activity have largely parallelled the introduction of new communication technologies.

The first period of Canadian political communication was marked by the lack of a pervasive national media. The problems of size and distance were paramount, and campaigns were rarely driven by national debates, but, instead, were usually a collection of local contests. Without national newspapers, television, or radio, the parties and their leaders were dependent upon personal contact to convey their messages to voters. As Michael Nolan has observed of this period, "platform speeches were probably the most important means of direct communication for politicians at election time."[3] The partisan newspaper, the public meeting, the political picnic, and the campaign train were the principal campaign tools available to parties. The newspapers were vitally important to the parties for they provided the main form of communication, linking their grass-roots supporters together, thus serving a purpose similar to that of a contemporary party newsletter.

The election campaign of 1878 has been described as a contest between Macdonald and Mackenzie as to who could attend the most political picnics.[4] Whistle-stop train tours allowed the leaders to travel to more parts of the country and to attract local media attention. Still, the only voters to actually see or hear the leaders were those who gathered at the train stations or in the parks to meet them personally. The parties relied upon local notables and supporters to help turn out the vote within the ridings. Recognizing the parties' limited ability to communicate directly with many voters, Paltiel and Van Loon concluded that "the organization of supporters and mobilization of voters took precedence over the communication of party platforms."[5]

The second period of campaign communication was marked by the advent of radio. While the parties continued to spend large amounts on newspaper advertising, the use of radio had a striking and significant impact on campaign communications. Radio made its debut in Canada in 1920, but it was not until the general election of 1930 that its presence was first felt in a national political campaign. Both the Liberals and the Conservatives purchased radio time to air speeches by their leaders. In fact, Conservative leader R.B. Bennett kicked off his 1930 campaign with a speech broadcast on radio from Winnipeg.[6]

Provincial politicians were quicker to recognize the power of the new medium. Alberta's William "Bible Bill" Aberhart used weekly radio broadcasts from the Calgary Prophetic Bible Institute to build popular support for his political ideas and eventually to lead his fledgling Social Credit Party to power in 1935.[7] In doing so, Aberhart revealed one of the important promises of radio: the ability to bypass a hostile press and communicate directly with voters. This was an especially important advance, given that many newspapers of the day were still often strongly partisan. While the partisan press was in decline, many newspapers were still dominated by reporters and columnists committed to a particular political and social ideology. Radio provided political leaders with the opportunity to present their views directly to voters without passing them through a media filter. For talented users of the medium, such as Aberhart, this proved a powerful new tool.

A second way in which radio changed the nature of political communication was by allowing party leaders to communicate simultaneously with voters in different communities. In the days of the old whistle-stop tours, a leader visiting different regions of the country might use a different text on each occasion. Radio meant that voters from different parts of a region, and sometimes even different provinces, would now be listening to the same speech. This resulted in leaders addressing more regional and national issues in their speeches, at the expense of local ones. Attendance at political meetings also began to drop as voters could remain at home and listen to the party leaders directly. Radio meant that it was no longer necessary to attend local meetings in order to learn about the issues and the parties' positions.[8]

Radio, and the increased use of advertising professionals, also allowed for the manipulation of a leader's image. Tom Axworthy cites the example of the Liberals' hiring the advertising agency Cockfield Brown and Co. of Montreal to create the "Uncle Louis" campaign of 1949.[9] Dalton Camp recalls how the "Liberal Party seized the new instruments of communication" to re-make St. Laurent – a sober, somewhat distant, corporate lawyer – into "everyone's handsomely aging uncle, doting on children, whimsical, a little patronizing and a whole lot more visible."[10] Camp identifies the power of the new medium and the increasing importance of image when he recalls that, while Conservative advisors carefully scrutinized the text of all of the prime minister's speeches, no one paid any attention to the Liberal leader's change in image. As Camp subsequently remembered, "I recall no one saying, for example, how devilishly clever it was to take this man, a wealthy corporation lawyer, and convert him into some Gladstonian version of 'The People's William,' so as to magnify the contrast with Mr. Drew."[11]

The third era of political communication, widely agreed to have begun in the late 1950s, is characterized by the widespread availability of television and advances in public-opinion polling. In many ways, radio set the stage for the introduction of television by establishing the trends of the increasing importance of the leader and his image, the necessity of talking in national terms, and the decline in emphasis on political organization at the local level.

The 1957 federal election between John Diefenbaker and Louis St. Laurent was the first Canadian election to be covered by television. From this very first television campaign, it became clear that this medium would fundamentally change election campaigns and have a significant influence on their outcomes. Changes were evident in both the way parties waged their electoral campaigns and the way the news media covered the campaigns. Diefenbaker understood the importance of this new medium and exploited it to his advantage, while St. Laurent was highly suspicious of it.[12] Indeed, whereas St. Laurent made only a couple of television appearances, Diefenbaker took advantage of every opportunity to appear. As a result, "a survey of homes with television sets in populous southwestern Ontario showed that Diefenbaker made the strongest impression."[13] As Reginald Whitaker has written, "television was an unmitigated disaster for the Liberals, a disaster so frightful that the party leadership itself was appalled and shaken."[14]

Television's fascination with personalities had a significant effect upon the parties. Television coverage of the parties' dramatic leadership conventions, the leaders' campaign tours, and leadership debates, with their emphasis on personality, all served to increase the pre-eminence of the party leader both during election campaigns and in the parliamentary caucus. While the questions of the relative electoral importance of the local candidate, the party label, and the national party leader have long been debated, the importance of the leaders markedly increased, as the television camera focused on them for much of the election campaign. In the third party system, leaders were always surrounded by entourages that included people skilled in the new technologies.[15] In many ways, the increased emphasis on mastering the use of new communication technology undermined the importance of having a locally based, nationally integrated campaign organization.

As television coverage of campaigns simultaneously reached Canadians from coast to coast, it encouraged "the trend begun by radio to regard elections as a national event, with the country seen as a single electoral district."[16] If the second period of campaigning began a shift from constituency-based emphasis to a regional and national one, this focus intensified in the third system, as "parties responded to the new context by shifting the focus of their attention from region to nation."[17]

The widespread use of the airplane also changed the nature of the leaders' tours. Rather than slowly crossing the country by train, and going where the tracks led, leaders were now able to travel back and forth across the country on a daily basis. This allowed campaign strategists to move the leader, and the accompanying press coverage, quickly from region to region, depending upon how an unfolding campaign shifted their strategic needs.

The other important advance marking the third period of campaign communication was the public-opinion poll. While the first public-opinion poll in Canada was conducted in 1941 by the Canadian Institute of Public Opinion, it was not until the early 1960s that national polling was commonly used by the Liberals.[18] The Pearson Liberals were the first to make systematic use of scientific polling. Prior to the 1962 election, US pollster Lou Harris was brought to Ottawa to take several polls for the party, and polling has been an integral part of the parties' campaign efforts ever since.

The primary function of public-opinion polling is to provide information to the parties on what voters are thinking. In doing this, the poll replaces the grass-roots party organization and MPs in filtering information from the constituencies to the party leadership. As Ward observed in 1970, it is the riding association that "transmits opinions, suggestions, and complaints from the party members to the elected representative in Parliament or in the Legislative Assembly, though this function is being superseded in part by the use of private opinion polls."[19] Today the traditional parties are almost completely reliant on opinion polling for gathering information on public opinion. As a result, "the traditional feedback role of party members and even MPs has become superfluous."[20]

Campaign Communication in the New Party System

Polling and Television Advertising
Party pollsters are assuming an increasingly important position among the parties' wartime personnel.[21] As the parties attempt to target specific groups of voters with tailored messages, the pollsters play a key role in identifying the regions of the country where the party should concentrate its resources, the voters to target in each region, and the message most likely to persuade these voters. While Canadian political polling has its roots in the United States, several prominent home-grown political pollsters have emerged in the last two decades, the Liberals' Martin Goldfarb and the Conservatives' Allan Gregg having been the most influential. Goldfarb was the Liberal party pollster from 1974 to 1984, and Gregg the Conservatives' from 1979 to 1993.[22] Many insiders in both parties give a significant amount of credit to these two men for the majority governments won by their parties during their tenure. Today a second generation of Canadian pollsters is working with the parties. This new group of wartime operatives includes the Liberal's Michael Marzolini, André Turcotte with Reform, Jim Matsui with the New Democrats, the Conservatives' Brian Owen, and Michel LePage of the Bloc Québécois.[23]

Successful political pollsters tend to have long roots in both polling and politics, and are keen observers of election campaigns. Unlike many others involved in electoral politics, pollsters occasionally work for different political parties – though not different competitors in the same election. Turcotte, for instance, worked for Marzolini on the 1993 Liberal campaign before switching to Reform. Similarly, the New Democrats' Matsui has previously done work for both the Liberals and the Conservatives, and the Liberal's Goldfarb did polling for the Ontario Conservatives and the British Columbia Social Credit. While all profess loyalty to their current clients, they also stress the need to retain a strong sense of objectivity in their work. Some degree of detachment is necessary in order to clearly interpret the information contained in polling data. In many cases, the pollsters are more committed to their craft than to any one political party.

It quickly becomes apparent when talking to these men and their clients that there is a great deal of truth to the popular adage that polling is both art and science. The pollster must have a solid technical training to ensure the drawing of representative samples and the proper wording of questions, as well as a sufficient understanding of statistical methods to be able to cull information from the raw numbers. But the good political pollster is also able to see beyond the numbers to decipher and understand the underlying voter sentiment. Perhaps most important, a good pollster must be able to interpret and translate voter sentiment into a prescribed course of action for the party campaign. The skilled pollster can predict how particular actions by the party will influence public opinion, and can identify which issues make particular voters more likely to vote for it. This ability is what makes the pollster of real use to a political party. As Marzolini puts it, being a party pollster is somewhat similar to being Sherlock Holmes, always searching for the one big clue that will help to make sense of everything else.

In successful campaigns the pollster works especially closely and effectively with the campaign's advertising team. One of the primary purposes of the pollster's research is to inform the campaign's advertising, but this method is effective only if the two teams work well together. The parties had different experiences in this regard in the 1997 campaign. In the most integrated operation, Matsui worked out of the same room as the New Democrats' creative team from Vancouver's Now Communications and played an important role in developing the party's advertising strategy. Marzolini has a long-established relationship with Gordon Ashworth, who coordinates the Liberals' Red Leaf advertising group; and Turcotte and Reform's advertising director, Bryan Thomas, from the London, Ontario, firm Thomas, Crncich and Partners, established a close working relationship. In contrast, the Conservatives experienced some difficulties in this regard in 1997. Changes were made at the senior level of the campaign on the eve of the election call, and the team never functioned smoothly. Even by the end of the campaign, advertising consultant Perry Miele, from Toronto's Gingko Group, had not developed a close working relationship with the party's pollster.[24]

The use of media agencies as specialists to oversee a party's media campaign dates back to the 1930s.[25] With the advent of television campaigning, the advice of media experts became essential, and for several decades all the major parties have entered into relationships with advertising agencies for the purpose of developing and executing their campaign media communications strategy. In the 1997 campaign, the New Democrats, Conservatives, and Reform all effectively brought one advertising agency into the campaign structure to consult on media strategies and hired them to make the campaign's advertisements. In many ways this relationship is similar to that between a media firm and its commercial clients.

For the last seven elections, the Liberals have taken a different approach. Liberal campaign advertising is managed under the umbrella of Red Leaf Advertising, the in-house advertising structure put together by the party every election cycle. Instead of contracting with a single firm, through the Red Leaf structure the party brings together a team of advertising experts from different agencies. For the 1997 campaign, long-time party operative and national-campaign director Gordon Ashworth recruited the Red Leaf creative team, attended its meetings, and served as a liaison between the campaign's political leadership and the advertisers. Through the Red Leaf structure, the Liberals' believe the campaign's political leadership is able to exercise more control over the advertising agenda and ensure that it is consistent with the campaign's overall message and objectives.[26]

Red Leaf was created after the party's dismal effort in the 1972 campaign, which centred on the infamously weak slogan "The Land Is Strong." According to Joseph Wearing, "the party felt it had not participated enough in advertising decisions that were being made by admen who spent most of their time selling soap."[27] In its early years, Jerry Grafstein "was the self-described 'political commissar' of the agency – working with the admen through all the stages of copy, design, layout and ensuring that the party's advertising adhered closely to the campaign committee's strategy."[28] Those recruited to serve on Red Leaf volunteer their time. However, as Ashworth points out, recruitment is not terribly difficult as the work is both interesting and prestigious and, perhaps most important for some, the Government of Canada is one of the largest advertisers in the country.

All of the parties now recognize the importance of recruiting advertising specialists who have experience in the political world. The parties' political leaders are quite wary of relying on extremely creative people who have no political antennae directing their advertising campaigns. The advertising persons themselves acknowledge the importance of involving politically savvy people in the process. Miele, for example, relied upon a small group of senior aides at Conservative campaign head-quarters who he felt had particularly strong political instincts to vet his advertising ideas and to spot potential problem areas. Owing to the par-ticularly regionalized nature of the 1997 election, the parties were careful to have regional input into their advertising campaigns. For example, Ashworth recruited an advisory committee of advertising specialists from the regions to consult with the Liberals' Toronto-based creative team.

All of the parties have different internal cultures, which is reflected in their attitudes towards political polling and advertising. The Liberals and Conservatives are the most experienced and comfortable with sophisti-cated research and advertising techniques. Both parties have been polling for more than three decades and have largely adopted a corporate mar-keting approach to their election campaigns. The New Democrats, while accepting the necessity of polling, are not as comfortable with it, nor as dependent upon it, as are the other two old-line parties. Matsui expresses some frustration with the New Democrats' more traditional election cul-ture, centred on a belief that elections are fought through personal con-tacts, such as door-to-door canvassing. With some limited success, he has made it his mission to get the party to adopt a more business-like approach and to use more sophisticated marketing strategies. For its part, the Reform Party's populist culture leads its members to be sceptical of all political professionals. Turcotte sensed this suspicion immediately and has encountered several senior party activists who wonder why the party needs political professionals at all. Many of the party's activists are partic-ularly suspicious of central Canadian political strategists who they fear will water down the party's platform in an effort to make it more accept-able to central Canadian elites. Pollsters are viewed as part of the problem with this "old-style" politics. Turcotte fights this by emphasizing his role in helping the party to target segments of the electorate and to frame its message in the most effective manner, as opposed to modifying the fun-damental message.

The relative financial strength of the parties also influences their views of the amount of polling that is necessary. Polling is extremely expensive, and none of the pollsters works for free. As discussed in Chapter 7, the Liberals and Conservatives regularly have considerably more funds at their disposal than do the other parties, and since polling expenses are explicitly exempted from the writ-period spending caps, the only limitation on the amount of polling a party may conduct is its capacity to pay for it.

The increased regionalism of the fourth party system has made polling more essential to the parties' electoral strategies than ever before. As the parties are now narrowing specific messages to focus on targeted groups, it is the pollsters' task to identify the key groups and the messages that will make them more likely to support the party. The pollsters' task is largely threefold: first, to identify regions of the country where their party has a sufficient concentration of potential supporters to offer the likelihood of winning a plurality of the vote in individual ridings; second, to identify the regional and socio-economic status of those voters who, though undecided or leaning to one party, may be persuaded to vote for their party (swing voters); and, finally, to determine which issue the party should emphasize in its conversation with each target group and what the best positioning of the party's policy is on that issue.

It is no longer sufficient for a pollster to report to the party client on which issues are of greatest importance to voters. The parties have limited resources and are competing in a fragmented market in which a vote share of 38 percent was enough to produce a majority government for the Liberals in 1997. Indeed, only the Liberals were aiming to win a majority in the 1997 campaign. Reform was aiming for Official Opposition status and knew that this would probably require winning less than 20 percent of the popular vote and about sixty parliamentary seats; the Bloc was hoping for a majority of Quebec's seats; and the New Democrats and Conservatives had as their most immediate goal the winning of at least twelve seats and regaining Official Party status in the House of Commons. This meant that no campaign team was concerned with winning the support of a majority of Canadians in the 1997 election – each was simply preoccupied with identifying and communicating with those swing voters in the key ridings that they needed to win to achieve their objective.

Canada's single-member electoral system ensures that geography is the first concern in developing an electoral strategy. The first step is for the pollster to identify regions of the country where there is a sufficient concentration of potential supporters to offer the likelihood of winning a plurality of the vote in individual ridings. For example, the Reform Party used its polling results to identify five regions where it concentrated its efforts in 1997: southwestern Ontario, Edmonton, the British Columbia lower mainland (but not Vancouver), Manitoba, and Saskatoon. Large portions of Alberta and British Columbia were not targeted, even though the party held almost all of those seats and was polling strongly in them at the outset of the campaign. Since parties need to focus their communication strategy on swing voters, they do not target those regions where they are already strong or have little voter support. Rather, they concentrate their efforts and resources where they see the potential to capture individual ridings.

The New Democrats have a long tradition of successfully concentrating their efforts in a relatively small number of ridings and thus maximizing their electoral yield. For example, the party received about a third as many votes as the Conservatives in 1993, yet elected four times as many members, and then again, in 1997, with approximately half the Conservative vote total, elected one more member than did the Conservatives. Learning from their 1993 experience, in an attempt to consolidate their support, and increase their representation in the House of Commons, the Conservatives concentrated their 1997 effort in parts of Ontario, Quebec, and Atlantic Canada. Even the Liberals, the only party running anything approaching a national campaign, expended few resources in large sections of the country – such as most of British Columbia outside of Victoria and parts of the lower mainland, and Alberta ridings outside of Edmonton.

Once the pollster has identified those regions of the country where the party is competitive and will focus its resources, attention is turned to the question of which market groups to target within these regions. The pollster is not able to come up with a list of voters to target, but, instead, develops composites of groups that are overrepresented in the "swing voter" category. The result is the identification of several different groups of voters with whom the parties want to communicate.

The pollster will identify the characteristics of voters who have not yet committed to voting for the client, but likewise have not ruled it out. A party does not want to waste resources talking to those who are ardent supporters of other parties, or with those who are already committed to supporting it (though some effort will be made to communicate with these voters to ensure that they actually vote). If voting participation rates continue to decline in Canada, we can expect to see the parties expending more effort on these committed voters as turnout will become a key factor in determining election outcomes. For the most part, though,

Canadian parties now tailor their message to the as-yet-unconvinced but still-persuadable swing voters.

The pollsters then determine which campaign themes are most effective in converting these specific voters into committed supporters of their party. The themes will differ by region, and by targeted group within the region. For example, in 1997, Reform decided that the following issues would be effective for the groups they had targeted in their key regions: in British Columbia and Alberta, national unity and political accountability; in Saskatchewan, tax relief, national unity, and political accountability; and, in Ontario, establishing Reform as a national party and national unity. Similarly, the Conservatives concentrated on different messages in their targeted regions: in Ontario, tax relief and health care; in Quebec, national unity and leadership; and, in Atlantic Canada, health care and social policy.

In determining which issues to concentrate on, the party is not simply mimicking the electorate, but is using opinion research to determine which of its various messages best resonates with their targeted voters. For example, prior to the 1997 election, Reform outlined dozens of policy positions in its "Fresh Start" campaign booklet. In deciding on its election themes, the party did not jettison those policy positions or make up new ones, but instead used opinion research to decide which of its positions it would emphasize where during the campaign. The pollsters' job was to tell the party which issue would generate the greatest positive impact on their targeted swing voters. In this instance, Reform learned through its opinion research that its policies on crime were not effective in convincing swing voters to support the party. While the party's research found that most Canadians agreed with Reform's crime-prevention policies, Turcotte's research found that highlighting the issue to targeted swing voters reinforced the "harsh edge" of the Reform image. Similarly, the party decided to downplay its positions regarding the need to reduce the size of government. This was particularly true in Ontario, where voters were just starting to feel the impact of the provincial Conservatives' "Common Sense Revolution" and were not receptive to a message promising more cutbacks and downsizing.

Accordingly, the party strategists decided not to revise Reform's policies, but simply chose not to include all of them in the campaign message delivered through advertisements and the leader's tour. Instead, the party concentrated its message on other issues, such as political accountability and national unity, that it believed would have a more positive effect on the voting decision of its targeted voters.

After determining which issues to concentrate on in each targeted region, the research turns to discovering the best positioning of the party's policy on the specific issues. Again, contrary to some popular opinion, this does not mean determining the party's position on the basis of poll results; rather, it means casting the party's predetermined position in the best light to make it persuasive to the targeted audience. For example, the Liberals were determined to make their fiscal accomplishments a centrepiece of their 1997 campaign. The party's researchers, however, learned that simply touting the fact that the government had balanced the budget, although widely acknowledged as a significant accomplishment, did not have a substantial effect on voting intentions. In part, this was the case because it was a past accomplishment, and elections are about the future, and it reminded voters of the heavy costs endured in balancing the budget but did not emphasize the accompanying benefits. Accordingly, the party discovered that it was more effective to sell its fiscal accomplishments in terms of future benefits. This led the Liberals to claim that their balancing of the budget provided the government the necessary fiscal room to modernize Canada's social programs for the twenty-first century.

The parties also use focus groups for purposes of gathering this type of information. Focus groups are small gatherings of voters (usually between ten and twenty) chosen to represent that cross section of the electorate being targeted by the campaign. These sessions are usually freewheeling discussion groups led by a professional moderator, and they generally last for about ninety minutes. Participants are paid a modest fee for their time and are not always told who is sponsoring the session. The campaigns use these events "to put flesh and emotion on the stark numbers of the polls."[29] Senior campaign operatives, sitting behind a one-way mirror, watch and listen to the discussion. The moderator will lead the group through a discussion of many topics, including the central issues in the campaign, the opposing parties' positions, and the positions of the sponsoring party. These sessions allow the strategists to hear what voters are thinking in far more detail than a poll allows. The information received is not scientific, in that the numbers are too small to offer any assurance of representativeness, but, if the same pattern recurs at several of these sessions, the parties can be confident that they are discovering something that may not be apparent from opinion polling. Besides helping to determine the best positioning of a party's policies, focus groups can assist a party in learning who its best spokespeople are on various issues. In 1997 the Liberals learned that Finance minister Paul Martin had great credibility with voters and was an effective spokesperson for delivering their economic message. As a result he was used as their public spokesperson on this issue.

Party polling does not begin with the drop of the election writ. All of the parties employ polls on an ongoing basis. For example, the Reform Party continues to conduct three or four national surveys each year, with sample sizes of approximately 1,500. The information received from these polls is utilized by the parliamentary party and in preparation for the next election. Reform used the results of its 1996 polls in developing its "Fresh Start" platform for the 1997 election.

Election polling normally begins with one or more large national baseline polls conducted in the months leading up to the election call. The Liberals, with significant funds in the bank and knowledge as to when the election would be called, conducted several large baseline polls in the months preceding the 1997 campaign, each with a sample size of approximately 2,400. These baseline polls are used in developing the strategic themes to be pursued during the election campaign and in creating the party advertising. With the permanent voters' list in place, the campaign period shrank in 1997, making pre-election polling more important than ever before. The shorter campaign period means the parties have less time for strategic adjustment, and accordingly more decisions need to be taken (and more television advertisements prepared), with only the baseline polls and focus group research to rely on.

For most parties, polling continues during the election campaign, primarily in the form of tracking polls. Tracking polls are used to measure changes in voter sentiment on an ongoing basis. A party conducting tracking polls will normally canvass a relatively small sample each night of the campaign. The results from any one day's polling are usually statistically insignificant because of the small sample size, so the pollster will pool the results from four or five sequential nights of polling to produce meaningful results. The following day, the numbers from the first night will be dropped and replaced by those from the current day. This gives the party ongoing data that track voter sentiment on a rolling basis. Daily sample sizes are usually in the low hundreds, though the Liberals, in 1997, were polling as many as 1,500 people a day by the end of the campaign. The Liberals were using this exceptionally large sample size in order to have significant tracking numbers for each region. Because the party was essentially fighting a series of regional campaigns, with a different constellation of opponents and salient issues in each, the overall national polling numbers were of little use to them in 1997. Marzolini found the regional tracking-poll numbers the most effective tool available to the party during the 1997 campaign. These numbers were used on a regular basis to make decisions regarding resource allocation, advertising strategies, and the leader's tour. Without this kind of sophisticated, detailed daily picture of the shifting electorate, the other parties were at a comparative disadvantage.

As tracking polls show shifts in voter opinion on a daily basis, they allow the parties to evaluate the effect of particular campaign strategies and events on voting intentions. For example, some parties use tracking to measure the effect of their television commercials. Bad results for a couple of days after the launch of a new advertisement in the absence of some other explanatory campaign event may result in the party pulling the advertisement.

Tracking polls are very expensive, and thus not used by all the parties. Tracking polls with daily samples of more than 1,000 would be out of the financial reach of many parties. The New Democrats limited their 1997 tracking to the few dozen ridings they were targeting. The tracking results were then used to continually narrow the list of targeted ridings that would receive much-needed funds, television advertising, and visits from the leader. By the end of the campaign, largely on the basis of the tracking numbers, the party had cut its list of targeted ridings in half, and was able to focus its campaign message and resources on very select groups of voters.

The Reform Party was the exception in 1997, as it conducted no tracking polls whatsoever. Reform Party strategists concluded that the short campaign period would not provide sufficient time to adjust their plans on the basis of tracking results. Faced with limited campaign funds, the party decided not to incur the expense of tracking polls. Turcotte believes this was a strategic mistake, and believes the party would have benefited from regional tracking that would have provided information concerning changes in voter sentiment in Reform's targeted regions. Instead, the party had to rely on data from its pre-election baseline and the information it picked up from focus groups during the campaign.

While quality polling research is essential to development and delivery of an effective advertising campaign, Conservative advertising consultant Miele warns against too much reliance on polling data. The danger is that, with the availability of daily tracking-poll results, nervous campaign officials may change direction on the basis of one or two nights' numbers. This may result in the party flailing around, from one issue to another, and never sticking with any strategy long enough to measure its real impact on voters. Miele suggests that it takes approximately fifteen days to see the full voter movement resulting from a campaign event, commercial, or party concentration on a particular issue. A short-sighted campaign team may panic after there is no voter movement recorded within the first few days of implementing a strategy and move on to another tack. The Conservatives experienced such a dilemma in 1997. Some party strategists became convinced fairly early on that they were not making substantial progress in Ontario by emphasizing tax relief – a key plank in the party's election platform. After Charest received favourable reviews for his performance in the English-language debate, they decided to drop their emphasis on the economic policies in their platform and, instead, concentrate on national unity. The problem with this strategy, according to Miele, is that there was never sufficient time given for the impact of the tax-relief issue to fully register in the polls. Furthermore, there was little quantitative evidence that a concentration on national unity would attract substantially more voters to the party. The Conservatives had faced a similar situation in 1988, when party support dropped midway through the campaign; that time, however, they stayed the course, stuck with their free-trade message, and recovered sufficiently to win a second majority government.

The parties also take different approaches with regard to riding-level polling. As described above, the New Democrats make the most strategic use of riding-level polling data. At the other extreme, the Reform Party conducted no polling at the riding level, and Turcotte discouraged individual candidates from commissioning polls. He advises candidates that riding-level polling is not a wise use of their funds, and that they would be better off spending their limited resources on advertising.

Marzolini conducted riding-level polls for Liberals in about fifty ridings during the 1997 campaign. In most instances these were commissioned by the local candidate, though on some occasions the national party had an interest in knowing what was happening in a particular riding. (For instance, senior Liberals were particularly interested in defeating star Conservative candidate Major General Lewis Mackenzie, and accordingly the Liberals polled in the Ontario riding of Parry Sound.) For a cost of about $7,000 to the local campaign, Marzolini conducted a riding poll, with a sample size of about 300 people, asking questions to determine which issues had local saliency, which strategic scenarios might benefit the Liberal candidate, and voter familiarity with the local candidates.[30] On the basis of these results, the candidate was provided with a canvassing, advertising, and get-out-the-vote plan.

While sympathetic to Turcotte's view that local polling is not a wise use of scarce local resources, Marzolini argues that it can occasionally mean the difference between victory and defeat, and illustrates this with the experience of the Toronto riding of Broadview-Greenwood in 1988. The New Democrats' Lynn McDonald was a popular incumbent who began her campaign with a substantial advantage over Liberal challenger Dennis Mills. In a poll for Mills, Marzolini asked voters how their voting intention might change if they knew that McDonald opposed Canada's participation in NATO. The result was a substantial number saying they would be less likely to vote for the incumbent – even among those who claimed to be committed supporters. This issue, which did not appear anywhere in the results of national polling and was not to be heard from any of the party leaders or national media covering the campaign, had particular saliency in this riding because of a large local Greek community concerned about possible Turkish aggression in the wake of a weakened NATO. On the basis of this information, Mills expended considerable effort informing voters about this rather obscure plank in the NDP platform rather than concentrating on free trade and the other issues dominating the national agenda. The result, Marzolini argues, was an upset victory for Mills on election night. While it is nearly impossible to attribute an electoral victory to any one tactic or strategy, this example does illustrate the potential usefulness of riding-level polling.

In successful campaigns, the pollsters are part of the campaign's strategic brain trust. The pollsters normally communicate their findings with only a very small number of senior party strategists (usually limited to three or four others, though the results are somewhat more widely disseminated in the New Democratic Party). And the numbers themselves are very highly guarded. In the case of the Liberals, Marzolini claims that the actual polling numbers never left his Toronto office, where they were guarded by motion detectors, and extra security personnel who swept the office for electronic bugs. The pollsters generally write brief memos summarizing their findings. It is important that they not simply report their findings but couch them in a strategic and proactive way. For instance, Turcotte is always cognizant of zeroing in on the key obstacles to increasing the Reform vote, and then recommending a target group and a message to be delivered to them. The pollsters limit their memos during the campaign to one or two pages, and present very few points so as to highlight the important information.

With the exception of data from specific riding polls, the numbers are not generally shared with riding campaigns or with regional or provincial campaign operatives. All of the pollsters are hard-pressed to come up with any connection between their national polling and local campaign efforts. The polling results are used almost exclusively for purposes of decision making regarding television advertising, resource allocation, and the leader's tour. The campaign as fought on the ground by local candidates and their scores of committed volunteers is almost completely disconnected from this work.

The principal use of the polling data is to inform the parties' communication strategies. It is through the mass media that the parties communicate their messages to large numbers of voters. If, for example, a campaign discovers that a large block of undecided eighteen- to thirty-year-old men primarily concerned with issues related to the budget deficit may be persuaded to vote for the party, they then turn to the mass media to communicate their deficit policies to that group. Ideally, the pollsters present their data to the media team, explain the underlying meaning to them, and work with them in developing a media campaign to communicate persuasively with the targeted group. This means that the relationship between the pollster and the media team is critical to the campaign's success.

Television remains the dominant method of campaign communication between parties and voters. More voters will see a party-sponsored television advertisement or watch an excerpt from a leader's stump speech on the evening news than will meet a candidate, attend a political meeting, or read a party mailing. Four factors have converged at the outset of the new party system to produce a significant change in the way parties are using television to communicate with voters. These factors are: (1) the increasing regionalization of party competition; (2) the use of more sophisticated polling techniques, providing the parties with detailed information on subsets of voters; (3) the explosive growth in the number of cable and specialty TV channels; and (4) the need to use "time buyers" to reach particular audience segments.

The first result of these changes is that parties no longer use television simply to send a single message to all voters, but, instead, as a primary tool in their efforts to send targeted messages to particular voting groups.

Party strategists put together a television marketing plan for each campaign that includes both paid and free advertising, the leader's tour, and participation in leaders' debates and town-hall forums, all aimed at communicating their message to their targeted voters.

Like their pollster colleagues, the media advisors of the national parties talk about the 1997 campaign in regional terms. Ashworth reports that it was the first time in his long experience with the Liberal party that the campaign was perceived in regional terms. It was also the first time that the party used regionally targeted advertisements. This tactic reflected the fact that the Liberals had different opponents attacking them on different issues, and from different directions, in each region. For instance, the party was being attacked from the right by the Conservatives and Reform on economic issues in Ontario, while both the New Democrats and the Conservatives were fighting the Liberals from the left on health care and social policy in Atlantic Canada; meanwhile, the party was fighting off Reform from the right and the New Democrats from the left in Western Canada. Given these electoral challenges, it quickly became apparent to the campaign's leadership that one set of national advertisements would not suffice. The party needed to tailor its advertisements to an electoral context of different opponents and different salient issues in each region. Of course, the parties have always treated French-speaking Canada differently, and 1997 was no exception.

The other parties all used regionally targeted advertisements for varying reasons. Reform had fewer campaign dollars than their principal opponents and needed to stretch these dollars – for them, regionally tailored advertisements promised more potential electoral bang for the advertising buck. Dollars spent on national advertisements were partially wasted as the party had no realistic hope of winning seats in Quebec and little chance in Atlantic Canada. Reform had set its sights on an electoral breakthrough in Ontario, and concentrated its advertising dollars to maximize its chances of holding its Western base and moving into Ontario. And, as discussed above, the party's polling revealed that different messages were needed in Ontario and in Western Canada.

The Conservatives also relied on regional advertising, as the party's research revealed two things. First, the party had little chance in Western Canada and would be wasting scarce resources by advertising heavily in those provinces. Second, different positioning was needed in Ontario and in Atlantic Canada. More than any other party, the Conservatives came the closest to offering contradictory messages to regionally distinct electorates. After the campaign, the Liberals' Ashworth was highly critical of the national media for paying little attention to the messages broadcast by the Conservatives outside of central Canada, and for not criticizing the party for an apparent contradiction in calling for tax relief in Ontario and increased spending in Atlantic Canada.

Advertisements are targeted not only by region, but also by socio-demographic group. For this purpose, the parties use "time buyers" who use computer programs to track the demographics of each television show's audience. These data are then used to match up a campaign's target audience with a television show's viewership. Generally, the parties contract out their time buying to specialty firms.[31]

This process becomes both more sophisticated and more effective as Canadians have more specialty channels available to them. Even if the technology had been available, and the electoral context appropriate, this type of campaigning would not have been exploited in Canada a decade ago. Before the widespread availability of cable television, most Canadians chose their television shows from among the offerings of the national networks. Today, the offerings have mushroomed to include all-sports networks, science and nature channels, cooking shows, country western music channels, and religious networks. The audience for the World Wrestling Federation on The Sports Network is certainly different from that for Martha Stewart on the Life Network, which in turn is significantly different from the Much Music viewership. Time buyers know the demographics of each show's audience and can purchase the party advertising time accordingly. The parties made some use of the specialty channels in 1997, though not a great deal. They do, however, suggest that this is the wave of the future, and foresee producing a much larger number of advertisements, with each one tailored to a particular audience targeted through the television specialty channels.

The parties' use of free media (i.e., print and electronic news and features coverage) is also part of their master communication strategies. For example the leader's tour is structured to complement and reinforce a party's paid advertising. Polling data influence decisions concerning which ridings the leaders visit, the theme of the visit, and the content of the leaders' speeches. For example, while the party leaders normally visit each province at least once, to provide the appearance of a national campaign, they spend most of their time in targeted ridings, where the party is concentrating its advertising efforts. The theme of the events the leaders participate in is often chosen to correspond with current advertising themes, so that, if a party is running commercials in British Columbia concerning the quality of health care, its leader may well visit a health-care facility during a visit to the province. The objective of this orches-trating of the leader's tour is to influence the free media coverage of the campaign in an attempt to reinforce the party's message to its targeted voters.

There is, then, a seamless connection between the work of the party pollster, the advertising consultant, the time buyer, and the tour director. The campaign relies on the polling and focus-group data to identify its target audience and the message to be delivered to that audience, the advertisers then develop an advertisement aimed at the targeted audience, the time buyers purchase advertising time for that particular spot on a tele-vision program with a large viewership among the targeted audience, and the tour director structures the leader's activity to reinforce the advertising message. While television initially had a nationalizing effect on campaign communication in that it encouraged and facilitated the simultaneous delivery of the same partisan message to Canadians from coast to coast, in its current manifestations it is increasingly being used to deliver substan-tively different targeted messages to particular subgroups of voters.

New Computer-Based Communication Technologies

While television offers parties the possibility of targeting groups of voters with a publicly delivered message, new computer-based technologies offer the promise of being able to deliver private, tailored messages to individ-ual voters. The parties' national strategists have become very enthusiastic about the campaign opportunities offered by these new technologies and generally have hired staff with computer skills to oversee their use.

There are three computer-based technological advances that parties are using to communicate with targeted groups of voters: increased capacity to use computer technology to collect and manage voter data; use of the Internet to communicate with voters; and use of advanced applications of telephone technology. These methods differ from tradi-tional means in their ability to facilitate the delivery of a targeted message with electronic speed to individual voters. Similar to television advertise-ments, these messages may be tailored to both region and a nearly endless number of sociodemographic characteristics. Unlike television advertise-ments, these "private" messages to voters are not readily available to other parties, the media, or other potential voters. Through these methods the parties can send private messages that may well remain below the radar screen of the national press and the opposing political parties. While the trend to national communication in the third party system strengthened the role of the press as campaign watchdogs, this task is made considerably more difficult by these fragmented and underground communications.

In his book on the 1988 election campaign, Robert Mason Lee describes an early application of this technology: the Conservative party's "Target 88" campaign.[32] In this project, the party used polling, telemarketing, and direct mail in a unified effort to deliver a personally tailored message to targeted voters. Polling data were used to identify forty close ridings, and then to identify 5,000 swing voters in each riding. The party then proceeded to communicate with these voters by mail and telephone. Returns from early mailings and telephone calls were used to personalize the message in subsequent communications. For instance, if a voter told a party caller that national unity was the most important issue, the party's position on national unity was highlighted in a future mailing to that voter.

"Target 88" allowed the party to enter into private communication with these 200,000 voters and to tailor their message to each voter in terms of the issue most important to that specific individual. Potentially, each of the 200,000 voters could receive a different, privately delivered message. Lee labels this the "electoral techno-massage."[33] The Conservatives concluded that the project was a success and credited it for increasing their vote total in the targeted ridings.

While "Target 88" was limited to forty ridings, the increased availability of computer technology and the accompanying increase in accessibility of computer hardware facilitated similar efforts on a much larger scale in the 1997 election. While the use of these technologies was only in its infancy in 1997, the parties are convinced that they are the way of the future. Though all of them experienced significant problems using these technologies in 1997, these difficulties were no more than growing pains. The real story is not how the technologies have been used, but the ways in which they will radically alter political communication in the fourth party system.

Electronic Voter Files
The parties' efforts in this regard have largely been manifested in their attempts to develop electronic data files on all voters, listing information such as their telephone number, address, sociodemographic characteristics, issues they are interested in, prior political involvement, and party

preference. The compilation of this type of voter data on computer software is now practicable as Elections Canada provides the parties with an electronic list of voters' names and street addresses. While the parties all use different software programs, they all generally attempt to merge the data provided by Elections Canada with commercially available electronic data, and then to supplement the information with data on individual voters collected by local campaigns.

For example, the Liberal party's software, "Electoral List Manager," allows for the merging of sociodemographic identifiers, known as "PSYTE codes," from Statistics Canada's census data. PSYTE codes provide sociodemographic information about the population by postal code. These data indicate, for example, which postal codes have a high concentration of senior citizens or new immigrants or single voters. To this general information about a neighbourhood, the software provides space for the campaign to add detailed information about each particular voter, such as which issues are of concern to him or her, whether the voter is or has been a party member, whether he or she had a yard sign in the last election, or whether he or she has contributed funds to the party. "Electoral List Manager" allows the local campaign workers to enter data collected during its voter canvasses. Entering this data is made easy as canvassers hand mark their findings on bar-code sheets, which are used by the campaign's computer volunteers, who scan them to enter the data directly into the voter files. After the results of a canvass are entered, the software can, for example, produce a personalized letter concerning the party's position on health care to all voters who have expressed an interest in health-care policy. Similarly, the campaign can, with little effort, produce a series of letters, each dealing with a different issue, and, using the information gathered about voters, send a mailing to those voters who have expressed an interest in a particular issue.

Riding campaigns must have computers, and personnel able to operate them, to use these programs. The national parties strongly encouraged their local associations to purchase or rent a personal computer for the 1997 campaign, and went to considerable lengths to ensure they were able to use them. For example, the Reform Party conducted training sessions in Toronto, Winnipeg, Edmonton, Kamloops, and Vancouver; and the Conservatives organized local "tech squads" through their Youth Federation, charged with overseeing ridings' computer operations. However, not all parties made equal use of the technology. Among New Democratic Party members, there was less enthusiasm for these programs at the national level, and, as the decision on whether and how to use their software package, "Enhanced Voter Data Base," was made at the provincial level, there was no uniformity in data collection across the country.

The use of these programs was riddled with problems in 1997. A campaign operative for the Conservative party in British Columbia reported that the party's software program was of limited use to its local campaigns in the province as most were badly understaffed and not sophisticated users of technology. Some of the party's riding associations that did purchase the necessary hardware had difficulty in finding computer-literate volunteers to manage the software. The Liberals found that the data provided by Elections Canada were not in the form they had expected, requiring the party to send a modification to their software to all riding associations in order for them to utilize the voters' list. At least one candidate found that, of the 68,000 names on the voters' list for his riding, only 6,000 matched with a telephone number on the purchased electronic telephone list. The British Columbia New Democrats' effort to merge their provincial supporter list with the electronic voting data posed another significant problem as the poll-area numbers for federal and provincial ridings were different. In one instance we witnessed a team of volunteers manually converting poll numbers for 12,000 names on one riding's supporter list so that the lists could be merged. These glitches, coupled with the need to look up manually and enter the missing telephone numbers, made what should have been an easy task – one intended to reduce the need for substantial volunteer time – into a very labour-intensive one.

As currently designed, the parties' databases require considerable volunteer strength if they are to be fully used. The software is not useful until data are added to it, and much of these data have to be collected by telephoning voters, or through door-to-door canvassing. Even a full database is of no value unless the campaign has the capacity to make use of the information. With only thirty-five campaign days and a limited volunteer pool, it is impracticable for parties to gather data on all their voters in time to use this information to send directed messages based upon the canvassing.

More than one riding campaign manager suggested that the real value of this software will be realized in future elections, when the data gathered and entered in previous elections will provide a local campaign with a significant jump start. Reliable lists will be available, containing information such as who contributed financially last time, who took a yard sign, who volunteered as a canvasser, what issues individual voters were concerned about. These lists will allow the campaign to begin on day one with a useful database of voter information. Riding associations can now also update the database between elections as Elections Canada will provide the parties with an updated version of the new permanent voters' list each year. Such updates will be necessary, since Elections Canada estimates that, in many urban ridings, as many as 50 percent of eligible voters will change addresses in the period between elections.

The national parties' excitement about the potential uses of the technology and their plans to exploit it in the future was apparent in recent testimony from party officials and MPs to the House of Common's Standing Committee on Procedure and House Affairs. In a draft 1998 report on electoral reform, the committee characterized some of the testimony it heard as follows: "Various witnesses before the Committee suggested that the Register of Electors and voting lists provided by Elections Canada should contain additional information, such as: telephone numbers, occupation, date of birth and gender."[34] The parties are clearly hoping that Elections Canada will facilitate their use of computerized databases and, in doing so, effectively provide them with another subsidy from the state.

In the future, parties may find it advantageous to spend considerable amounts of money (all pre-writ, and thus not allocated against their campaign-spending limits) to purchase electronic data on voters. Mounds of electronic personal data are available on virtually every Canadian. For example, many retailers now keep electronic records of all purchases made by their customers, many magazines offer electronic subscriber lists for sale, and telephone companies sell computerized lists of telephone numbers. This information could be centrally loaded by the parties' national offices into their software before it even reaches the local campaign headquarters. Without the need first to gather and input substantial data during the campaign period, the local parties would be able to make substantially greater use of these programs. In effect, local candidates could have at their disposal an electronic profile of each voter in the riding. The first round of telephone calls and door-to-door canvassing (the only round in many campaigns) would not need to be aimed at gathering information from the voter but could be a targeted sales pitch tailored to the individual voter.

This type of centralized data gathering could have a profound effect on intra-party democracy and the balance of power between riding associations and the national campaign. Rather than relying on local volunteers in each riding, parties might decide to keep one centralized voters' list for these purposes. Purchased electronic data could be centrally merged, and targeted communications could be centrally produced and mailed. Parties could even decide to centrally canvass swing voters in targeted ridings (echoing "Target 88") with national campaigns, overseeing delivery of tailored communications with these voters and thus eliminating the need for local volunteers. The result could well be a takeover of local campaign efforts by the national office in targeted ridings.

The Internet
Prior to the 1997 election campaign, the parties all introduced home pages on the World Wide Web. The Reform Party was the first of the major parties to go on-line in January 1995, and their competitors quickly followed suit. Several of the parties now have full-time staff assigned to maintain their home pages and oversee Internet use.

The Bloc Québécois had the most basic 1997 site, providing details of its electoral platform, information on leader Gilles Duceppe, the names and ridings of all seventy-five party candidates, and a history of the party. The Reform and Conservative parties had the most sophisticated sites. The Conservative pages included daily notes from the campaign trail, an issue of the day, reports of favourable news headlines, and a detailed daily itinerary for their leader. Party leader Jean Charest also went live on-line regularly to answer questions and deliver the party's message. The Reform Party, reflecting their view of the Web as being essentially an opportunity for interactive communication, included an "Interactive Fresh Start Survey" on their pages. Browsers were asked to agree or disagree with eight statements concerning the party's platform, and were given an opportunity to make additional comments.

Many individual candidates had their own Web pages. Most of these were basic pages that included a short biography of the candidate, provided information on how to contact the candidate, and invited browsers to send an electronic mail message (e-mail). The Conservatives estimate that one-third of their candidates had Web pages. The party provided candidates, free of charge, with "PC Web Expert," a basic template to help set up standardized candidate home pages. Some candidates included their own and their party's e-mail and Web page addresses on their printed campaign promotional material, believing that this provided an opportunity for the interested voter to learn more about issues and the background of the candidate. An example of a candidate making use of a Web page is Lynne Woolstencroft from Waterloo, Ontario. Figure 9.1

Figure 9.1

Web advertising on a candidate's calling card, 1997

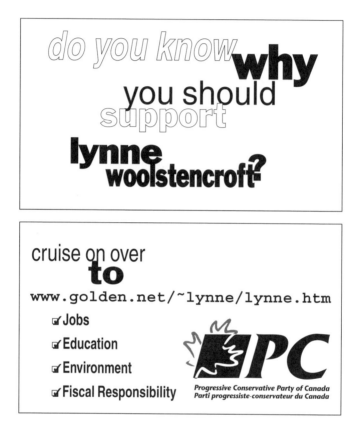

Source: Reprinted with permission of Lynne Woolstencroft.

shows both sides of a business card that Woolstencroft distributed during the campaign.

Reform leader Preston Manning made reference to his party's Web page during media appearances. On at least one occasion, when challenged during a televised debate, Manning encouraged voters to check the party's Web page, where, he promised, independent reports supporting Reform's economic policies would be made available to voters.[35] The Web would seem to have potential as a useful campaign adjunct in this fashion. Party leaders challenged in debate might make reference to it for supporting documentation, or encourage viewers to consult the Web for their party's position on issues not covered during the debate. The parties also highlight their presence on the Web to advertise their use of this new technology (at least two of the parties had their home page URL (Web address) pasted onto the sides of their leader's bus, and some included it with the paid advertising).

Information on the number of voters visiting the parties' Web pages is sketchy as the parties count hits in different ways – some tracking all pages entered by browsers, and others tracking only the number of visits. The Liberals, Conservatives, and Reform all report substantial increases in the use of their Web pages immediately prior to and during the campaign. The Conservatives were getting about 1,000 visits a day just prior to the election, and this increased to about 10,000 during the campaign (apparently somewhat more visits than the Liberals recorded, and fewer than Reform's). Several of the parties suggested that many of these visits may be coming from media personnel. This is not surprising, considering that representatives of fewer news outlets travelled with the leaders in the 1997 campaign than in previous elections. It is possible that some reporters instead relied on the parties' Web pages to supplement their stories. At least some of the parties, anticipating this, sent technical staff on their leader's tour to ensure rapid updating of their pages. The Conservatives found that the pages accessed most frequently were those containing the party platform, daily updates from the tour, campaign notes, and the leader's itinerary.

The parties' technology staff report a dilemma. They receive increased news coverage of their Web pages when they employ very sophisticated applications. This publicity inevitably presents the party in the favourable light of having mastered cutting-edge technology and increases voter awareness of the site. At the same time, however, the parties report receiving complaints from voters that the pages are too high-tech, and thus not accessible to those without the most advanced hardware and software. An example would be Jean Charest's live daily appearance over the Internet. The "appearance" attracted substantial media coverage, but only a small proportion of all Internet users would have the computer applications necessary to view it. This raises the issue of whether some parties were truly trying to communicate with voters through the Internet or are primarily interested in catching the national media's attention with these high-tech practices.

While political party use of the World Wide Web was very much in its infancy in the 1997 campaign, the parties were aware of the potential use of this new medium in targeting specific audiences. Former Liberal party national director George Young, who oversaw the party's use of the Web in the 1997 campaign, views the technology as essentially an extension of direct mail, in that the message can be tailored to the demographics of the likely user group. Both the Conservative and Reform technical directors echoed this view, suggesting that the Web offered a unique opportunity for the parties to reach young voters. Both parties tailored their home pages to be attractive to members of Generation X, who they believe are overrepresented among those browsing the Web. These potential voters are generally underrepresented among actual voters, and the Web may be a vehicle for increasing their participation in election campaigns.

The New Democrats also invested in a Web page during the 1997 campaign, which featured its "Untaxed Corporate Profit Clock" ticking away on-line and tallying what the party claimed was the total of unpaid corporate taxes since the Chrétien government came to power. However, the party may have missed an opportunity to tailor its message to likely Web surfers. The NDP federal secretary, David Woodbury, did not share the enthusiasm of the other parties for the World Wide Web, saying that it made little sense for the party to expend much time or resources on Web communication since so few voters have access to it. While this is generally true, it is widely believed that a substantial percentage of Generation Xers are regular users of the Web.

Another use of the Internet is e-mail communication. The parties' Web pages generated thousands of electronic messages from voters during the campaign. Some parties attempt to respond to every e-mail, while others respond only to selected inquiries. Staff and volunteers were seconded to this activity during the 1997 campaign. This proved very time-consuming as many of the inquiries asked detailed policy questions requiring some research by the respondent. For the most part, the parties do not mind this task as they feel they are communicating with real voters about issues that they are concerned about.

As do the software packages discussed above, e-mail offers the parties yet another way of delivering targeted messages to selected groups of voters. Newly emerging in the commercial sphere is an electronic direct-mail industry. Similar to traditional direct-mail practice, electronic address lists are available for purchase from providers in various commercial fields that have compiled lists of users with particular sociodemographic traits.

Commercial users are now beginning the practice of sending unsolicited messages, using these lists. While the parties have not yet made use of this technology, there are suggestions that it may be part of future campaigns. For example, a party may purchase a list from an Internet provider of the e-mail addresses of its customers who have recently visited Web pages concerning alternative forms of medicine, and then send all of these voters an unsolicited e-mail message detailing its policy position on the regulation of herbal remedies. While this technology is similar to the traditional direct-mail practice, it is substantially less expensive and much quicker, and provides new sources of information on voters. As more and more Canadians become Internet subscribers, this practice will inevitably become more appealing to the parties.

Democratic Dialler
Another method the parties used in the 1997 campaign to communicate with discrete groups of voters is an advanced use of the telephone that the Reform Party calls "democratic dialler." Democratic dialler is an automated telephone system that delivers up to 8,000 prerecorded messages a day. The user prerecords a message and programs the system to deliver it to specific telephone numbers. The telephone numbers may be from a list developed by the user, such as a party's membership list; alternatively, the machine can be programmed to call everyone with a particular telephone prefix. Reform has used this technology to communicate with its own members and to advertise major party events.

More sophisticated uses of this technology are probably not far away. The system allows the user to send a tailored message to voters selected on the basis of some identified characteristic. For example, a party may use the system to send a partisan message to all voters who reside in a particular city, or may choose to target only those who live in an upscale neighbourhood with its tax-relief message. Future uses of the system may also include the parties' purchasing of telephone lists from vendors in niche markets and then sending a tailored message to these voters. For example, a party may purchase a list of members of the Audubon Society and send each of them a telephone message outlining their policy for protecting endangered owls. US parties have used this technology to send targeted messages from famous persons associated with the particular cause. In the 1998 midterm elections, recorded telephone messages from Hillary Clinton and Jesse Jackson were credited with raising voter turnout among targeted Democratic constituencies. Again, this method is similar to traditional direct mail, except that it is considerably quicker, requires fewer campaign workers, in the long term is considerably less expensive, and is far more difficult to regulate publicly. These communications leave no paper trail, making it more difficult to ensure compliance with various campaign regulations such as financing laws.

"National" Campaigns?

While the use of many of the technological applications described in this chapter was rather benign in the 1997 campaign, their potential raises one of the most fundamental and long-standing concerns in Canadian politics – the necessity of creating national consensus. While television initially facilitated a national public political discourse, it is now being used increasingly to send regionally targeted messages to voters. The democratic dialler, Internet, and computerized voters' lists and databases allow the parties to enter into essentially private conversations with individual voters. These conversations occur beyond the radar screens of the community's national political dialogue. Parties can deliver different messages to voters in different regions or provinces, and do so without the transparency and accountability inherent in the traditional media. Even within a province – indeed, within a single neighbourhood – parties are able to send different messages to different voters. While this has always been true through door-to-door canvassing and through direct mail, the new methods vastly increase both the amount and the types of information the parties may have about individual voters, and the number of voters they can contact during the short campaign period. When parties are able to communicate privately with most voters and send each a tailored message, one must wonder whether there will be any national or communal dialogue left with the capacity to create and sustain a democratic consensus on the difficult issues.

The use of these technologies also makes the role of the media as watchdog of the parties during election campaigns more difficult. Given the private nature of many of these forms of communication, voters will no longer be able to count on the media to scrutinize the accuracy of the parties' messages or to expose any contradictions in the messages they are delivering to different groups of voters across the country.

10
Rebuilding the Canadian Party System

For its first one and a quarter centuries, Canadian party politics was dominated by Liberals and Conservatives. Other parties appeared and made their mark, some quickly disappearing, others persisting, but none long challenged the two old parties' hold on the country's political agenda or their grip on Parliament and the national government. This is not to say that Canadian parties or the Canadian party system has been little changed over thirteen decades. While there have been long periods of continuity and stability, these have been broken by short periods of intense change in which almost all aspects of party organization and life – their structures, membership, leadership politics, financing, and communications – have been quickly overthrown, then rebuilt. The result has been a series of distinctive party systems. Our argument is that the party system collapsed for the third time in the 1990s and is once again being rebuilt. It is less clear that the Liberals and Conservatives will once again manage to transform themselves and find a way to dominate national politics in the fourth Canadian party system, as they did in the first three.

If the continuing pre-eminence of the Liberals and Conservatives sometimes obscured the extent to which the successive party systems differed from one another, it is also true that the parties' basic, defining activities changed little over the cycles of the changing party systems. Canadian political parties continued to nominate candidates and mount local campaigns on their behalf, much as they always had. In part, this was the case because the electoral system was not changed, and the imperatives of mobilizing political support in geographically defined, single-member, districts kept the parties replaying an old game, one that gave the two big parties a significant advantage. No less important to the continuity of the rhythms of Canadian party politics was the well-entrenched formula that governed the parties' own internal political balances: local organizational autonomy for national parliamentary discipline. This formula persisted because it provided a coping mechanism for the parties as they struggled to manage the electoral politics of a growing, geographically sprawling Canadian polity. But it also often deceived observers of Canadian elections into thinking that little about the country's parties ever changed. Thus there is probably little in our account of the parties' politics on the ground at the end of the twentieth century that would surprise Siegfried, who wrote about these same patterns at its beginning.[1]

But if the electoral activity of parties in the constituencies has continued so unchanged since Confederation, why has the party system gone through cycles of collapse and rebuilding, in which the parties had to reinvent themselves in wholly new ways? To answer this question we must look beyond the parties' electoral activities to explore what role they play in the governance of the country. Simply put, parties provide the central political linkage of a democratic system between the society and its governing institutions. In doing so, they give citizens an instrument by which to press and check and change their government. But they also give the government's political leaders a tool for mobilizing support, managing conflict, and legitimating decisions. This critical network of symbiotic relationships flows naturally from the privileged position that the parties' nominating and campaigning activity provides, but its shape and character depend upon the wants and needs of the society, and the nature of its government structures. As either or both of these change, so must the parties if they hope to remain vital and relevant political linkage tools. In short, changing forms of governance have prompted changes to the party system.

Over the course of Canadian history, the parties have always had to struggle to link society to government. The open, growing, pluralistic society and economy continued to make new and changing demands, on the government but also on the very processes of governing. Canada's simple cadre-style parties, organized as flexible electoral machines, exhibited a remarkable capacity to bend and respond to their changing environment. But no party system is infinitely malleable. When the politics of the changing country outruns its governing formulas, then the party system that links the two snaps, and whole new patterns of competition and linkage need to be built. In this rebuilding, the parties must learn new ways of operating and develop new structures that will allow them to do so successfully. The result is not only new parties, but also new norms and forms of political linkage, as the transformed party system provides for a whole new Canadian politics.

Twice before, Canadian parties have snapped, no longer able to manage the political linkage demanded of them. Each time the system was rebuilt. Despite the apparent continuities represented by the survival of the Liberals and Conservatives and the persistence of constituency-organized electoral politics, each successive Canadian party system differed from its predecessor in style, substance, balance between local and national forces, and place in the governance of the country.

The post-Confederation two-party system lasted for half a century because it was well adapted to linking the demands of the small, rural, three-region Canada of its day to the new government that had been created. The political settlement of Confederation and the economic bargain of the national policy structured party competition. The parties rooted in the representational demands of local constituencies were partisan cliques gathered around their parliamentary leaders. They depended upon patronage to mobilize electoral support and satisfy local demands; they exploited the networks of patronage to raise political money and to manipulate the media; and they used patronage both to build and to discipline the public service, and as their principal instrument of government. In all this activity, the parties were engaged in state-building, operating as the recruitment agencies of the institutions of the new state they were struggling to create. As the parties consumed the state, this mature party system blurred any working distinction between politics and administration.

Changes to both Canadian society and its governing institutions in the early years of the twentieth century vitiated this pattern of political linkage and led to the collapse of the party system. The enormous expansion of the electorate on the Prairies, and demands for a greater degree of democratic participation and accountability, on the one hand, and the pressure to replace partisanship with expertise as the dominant criteria in the public service, on the other, stripped the parties of their old roles and forced them to find new ones. Responding to these imperatives, the parties built national extra-parliamentary associations that assumed the tasks of choosing leaders and raising money, and they developed political organizations around a set of powerful regional chieftains. This allowed the parties to operate as national brokers in a system in which the parties' key political linkage challenge was to develop the interregional public policy accommodations necessary for Canadian nation-building.

Judged by its capacity to provide the needed political linkages between a set of discordant regional demands and the national government, this second party system worked well. It allowed the centre to strike the compromises necessary for effective policy making. Judged by its capacity to generate the electoral alternatives necessary to ensure accountability, the party system didn't work well, because only the Liberals had sufficient strength in all regions to operate as genuine interregional brokers. Over time, their long years of easy dominance led to another blurring of the lines between administration and politics as the party was captured by the state (an ironic reversal of the previous system's dynamic) and the Liberal party became the "Government party."[2]

By the early 1960s, with growing government involvement in the economy and society, the tasks of interregional accommodation and national policy making began to be assumed by a system of intergovernmental bargaining between Ottawa and the provinces that soon came to be known as executive federalism. At much the same time, the Quiet Revolution was transforming Quebec society, and English Canadians were embracing calls for a more participatory democracy. Taken together, these changes broke the party system by depriving it of its central tasks and challenging the legitimacy of its operating practices. The result was a number of minority governments, and over two decades in which no party was able to fashion successive majority governments.

The new parties that emerged out of these political dislocations created new patterns of political linkage that connected individual Canadians to the national government in terms of their common support for distinctive visions of a pan-Canadian community. With greatly weakened or severed ties to their provincial namesakes, the large national parties freed themselves to pursue their own agendas. The new party organizations that did this were more national and more centralized than ever, using the capacities of survey research to gather information, and of national television to propagate their programs. But these parties were also more open: their members met regularly in national conventions and seized the power to remove the leadership, and the parties' election finances were regulated and subject to public scrutiny.

Effective as it may have been for articulating a national agenda, this party system's capacity to link Canadians to their government was always brittle. Though it appeared to sharpen partisan public choice, the country's governance was actually becoming increasingly apartisan, as the most important political decisions were taken in private meetings between representatives of the federal and provincial governments. The result was political decision making whereby partisanship was ignored in the interests of making agreements. Rather than linking central governing elites to the population, this system came to pit them against one another. Citizens responded in a variety of different, and sometimes contradictory, ways: they used the new Charter of Rights and Freedoms to pursue political goals through the courts, they increasingly channelled their political participation through interest groups, they supported different parties in the federal and provincial arenas, they started record numbers of new parties, and some stopped voting.

Ultimately, the pan-Canadianism of the third party system proved unsustainable. The very essence of the pan-Canadianism of this era was big national programs, designed to win Canadians' allegiance to their national government. These programs were costly, and ultimately proved to be the undoing of the third party system. By the time the Liberals formed a government in 1993, the indebtedness of the federal government was reaching serious proportions, with some thirty cents of every tax dollar going to service the national debt. Despite their inclination and 1993 election promises to do just the opposite, the Chrétien Liberals had no choice but to usher in an era of smaller government and substantially reduced program spending in their first mandate.

Ironically enough, the pan-Canadian focus of the third party system also served to exacerbate regional tensions and fuel regional discontent. The constitutional negotiations that became semi-permanent fixtures of the third party system resulted not in a more unified country, but, rather, in the reverse. Patriation in 1982 took place without the consent of the government of Quebec, and subsequent efforts to remedy this were failures that served only to highlight ongoing regional tensions. Moreover, because the ethos of pan-Canadianism meant that Quebec nationalist and Western decentralist voices were not heard at the centre, regional tensions mounted until they reached crisis proportions in the early 1990s.

The pan-Canadian dynamic of the dominant national parties increasingly came into question as substantial segments of the electorate found themselves alienated from the processes of the country's electoral democracy. Decades of conflict over the Constitution, and Quebec's role in the federation, drove all the major parties to adopt essentially similar positions on the national/constitutional question in an attempt to deflate the electoral power of the bicultural cleavage. This left substantial segments of the electorate without representation within the party system: Canadians whose primary political orientations were regional, Quebecers who sought independence for their province, neo-conservatives who argued for a substantial devolution of power from the national government, English Canadians whose belief in the equality of the provinces caused them to reject any sort of recognition of Quebec's distinctiveness – all found themselves without a voice in Parliament. The system of executive federalism that predicated the third party system broke down when the Charlottetown Accord was rejected by a majority of Canadians in a national referendum. With the demise of executive federalism and with the national state constrained by fiscal pressures, the third party system inevitably crumbled.

The emergence of the Reform Party and the Bloc Québécois as more than trivial nuisance parties signalled that powerful representational impulses were determined to break into the party system and create new patterns and institutions of political linkage. When these two parties had their different, anti-establishment positions prevail in the Charlottetown constitutional referendum, it was clear that the three old parties had lost their oligopolistic control over the party-system channels that linked citizens to the national government. But the Charlottetown referendum was not simply a rejection of the old parties' commitment to keeping distinctive representational positions off the agenda. It was also a rejection of the elitist practices of executive federalism that had got the country to Charlottetown in the first place.

The increasing pluralism of Canadian society, and the recognition and acceptance of the interests and claims of Aboriginal people, women, and visible minorities, challenged the legitimacy of the closed system of public decision making by a small number of middle-aged white men in grey suits. These groups argued that their interests would be represented only if they participated directly in the country's central decision-making forums. Their claims were so persuasive that they called into question for many Canadians the validity of deals made by the first ministers behind closed doors. In the case of Aboriginals, demands for inclusion resulted in Aboriginal groups being invited to join the constitutional negotiations that resulted in the Charlottetown Accord.

In addition to these claims, an increasingly well-educated and assertive population was demanding a more egalitarian politics in which their voices would be heard and in which they would not be expected to defer to elites of any sort. The third party system had evolved to suit the requirements of a country with a relatively deferential electorate. This was reflected in the internal workings of parties: they were internally democratic, but this democracy was limited to electing candidates at the local level and periodically voting to elect or remove a leader. With the exception of the New Democrats, party members were seldom able to affect party policy, given the parliamentary caucus's well-established role in this regard. In recent decades, however, the Canadian electorate has become substantially less deferential and increasingly egalitarian in its outlook.[3] As the electorate has become better educated, more informed about politics, and, in fact, more interested in politics, it has become less tolerant of political bosses dictating the affairs of state. Within the parties, these pressures translated into challenges to leaders, a propensity to look outside the caucus for new leaders, and calls for a participatory process in which all members would have a direct vote for the leader. It also translated into a thirst for more direct representation of citizens' views in Parliament. Canadians have grown increasingly critical of the strict party discipline practised in the House of Commons, calling on members of Parliament to represent the views of their constituents, regardless of party policy.

The pan-Canadian parties, eager to promote a nationally coherent but electorally appealing image, had become heavily reliant on a small cadre of national figures skilled in the magic arts of opinion polling and television advertising. These figures, clustered around the party leaders, practised a centralized, disciplined politics that was heavily technocratic and relatively impervious to messages from the grass roots. This, too, was a style that was increasingly at odds with the values of the electorate, and it fed the growing cynicism about politicians and the declining affection for the parties.

When Reform argued for more participatory structures, increased accountability of MPs to their constituents, and a loosening of the reins of party discipline, they successfully tapped into this well of anti-party sentiment. While these changes in the social and representational fabric of the country were eroding one set of bases for the party system, the limitations of an executive-federalism mode of pan-Canadian governance were eroding the other. The politics of this era was characterized by the development of ambitious and expensive national programs marked by a lack of easy public control or clear accountability. Not only did this program expansion often exacerbate regional tensions and stimulate intergovernmental disputes, but it also contributed to a mushrooming public debt. By the late 1980s and early 1990s, governments of all partisan colours began to respond by making major cuts to their spending on these very programs. With individual governments acting independently to defend their own fiscal balance sheets, this spelled the beginning of the end of executive federalism, and made the survival of key elements of the whole system of transfers that underlay and supported the national welfare state an item on the public agenda.

Given these substantial changes in the demographic composition, basic values, and political beliefs of the Canadian electorate, as well as the decay of the dominant governing mechanism, it is no wonder that the party system linking Canadian society to its government was stretched to the breaking point. In 1993 it snapped. New parties entered the system, and the old parties have had to begin to rebuild themselves. Together, the new and old parties are restructuring the party system that contains them. If past experience is a reliable guide, these transformations will see little change at the constituency level, where candidates are nominated and local campaigns mounted. As in earlier transitions, the Liberal party retains its place as the country's governing party. Only a major overhaul of the electoral system is likely to alter those patterns.

On the other hand, the lessons of earlier party-system transformations suggest that the parties' organizational structures, leadership politics, finances, and modes of communication are all likely to be reshaped, assuming forms that will serve the political linkage needs of the country's fourth political incarnation. There is no easy way to delineate the exact shape that this new party system is adopting. While executive federalism may be surrendering its place as the country's dominant governing mechanism, many of its forms will persist (as do those of patronage and brokerage from earlier Canadas) to confuse and obscure the direction and extent of the transformation. With the country still grappling with the problem of inventing new patterns of governance, the task of linking these institutional arrangements to the society must inevitably remain open. Quite what the latent functions of the fourth Canadian party system will be is still unclear. What we can more confidently identify are some of the key characteristics that will help define the new party system.

Characteristics of the Emerging Party System

Although there are substantial continuities between the third party system and the system that is currently taking shape, five characteristics that distinguish the emerging system can be identified. Most immediately evident is the entry of two new parties, which have eclipsed both the

Conservatives and NDP in Parliament. Closely related to this is a pattern of party competition that is highly regionalized. Compounding the fragmentation of greater regionalization is the tendency towards private and highly segmented campaign communications, which effectively break up the mass national electorate that formed the basis for the pan-Canadian appeals of the third party system. The emerging system is characterized by a new diversity in terms of the societal basis, ideology, and internal organization of the parties that constitute it. Finally, the participatory demands of an assertive citizenry contributed to the decline of the third party system and have left a mark on the emerging system as all the parties have tried to become more internally democratic.

The Entry of Two New Parties
The first, and most readily apparent, defining characteristic of the emerging party system is a change in the cast of characters. While the old party system was dominated by the Liberal and Conservative parties, with the NDP as a perpetual third party, the emerging party system encompasses five parties. This situation presents a serious threat to the Liberal and Conservative parties' historic domination of Canadian politics. Although it is not clear which of these five parties will persist and which will fade away or merge with others, it is evident that the Conservatives no longer enjoy the security of being one of two dominant parties in a relatively stable party system.

With the breakdown of the Mulroney coalition in 1993, substantial segments of the electorate in both Alberta and British Columbia, on the one hand, and in Quebec, on the other, opted to support regionally based parties certain to be in opposition. The Western voters who decided to cast their ballots for a regionally based protest party were following a long-standing Western Canadian tradition. Voters in Alberta have seldom chosen to support governing parties in order to be represented in governing circles in Ottawa. Since the First World War, Alberta voters have supported governing parties on only three occasions. It was only when voters in the rest of the country shifted their support to the Conservatives under Diefenbaker in 1958, and later Mulroney in 1984, that Alberta was represented in majority governments. In this sense, Alberta voters steadfastly waited for the rest of the country to come to them. This willingness to be excluded from governing coalitions, coupled with an apparent sense of satisfaction at having their views represented by a regional party, suggests that little will discourage Reform supporters in Alberta and parts of British Columbia from continuing to support the party. For the foreseeable future, then, the Reform Party will remain a significant presence in Canadian politics.

This assumes that Reform's United Alternative campaign will fail. Since becoming the Official Opposition in 1997, the Reform Party has tried to increase its appeal outside its original base of support by taking on the outward trappings of a traditional, ideologically flexible, party. At the same time, Preston Manning has launched his United Alternative campaign, intended to create a party less ideologically coherent than Reform, and with the capacity to unseat the governing Liberals. The effort to disband Reform and create the United Alternative has opened fissures within the Reform Party and its caucus. On the one hand, Manning and a substantial segment of the party seem willing to sacrifice the party's regional orientation and coherent policy stances for a chance to govern. On the other hand, a substantial segment of both the party and the caucus are reluctant to abandon Reform's founding principles in an effort to unseat the Liberals. The unwillingness of the Conservative party establishment to consider any sort of merger or cooperation with Reform, coupled with a widespread perception from Ontario eastward that Reform is a regional party that espouses extremist policies, serve as substantial constraints on Manning's ability to form a new political grouping.

It is not clear what Reform's place will be in the fourth party system. It is possible, although unlikely, that the United Alternative effort will allow Reform to eclipse the Conservatives as the alternative governing party. It is also possible that Reform's permanent place in the fourth party system will be as a predominantly regional protest party with no prospect of unseating the Liberals. Like the Social Credit Party before it, Reform could well hold onto its seats in Alberta and parts of British Columbia, and thereby remain a constant, but relatively uninfluential, presence in Parliament. If the Conservative party is unable to substantially improve its electoral fortunes but is not decimated entirely, it is possible that some sort of cooperative relationship between the Conservatives and Reform might be reached. If this is the case, a Reform-Conservative alliance could eventually emerge as an alternative governing party or coalition. This is not an inevitable outcome, however. It is equally possible to imagine the Conservatives entering into an alliance with the Liberal party, allowing the Liberals to govern without a parliamentary majority. In all of these scenarios, Reform remains a significant element of the new party system.

By the same token, it is difficult to imagine a scenario in which the Bloc Québécois entirely disappears in the foreseeable future. Committed sovereigntists remain a significant force in Quebec politics, and these voters are unlikely to support the Liberals or Conservatives. The Conservative party was able to win the support of soft sovereigntist voters in Quebec in the 1980s when it had a leader from that province. With Joe Clark at the helm, the Conservatives are unlikely to maintain much of a base in Quebec. This leaves sovereigntist voters with only two viable options: voting for the Bloc or not voting at all. Barring significant changes on the constitutional front, then, the Bloc appears to be another more or less permanent fixture within the emerging party system.

The continued presence of these two regionally based parties will ensure that patterns of political competition remain highly regionalized. The presence of these two new parties creates a dynamic in which the new regionally based parties are pitted against the older parties, which are trying to maintain their pan-Canadian scope and basis of support. Even if the Bloc and Reform do not survive the transition into the new party system, they will have played a significant role in shaping the system in general, and the specific practices of the parties within it. Most notably, the Reform Party's populism and claims of internal democracy have forced the other parties to respond with reforms to their internal organization.

Of the three old parties, the Liberals alone emerged from the electoral earthquake of 1993 unbroken. The emergence of two new parties has virtually guaranteed that the party will continue to govern until such time as one of the other parties is able to muster a more geographically diffuse basis of support or engineer a merger. That said, the emerging party system presents the Liberals with a number of significant challenges. First, the party's geographic basis of support has narrowed considerably, making the party heavily reliant on Ontario. With almost two-thirds of its seats in Ontario, the Liberal caucus lacks the breadth of regional representation that a governing party wants, and faces difficulties in managing its large and powerful Ontario caucus. Second, in both the 1993 and 1997 elections, the party's basis of support was very narrow: 41 percent and 38 percent of the popular vote, respectively. Should this gradual erosion of the party's support continue, its already tenuous hold on government will weaken, producing a series of minority governments in which the party could govern only with the support of either the NDP or the Conservatives.

Although the Liberal party has changed less than its opponents in responding to the changes in the party system, its central governing position has nevertheless been affected.[4] Underlying social and economic forces, coupled with the rise of Reform as the dynamic element of the party system, have forced the Liberal party to abandon its economic nationalism and commitment to a strong central government. Although adherents of these policies remain present within the party, they are unable to determine the party's direction on crucial issues of the day. And as the sole remaining national party, the Liberal party can no longer run one national campaign, but rather must run several regional campaigns, competing against different parties in each part of the country.

In the aftermath of 1993, both the Conservatives and the New Democrats were devastated organizations. Not surprisingly, given the cataclysmic scale of their setbacks, both parties launched significant processes of internal reform, but neither appears to have resolved its fundamental dilemma. The Conservatives, under the leadership of a Western Canadian former prime minister, have no geographic basis of support and little prospect of quickly building one. The New Democrats may have been saved from oblivion by their new-found support in Atlantic Canada, but they have not resolved the question of their relationship to the labour movement, nor have they found a solid basis of support from which to launch a process of rebuilding. Although unlikely to disappear entirely, neither party appears poised to present a credible challenge to the governing Liberals.

A Regionalization of Party Politics
The second, and related, defining characteristic of the emerging party system is a greater regionalization, in terms of both the basis of party support and the patterns of party campaigning. This trend is a function of the entry of two regionally based parties and the breakdown of the pan-Canadianism of the old system. As substantial numbers of Westerners and Quebecers opted to have a regionally based party represent their interests in the federal arena, the party system was transformed from a system with a pan-Canadian scope and cast to one with a highly regionalized character. One of the ongoing tensions of Canadian politics – a strong centre versus decentralization – has now become vividly captured within the party system, in a dynamic pitting the two new, and radically decentralist, parties against the older pan-Canadian parties.

In both 1993 and 1997, national elections were anything but national.

In the 1993 campaign, the two regionally based parties' unanticipated surge in strength caught the old parties by surprise, and their national, pan-Canadian, strategies were dramatically unsuited to meet the challenges of a new kind of campaign. In 1997, the old parties were better prepared for the terrain: the Conservatives and New Democrats conducted regionally targeted campaigns, while the Liberals, the only party to compete aggressively in all parts of the country, prepared different strategies and messages for each region. The result was the development of a number of distinct regional party systems, each with its own campaign and political dynamic.

The emergence of Reform and the Bloc forced the other parties in the system to endeavour to establish some sort of a regional basis of electoral support. This was a particular problem for the Conservatives and New Democrats as the emergence of Reform had eroded both parties' bases in Western Canada, while the Bloc had drained the Conservatives of their newly found support in Quebec. It was the small provinces of Atlantic Canada that ultimately bolstered both in 1997. Thirteen of the Conservatives' twenty seats were in the Atlantic provinces; were it not for this recovery, the party would once again have failed to achieve recognized party status in the House of Commons. More remarkable was the NDP's success in winning one-quarter of the region's seats. Ironically, just as the third party system's structure of competition disappeared elsewhere in Canada, it seemed to arrive in the Atlantic provinces. Prior to the 1997 election, the NDP had been unable to make any significant inroads in the region. In 1997, however, with the Liberal government falling into disfavour across Atlantic Canada as a result of its deficit-cutting policies and perceived mismanagement of the fishery, and with the NDP led by a popular Nova Scotian, Alexa McDonough, the NDP was finally able to break through into the region. Given that the NDP breakthrough may well have been led by a favourite-daughter phenomenon, we are left to speculate whether the party's showing in the region will outlast her leadership. Nonetheless, the entry of the New Democrats into the region demonstrates the new regional dynamic characteristic of the emerging system.

Regionalization did not entirely extinguish the pan-Canadianism of the third party system. Although the Liberal party was reduced to looking like a regional party from Ontario, it maintained the pan-Canadian ethos that was its trademark. During the 1997 campaign and subsequently, the Liberals have made tentative moves to reassert their pan-Canadian vision.

Notable among these is the Millennium Fund scholarship program, a reassertion of the federal government's entitlement to use its spending power to create a major national program in an area of provincial jurisdiction. In this sense, pan-Canadianism seems alive and well, albeit only in Ontario and within the large urban centres – Vancouver, Montreal, Edmonton, and Winnipeg – where the Liberals are still able to win seats. Liberals remain a national party, or at least a national metropolitan party, appealing to Canadians who reject the decentralizing thrust of both Reform and the Bloc.

It was not coincidence that the party system became far more regionalized in the immediate aftermath of the failure of the constitutional rounds of the late 1980s and early 1990s. The Canadian electorate's rejection of the Charlottetown Accord in a national referendum marked the end of the era of uncontested executive federalism in which regional conflicts were brokered, not within the governing party, but within the first ministers' conference. In the emerging party system, the articulation of regional claims is being made within the party system, with regionally based parties increasingly acting as representatives of regional interests within the national political arena. This marks a significant departure from the third party system, in which the articulation of regional claims was largely made within the federal-provincial arena.

Fragmentation of the Electorate
The emergence of the Bloc and Reform effectively shattered the pan-Canadian appeals of the third party system by forcing a regionalization of political discourse. Although this is most immediately apparent in the fragmentation of the national political agenda and debate, technological advances have fostered a further fragmentation. New communication technologies, coupled with increasingly rich sources of sociodemographic data, have allowed parties to make their appeals to the electorate in increasingly targeted and private ways. Rather than a mass appeal to the Canadian electorate through network television, parties are able to communicate with voters through direct mail, over the telephone, or via the Internet, delivering a message targeted to the voter's demographic grouping or general interests. As this sort of political communication proliferates, the national discussion of politics during an election campaign will increasingly be replaced by a series of highly focused, private conversations. When coupled with the regional dynamics of campaigns, this trend is contributing to the end of pan-Canadian politics.

This trend towards fragmentation of political communications enhances and further entrenches the place of political professionals within the party organizations. Despite calls for further democratization of political parties, these new communication patterns ensure that pollsters, advertising and marketing specialists, and those skilled in the management and manipulation of data sets will retain a central role within campaign organizations. Fragmented and private political communication requires the skills and technology of these professionals, reinforcing their place within the party structure. As recorded messages from the party leader delivered through automatic-dialling machines replace the personal call from a local volunteer during election campaigns, the role of the party regular will be further diminished, and parties will be, to an even greater extent, animated by professionals.

Greater Diversity among Parties
The fourth distinguishing characteristic of the emerging party system is its diversity in terms of the societal basis, ideology, and internal organization of the individual parties that constitute it. In the third party system, there was remarkable uniformity among the three major parties in terms of their efforts to develop or maintain a pan-Canadian focus, their efforts to promote inclusiveness through representational quotas of various kinds, and even their internal organization. The NDP diverged somewhat from the other two parties with its organic ties to organized labour and its slightly different mechanism for leadership selection, but, beyond these differences, the parties were remarkably similar. This similarity, we have argued, contributed to the downfall of the third party system as it left too many interests and perspectives unrepresented.

Unlike its predecessor, the new party system is characterized by considerable diversity among the parties. The first source of this is the division between the new, regionally based, parties, with their decentralist views, and the old, pan-Canadian, parties, with their continuing attachment to the central government. The second, and related, source of diversity is in the new parties' rejection of the basic principles of pan-Canadianism: bilingualism, multiculturalism, and a politics of accommodation. Although somewhat on the defensive, the old parties have tried to maintain their commitment to these ideas. The third source of diversity is in terms of conceptions of representation: the Reform Party explicitly rejects the old parties' efforts to promote inclusion by recognizing difference. Reform has eschewed the old parties' practice of guaranteeing representation for linguistic groups, regions, women, youth, and others, choosing instead to treat all its members as equal, undifferentiated individuals.

Certainly, this new diversity of principle and form presents a profound challenge to the kind of party politics and, in fact, the kind of governance, Canadians have been accustomed to in the past half-century. For many, this challenge is understood as presenting a threat to the Canada and the way of life that they value highly. Much more is at stake in contemporary Canadian electoral politics than has been for a long time. The shape of the emerging party system will ultimately affect the politics of the first decades of the twenty-first century, and it is clear that many fundamental principles of the governing regime will be contested by the new political actors. From the point of view of democratic politics, this is a positive development. The debate over fundamentals may invigorate a national polity that has suffered a malaise in recent years. A new diversity of parties offers more Canadians political choices that satisfy their desire for representation. In this sense, the emergence of the new party system offers the potential for a reinvigorated democratic life in Canada.

Democratization

One of the most apparent factors that contributed to the demise of the third party system was the rising assertiveness and populism of the Canadian electorate. Once largely content to defer to the decisions of political elites, Canadians have increasingly come to distrust political institutions and the individuals who animate them, and are calling for citizens to have a direct input into political decision making. These changing attitudes created significant pressures for change within the political system writ large, and within each of the political parties.

As a result, we have seen changes both to the party system and to the internal practices of parties within the system. This populist discontent is manifested most clearly by the emergence of the Reform Party, which criticized both the structure of Canadian political institutions and the top-down practices of the old parties. Reform has attempted, with some success, to conduct its internal party affairs in such a manner as to demonstrate its commitment to populist and democratic principles. This has prompted the other parties within the system to respond as they have in the past, most notably by changing their method of leadership selection to some variation of universal membership voting. This shift represents the essence of the changing norms of internal party democracy, as it will allow more party members an opportunity for direct, unmediated participation in what is arguably the party's most important decision.

With the shift to direct election of party leaders also comes a blurring of the distinction between party members and non-members. When individuals can join the party and then almost immediately cast a ballot for the party leader, the meaning of party membership changes. Unlike the mass party model, in which party members are given a say in party decisions in return for their labour on behalf of the party, this new form of party membership imposes no obligations on the party member beyond paying a nominal membership fee. In this sense, we are moving rapidly in the direction of US-style primaries, in which citizens may vote in primary elections without belonging to the party. This raises the prospect of significant changes to the regulatory framework for political parties. To date, parties have regulated their own internal affairs. As public funds are increasingly used to conduct leadership campaigns, and as a growing number of citizens can participate in leadership votes, there may be pressure from the public, or even from inside the parties, for state regulation of these contests.

Rebuilding the Canadian Party System

The Canadian party system is once again in transition. Changing representational demands have created pressures on the system, leading indirectly to the formation of new parties. Populist impulses have forced the parties once again to reform their internal practices in the name of democratization. And leader-follower relationships, and the organizational imperatives that flow from them, are being restructured as universal membership voting has become the accepted practice for selecting party leaders. Although the conduct of election battles remains much the same, significant changes in technology appear to be transforming political communication, making the conversation between voters and parties increasingly fragmented and privatized. Moreover, elections have reverted from being national contests to become increasingly regional ones as the party system has fractured along regional lines. Finally, just as previous periods of transition were associated with changes in the basic structure of governance, so, too, is this one. Fiscal and international pressures have significantly constrained the Canadian state, as has the tendency towards decentralization. Although the shape of the emerging party system is not yet clear, it appears to serve the functional requirements of this new and limited form of governance.

Some elements of the contemporary transition fit tidily into historical patterns. The pressure for internal party democracy and the consequent change in the method of selecting the leader provide precise parallels with developments during earlier transitions. Although less clear, changes in campaign communication technologies appear to hold the same transformative promise as did radio and television in earlier transitions.

Other elements of the contemporary transition appear somewhat different from earlier cycles of change. Most notably, this is the first transition in which the fate of one of the two parties that have governed appears in question. Although the place of the Liberal party within the party system has changed little, it is not so clear that the Conservative party will survive the current transition intact. This is also the first transition in which the party system is under a perceived threat from alternative modes of political representation – interest groups and social-movement organizations. Even though the perception of threat in this regard may exceed the reality, it is noteworthy that the primacy of parties on the Canadian political landscape is being questioned by many.

Nonetheless, it is clear that Canada remains a party country. As the composition of Canadian society, and the values and political beliefs of Canadians, evolve, these changes are being reflected in the structure of the party system. New parties form, and older parties try to adapt to the new landscape. As the fourth party system takes shape, political parties remain as essential to democratic life in Canada as they were at Confederation.

Appendix:
Formal Interview Schedule

Titles represent the position held at time of interview. Informal interviews were also conducted with many campaign volunteers, candidates, and party activists.

Michael Allen, National Director, Progressive Conservative Party of Canada, 23 April 1997, Ottawa, Ontario

Bruce Anderson, 1997 Senior Campaign Advisor, Progressive Conservative Party of Canada; Earnscliffe Communications, 4 July 1997, Ottawa, Ontario

Gordon Ashworth, 1997 National Campaign Director, Liberal Party of Canada, 2 July 1997, Toronto, Ontario

Brad Farquhar, Technology Strategist, Reform Party of Canada, 10 April 1997, Calgary, Alberta

Robert Fielder, National Membership Program Coordinator, Progressive Conservative Party of Canada, 23 April 1997, Ottawa, Ontario

Pierre Fortier, President, Progressive Conservative Party of Canada, 23 April 1997, Ottawa, Ontario

Peter Grant, Broadcasting Arbitrator, 20 June 1997, Toronto, Ontario

Steve Kukucha, 1997 Campaign Director, Liberal Party of Canada (BC), 3 April 1997, Vancouver, BC

Ron Leach, President, Alliance to Preserve English in Canada, 17 June 1997, Toronto, Ontario

Dr. Kellie Leitch, Training Coordinator, Progressive Conservative Party of Canada, 23 April 1997, Ottawa, Ontario

Michael Marzolini, Liberal Party of Canada Pollster; Chairman, Pollara Strategic Opinion and Market Research, 3 July 1997, Toronto, Ontario

Jim Matsui, New Democratic Party Pollster; President, ComQuest Research, 14 July 1998, Toronto, Ontario

Glenn McMurray, Executive Director, Reform Party of Canada, 10 April 1997, Calgary, Alberta

Terry Mercer, National Director, Liberal Party of Canada, 25 April 1997, Ottawa, Ontario

Perry Miele, 1997 Advertising Director, Progressive Conservative Party of Canada; Partner, The Gingko Group, 3 July 1997, Toronto, Ontario

David Miller, 1997 Tour Director, Liberal Party of Canada; Senior Vice-President, Hill and Knowlton, 4 July 1997, Ottawa, Ontario

Ian Morrison, President, Friends of Canadian Broadcasting, 27 June 1997, Toronto, Ontario

Harry Myers, President, Reform Party of Canada, 10 April 1997, Calgary, Alberta

Bruce Pollock, 1997 British Columbia Campaign Director, Progressive Conservative Party of Canada, 4 June 1997, Vancouver, BC

David Robinson, Research Coordinator, Council of Canadians, 24 June 1997, Ottawa, Ontario

Jennifer Robinson, Communications Director, Progressive Conservative Party of Canada, 23 April 1997, Ottawa, Ontario

David Salmon, Executive Councillor, Reform Party of Canada, 10 April 1997, Calgary, Alberta

David Smith, 1997 Campaign Chairman, Liberal Party of Canada; Managing Partner, Fraser and Milner, 14 July 1998, Toronto, Ontario

Ron Stipp, Director of Operations – British Columbia, New Democratic Party, March 1997, Burnaby, BC

Brian Thomas, 1997 Advertising Director, Reform Party of Canada; President, Thomas Crncich and Partners, 7 July 1997, London, Ontario

Dr. André Turcotte, Reform Party Pollster; President, Feedback Research, 15 July 1998, Toronto, Ontario

Ed Wark, Campaign Manager for Bill Siskay – New Democratic Party Candidate, Vancouver Centre, 16 May 1997, Vancouver, BC

Artur Wilczynski, Campaign Manager for Hedy Fry – Liberal Candidate in Vancouver Centre, 16 May 1997, Vancouver, BC

David Woodbury, Federal Secretary, New Democratic Party of Canada, 24 April 1997, Ottawa, Ontario

George Young, Former National Director, Liberal Party of Canada, Vice-President, Pollara Group, 23 June 1997, Ottawa, Ontario

Notes

Chapter 1: Party Politics at Century's End

1 For the American case, see William Nesbet Chambers and Walter Dean Durnham, eds., *The American Party Systems: Stages of Political Development* (New York: Oxford University Press, 1967), or John H. Aldrich, *Why Parties?: The Origin and Transformation of Party Politics in America* (Chicago: University of Chicago Press, 1995). For stimulating comparative analyses, see Byron E. Shafer, ed., *Postwar Politics in the G-7: Orders and Eras in Comparative Perspective* (Madison: University of Wisconsin Press, 1996).

2 See R. Kenneth Carty, "Three Canadian Party Systems," R. Johnston, André Blais, Henry E. Brady, and Jean Crête, "The Electoral Basis of the Canadian Party Systems, 1978-1984," and David E. Smith, "Party Government in Canada," all in *Canadian Political Party Systems: A Reader*, ed. R. Kenneth Carty (Peterborough, ON: Broadview Press, 1992), part 4.

3 It was during the third party system that the country came to be defined in terms of five distinct regions: British Columbia, the Prairies, Ontario, Quebec, and Atlantic Canada. On that subject, see R. Kenneth Carty, "The Electorate and the Evolution of Canadian Electoral Politics," *American Review of Canadian Studies* 26, 1 (Spring 1996): 7-29. It may be that one of the impacts of Reform will be to reorder this pattern, splitting Alberta from its Prairie neighbours and tying it, for national political purposes, more closely to British Columbia.

4 Alan Cairns, "The Electoral System and the Party System in Canada, 1921-1965," *Canadian Journal of Political Science* 1 (1968): 55-80; J.A.A. Lovink, "On Analysing the Impact of the Electoral System on the Party System in Canada," *Canadian Journal of Political Science* 3 (1970): 497-516; and R. Johnston and J. Ballantyne, "Geography and the Electoral System," *Canadian Journal of Political Science* 10 (1977): 857-66.

5 For an example of a provincial party doing much the same thing, see Peter Woolstencroft, "Reclaiming the 'Pink Palace': The Progressive Conservative Party Comes in from the Cold," in *The Government and Politics of Ontario*, 5th ed., ed. G. White (Toronto: University of Toronto Press, 1997).

6 André Siegfried pointed to the comparatively strong position of Canadian party leaders a century ago in *The Race Question in Canada* (1907; reprint, Toronto: McClelland and Stewart, 1966). For the standard contemporary account of leadership politics, see John C. Courtney, *Do Conventions Matter? Choosing National Party Leaders in Canada* (Montreal and Kingston: McGill-Queen's University Press, 1995).

Chapter 2: The Party Question in Canada

1 The Liberals had also managed to win a majority with just 41 percent in 1945. They would squeak out a majority government with an even smaller vote-share (38.5 percent) four years later, in the 1997 election.

2 The argument of next few paragraphs draws on R. Kenneth Carty, "For the Third Asking: Is There a Future for National Political Parties in Canada?," in *In Pursuit of the Public Good,* ed. Tom Kent (Montreal and Kingston: McGill-Queen's University Press, 1997).

3 On the parties in the individual pre-Confederation colonies, see Gordon T. Stewart, *The Origins of Canadian Politics: A Comparative Approach* (Vancouver: University of British Columbia Press, 1986).

4 Canada, Royal Commission on Electoral Reform and Party Financing, *Reforming Electoral Democracy,* Vol. 1 of the *Report of the Royal Commission on Electoral Reform and Party Financing* (Ottawa: Minister of Supply and Services, 1991), 226.

5 Stewart, *The Origins of Canadian Politics,* 74.

6 On cadre-style party organization, see M. Duverger, *Political Parties* (London: Methuen, 1964), 64.

7 R. Johnston, André Blais, Henry E. Brady, and Jean Crête, *Letting the People Decide: Dynamics of a Canadian Election* (Montreal and Kingston: McGill-Queen's University Press, 1992), 45-6.

8 André Siegfried, *The Race Question in Canada* (1907; reprint, Toronto: McClelland and Stewart, 1966), 114, 113.

9 Reginald Whitaker, *The Government Party: Organizing and Financing the Liberal Party of Canada, 1930-1958* (Toronto: University of Toronto Press, 1977).

10 On the shifting equation base, see R. Kenneth Carty, "The Electorate and the Evolution of Canadian Electoral Politics," *American Review of Canadian Studies* 26, 1 (Spring 1996): 7-29. Towards the end of the second party system, the eastern region changed when Newfoundland and Labrador joined Canada in 1949. The new region, the Maritimes and Newfoundland, became known as Atlantic Canada.

11 The Liberals were in power from 1921 until 1957, with the exception of a few weeks in the summer of 1926 (the King-Byng affair) and the years of the Great Depression (1930-5). For an excellent account of the 1930 Conservative government, and its failure to establish a ministerialist organization and to practise the necessary brokerage for a governing party, see Larry A. Glassford, *Reaction and Reform: The Politics of the Conservative Party under R.B. Bennett, 1927-1938* (Toronto: University of Toronto Press, 1992).

12 Walter D. Young, *The Anatomy of a Party: The National CCF* (Toronto: University of Toronto Press, 1969).

13 The phrase is Donald Blake's. See his *Two Political Worlds: Parties and Voting in British Columbia* (Vancouver: University of British Columbia Press, 1985). Some individual parties managed to maintain an integrated form in provinces where separation was becoming the norm. The Saskatchewan Liberals were a case in point, as was the CCF in the provinces where it existed.

14 For the classic account, see Richard Simeon, *Federal-Provincial Diplomacy: The Making of Recent Policy in Canada* (Toronto: University of Toronto Press, 1972).

15 The development of many of the pillars of the current Canadian welfare state in the

1960s took place in this structure and involved politicians from the CCF/NDP, Liberal, Conservative, Social Credit, and Union Nationale governments. For three policy cases – pensions, finances, and the Constitution – see ibid.

16 Johnston et al., *Letting the People Decide.*

17 See Stephen Clarkson, "Democracy in the Liberal Party: The Experiment with Citizen Participation under Pierre Trudeau," in *Party Politics in Canada,* 4th ed., ed. H.G. Thorburn (Scarborough, ON: Prentice-Hall, 1979).

18 David E. Smith, "Party Government, Representation and National Integration in Canada," in *Party Government and Regional Representation in Canada,* ed. P. Aucoin (Toronto: University of Toronto Press, 1985).

19 Ibid., 31.

20 "Leadership review" was the euphemism Canadian parties adopted to refer to the power of members to fire their leader.

21 George C. Perlin, *The Tory Syndrome: Leadership Politics in the Progressive Conservative Party* (Montreal and Kingston: McGill-Queen's University Press, 1980). As Perlin notes in Chapter 3, such conflicts had long bedeviled the Conservatives during their long years in opposition after the First World War.

22 For a portrait of local party-association competition and democracy, see Chapter 4 of R. Kenneth Carty, *Canadian Political Parties in the Constituencies* (Toronto: Dundurn Press, 1991).

23 The smaller parties had little access to these sources, and consequently had comparatively little money. The CCF relied on gifts from its supporters and provincial affiliates. Social Credit depended to a considerable extent on the goodwill of the (Social Credit) Alberta government.

24 Joseph Wearing, *The L-Shaped Party: The Liberal Party of Canada, 1958-1980* (Toronto: McGraw-Hill Ryerson, 1981), 68-72.

25 Leslie A. Pal, *Interests of State: The Politics of Language, Multiculturalism and Feminism in Canada* (Montreal and Kingston: McGill-Queen's University Press, 1993).

26 Trudeau spent more time than Laurier in office, to become the third-longest-serving prime minister in Canadian history. He was out of office for a few months in 1979 and early 1980, after the Conservatives managed to win more seats in Ontario than the Liberals in the 1979 election, a pattern quickly reversed in early 1980, after the minority Conservative Clark government fell.

27 Alberta and Quebec were two (of the four) provinces that had given the free-trade Liberals a majority of seats in 1911.

28 Johnston et al., *Letting the People Decide,* 102-10, especially Figure 3.2.

29 For details of the changing electorate, see Carty, "The Electorate."

30 Donald Blake, "Party Competition and Electoral Volatility: Canada in Comparative Perspective," in *Representation, Integration and Political Parties in Canada,* ed. H. Bakvis (Toronto: Dundurn Press, 1991).

31 See Johnston et al., *Letting the People Decide,* Chaps. 2 and 3.

32 Clarkson, "Democracy in the Liberal Party."

33 Harold D. Clarke and Allan Kornberg, "Evaluations and Evolution: Public Attitudes towards Canada's Federal Political Parties, 1965-1991," *Canadian Journal of Political Science* 26, 2 (1993): 290, 297, 307.

34 The exception to this was in 1993, when Reform's score was slightly higher than that

for the Conservatives and New Democrats. It was lower than both by the time of the 1997 election.

35 The enumeration to construct the first modern permanent national electoral register was conducted in April 1997, and the election was called soon after it was completed. This meant that, while little time elapsed between the two events, for the first time since the 1930s the enumeration was carried out under different conditions and in the absence of ongoing electioneering. When the initial register was completed, it was announced that there were 18,753,094 names on the list, more than a million fewer than had been on the final register for the 1993 general election. Although another 495,000 were enrolled during the campaign period, and 415,000 registered on election day, the final total, 19,663,478, was still almost a quarter of a million fewer than in 1993, despite the fact that the country's voting-age population had grown by more than a million. It seems clear that the first round in compiling the permanent national electoral register was not a complete success. Given that about 20 percent of the list needs to be modified or changed every year, it is going to be a major challenge to make the new system work.

36 Donald Blake and Lynda Erickson, "New Party Insurgency and Party System Change: The 1993 Canadian Election," unpublished manuscript, 1998.

37 Stefano Bartolini and Peter Mair, *Identity, Competition, and Electoral Volatility: The Stabilisation of European Electorates, 1885-1985* (Cambridge: Cambridge University Press, 1990). Peter Mair, in his subsequent *Party System Change: Approaches and Interpretations* (Oxford: Clarendon Press, 1997), notes that Germany in 1919 and Greece in 1950 and 1951 had higher volatility scores than Canada in 1993 (216, n 10). As those three elections can hardly be considered to be part of a set of normal democratic contests, it seems reasonable to conclude that the 1993 Canadian contest was the most volatile democratic election yet held.

38 The House of Commons requires that a parliamentary group have twelve members to be recognized as a party. The number is arbitrary and was arrived at in the 1960s, when the minority Liberals needed to recognize the Créditistes, who had just fourteen members after the 1965 election.

Chapter 3: Challenging the Consensus

1 The Progressives won twenty-four seats in Ontario in 1921, but were reduced to only two seats in the subsequent election.

2 Some observers suggest that the rise of Reform and the Bloc in 1993 are parallel developments to the rise of the Créditistes. Based on his study of the rise of Social Credit in Quebec, Maurice Pinard argued that where a one-party-dominant system exists, when voters are driven to seek an alternative to the governing party the opportunity arises for the emergence of a new party (see Hugh Thorburn, "Interpretations of the Canadian Party System," in *Party Politics in Canada,* 7th ed., ed. Hugh Thorburn [Scarborough, ON: Prentice-Hall, 1996], 125). Thorburn suggests that this theory could explain the rise of the Bloc and Reform in 1993. Given that the Liberals remained a significant party in Quebec, and that the NDP and Liberals both maintained some support in the West, this explanation does not seem convincing. The rise of the two new parties is better understood as a consequence of the breakdown of the fragile Mulroney coalition.

3 When the NDP first formed, it might have been characterized an ideological party, as it adhered to a coherent social-democratic platform. Over time, it took on much of the ideological flexibility that characterizes the two traditional parties.

4 By definition, an ideological party is inflexible on its core issue. For the Bloc, sovereignty – not the economy or other issues – is central to its mission.

5 Tom Flanagan, *Waiting for the Wave: The Reform Party and Preston Manning* (Toronto: Stoddart, 1995), 40-1.

6 See Sydney Sharpe and Don Braid, *Storming Babylon: Preston Manning and the Rise of the Reform Party* (Toronto: Key Porter, 1992), and Murray Dobbin, *Preston Manning and the Reform Party* (Toronto: Lorimer, 1991).

7 See Flanagan, *Waiting for the Wave*, 40-1.

8 A more problematic group has been the evangelical religious right, a group to which Manning and many prominent figures in the party belong, but an association that they downplay.

9 See Peter Russell, *Constitutional Odyssey: Can Canadians Become a Sovereign People?* 2nd ed. (Toronto: University of Toronto Press, 1993).

10 Manon Cornelier, *The Bloc* (Toronto: Lorimer, 1995), 7-9.

11 Ibid., 47.

12 The Bélanger-Campeau Commission, formed to advise the provincial Liberal government on its constitutional strategy in the aftermath of the failure of the Meech Lake Accord, had recommended that the provincial government hold a referendum on sovereignty in 1992. This did not take place, as a referendum on the Charlottetown Accord was held in its stead.

13 Cornelier, *The Bloc*, 57.

14 Ibid., 64.

15 Ibid., 68.

16 Richard Johnston, André Blais, Elisabeth Gidengil, and Neil Nevitte, *The Challenge of Direct Democracy: The 1992 Canadian Referendum* (Montreal and Kingston: McGill-Queen's University Press, 1996), 68.

17 Ibid., 131.

18 Ibid., 265.

19 Ibid., 263.

20 Cornelier, *The Bloc*, 68.

21 Ibid., 88.

22 Ibid., 78.

23 Ibid., 83.

24 Flanagan, *Waiting for the Wave*, 161-2.

25 Cornelier, *The Bloc*, 92.

26 Ibid., 97.

27 Lysiane Gagnon, "The Bloc Is a Very Versatile Power Tool," *Globe and Mail*, 15 March 1997, D3.

28 Flanagan, *Waiting for the Wave*, 174.

29 Faron Ellis and Keith Archer, "Reform at the Crossroads," in *The Canadian General Election of 1997*, ed. Alan Frizzell and Jon Pammett (Toronto: Dundurn Press, 1997), 117.

30 The 1995 referendum on Quebec sovereignty was the second provincial referendum

on the subject.The first was held in 1980.The 1980 referendum result was 40 percent in favour of sovereignty, while the 1995 referendum result was 49.4 percent in favour.
31 André Bernard, "The Bloc Québécois," in *Canadian General Election of 1997*, ed. Frizzell and Pammett, 135-48.
32 Gagnon, "The Bloc Is aVeryVersatile PowerTool."
33 Philip Authier, "Liberals Rip Bouchard's Fund Raising for the Bloc," *Montreal Gazette,* 5 May 1997.
34 These data, and those in Figure 3.1, are calculated from the Canadian Election Study. Data from the 1997 Canadian Election Study were provided by the Institute for Social Research,York University.The survey was funded by the Social Sciences and Humanities Research Council of Canada (SSHRC), grant number 412-96-0007, and was completed for the 1997 Canadian Election Survey Team of André Blais (Université de Montréal), Elisabeth Gidengil (McGill University), Richard Nadeau (Université de Montréal), and Neil Nevitte (University ofToronto).The Institute for Social Research, the SSHRC, and the Canadian Election Survey Team are not responsible for the analysis and interpretations presented here.
35 Ellis and Archer, "Reform at the Crossroads," 128.
36 Preston Manning, "Leadership for a New Generation," address to the Reform Assembly '98, 29 May 1998.
37 Ibid.
38 The party had about 65,000 members at the time of the vote.This was about 25,000 fewer than the Conservatives had during their leadership vote only a few months earlier.The comparison is instructive and indicates that the Conservatives may not be the easy takeover target Reformers often paint them as.
39 Brian Laghi, "Manning's Big Gamble," *Globe and Mail,* 29 May 1999,A1.

Chapter 4: Struggling to Survive
1 R. Kenneth Carty, "For the Third Asking: Is There a Future for National Political Parties in Canada?," in *In Pursuit of the Public Good,* ed. Tom Kent (Montreal and Kingston: McGill-Queen's University Press, 1997).
2 Canada, Royal Commission on Electoral Reform and Party Financing, *Reforming Electoral Democracy,*Vol. 1 of the *Report of the Royal Commission on Electoral Reform and Party Financing* (Ottawa: Minister of Supply and Services, 1991), 6, 11-13.
3 One of the few issues Parliament did attempt to deal with was the regulation of independent (i.e., non-political party) election spending.The courts promptly declared the legislation unconstitutional.
4 The Conservatives' 1917 vote-share was won under the Unionist government label, and therefore undoubtedly included some Liberal votes.
5 R. Kenneth Carty, *Canadian Political Parties in the Constituencies* (Toronto: Dundurn Press, 1991), 98-102, 240-3.
6 Neil Bradford and Jane Jensen, "Facing Economic Restructuring and Constitutional Renewal: Social Democracy Adrift in Canada," in *Labor Parties in Postindustrial Societies,* ed. Francis Fox Piven (New York: Oxford University Press, 1992).
7 Alan Whitehorn, "The NDP Election Campaign: Dashed Hopes," in *The Canadian General Election of 1988,* ed. Alan Frizzell, Jon H. Pammett, and Anthony Westell (Ottawa: Carleton University Press, 1988), 48.

8 Keith Archer, "Leadership Selection in the New Democratic Party," in *Canadian Political Parties: Leaders, Candidates and Organization,* ed. H. Bakvis (Toronto: Dundurn Press, 1991), 36-8. Archer's data indicate that gender did not influence delegates' voting decisions on the final, decisive ballot. The issue was significant, for there is little doubt but that its salience in the party put McLaughlin on the ballot in the first place.

9 Robinson, a maverick MP, has never publicly explained why he withdrew, but it is generally thought that he believed he couldn't win, so didn't force a final ballot.

10 Less than 9 percent of the electorate are in the region.

11 Edward Greenspon and Jeff Sallot, "Pragmatic McDonough Nudges NDP to Centre," *Globe and Mail,* 21 September 1998.

12 Though the Conservatives' Quebec support didn't fall below BC levels until the 1972 general election.

13 On the role of the caucus in forcing Clark out, see P. Martin, A. Gregg, and G. Perlin, *Contenders: The Tory Quest for Power* (Scarborough, ON: Prentice-Hall, 1983), Chap. 1.

14 George C. Perlin, *The Tory Syndrome: Leadership Politics in the Progressive Conservative Party* (Montreal and Kingston: McGill-Queen's University Press, 1980).

15 W.T. Stanbury, *Money in Politics: Financing Federal Parties and Candidates in Canada* (Toronto: Dundurn Press, 1991), Table 3.1.

16 P. Martin et al., *Contenders.* For evidence of the importance of winning to the leadership convention delegates, see ibid., Table 9, in Appendix B.

17 Alberta, now the region's largest province, had delivered every one of its seats to the Conservatives after 1972. In the second party system, the region's largest province had been Liberal Saskatchewan.

18 R. Johnston, André Blais, Henry E. Brady, and Jean Crête, *Letting the People Decide: Dynamics of a Canadian Election* (Montreal and Kingston: McGill-Queen's University Press, 1992); G. Fraser, *Playing for Keeps: The Making of the Prime Minister, 1988* (Toronto: McClelland and Stewart, 1989).

19 On the importance of the leader, see André Siegfried, *The Race Question in Canada* (1907; reprint, Toronto: McClelland and Stewart, 1966); on the utility of changing leaders, see David K. Stewart and R. Kenneth Carty, "Does Changing the Party Leader Provide an Electoral Boost? A Study of Canadian Provincial Parties, 1960-92," *Canadian Journal of Political Science* 26, 2 (1993): 313-30.

20 David McLaughlin, *Poisoned Chalice: The Last Campaign of the Progressive Conservative Party?* (Toronto: Dundurn Press, 1994), 74-83. McLaughlin titled his chapter on the leadership selection "Leadership '93: The Race That Never Was."

21 Peter Woolstencroft, "On the Ropes Again? The Campaign of the Progressive Conservative Party in the 1997 Federal Election," in *The Canadian General Election of 1997,* ed. Alan Frizzell and Jon Pammett (Toronto: Dundurn Press, 1997), 73-5. See also Heather McIvor, "The Politics of Revival: The Progressive Conservative Party of Canada, 1993-1998," unpublished ms.

22 Woolstencroft, "On the Ropes," 76-7.

23 See the discussion of the dynamics of party membership in Chapter 8.

24 Peter Woolstencroft, "Democracy and the Selection of Party Leaders: The Case of the Progressive Conservative Leadership Election" and Roy Norton, "The P.C. Leadership Selection Process: A New Model for National Political Parties," papers presented to the Canadian Political Science Association annual meeting, June 1999.

25 See Joseph Wearing, *The L-Shaped Party: The Liberal Party of Canada, 1958-1980* (Toronto: McGraw-Hill Ryerson, 1981), for an account of the building of the Liberal party under the third party system.

26 R. Kenneth Carty, "Campaigning in the Trenches: The Transformation of Constituency Politics," in *Party Democracy in Canada: The Politics of National Party Conventions,* ed. G.C. Perlin (Scarborough, ON: Prentice-Hall, 1988); R. Kenneth Carty, "Transforming the Politics of Leadership Selection," paper presented to the annual meeting of the Atlantic Provinces Political Science Association, October 1984.

27 See Perlin, *The Tory Syndrome,* and M. Graesser, "Leadership Crises in an Opposition Party: The Liberal Party of Newfoundland," in *Leaders and Parties in Canadian Politics: Experiences of the Provinces,* ed. R. Kenneth Carty, Lynda Erickson, and Donald Blake (Toronto: Harcourt Brace Jovanovich, 1992).

28 Carty, "Transforming the Politics of Leadership Selection."

29 George C. Perlin, "Leadership Selection in the PC and Liberal Parties," in *Party Politics in Canada,* 7th ed., ed. H.G. Thorburn (Scarborough, ON: Prentice-Hall, 1996).

30 The other figure involved in the defeat of the Meech Lake Accord was the NDP Aboriginal member of the Manitoba legislature Elijah Harper. Harper was later recruited into the Liberal party in an attempt to bolster the party's support in the province and was elected to the Commons in the 1993 election.

31 The leader's ability to name local candidates serves a number of distinctive purposes. See the discussion in Chapter 8.

32 Arguments made in favour of this system by Ontario Liberals who testified to how well it had worked for them only weeks earlier persuaded many delegates unsure of what sort of every-member system to support.

33 For accounts of earlier policy-making cycles, see Wearing, *The L-Shaped Party,* 19-20, 206-14.

34 However, by third-party-system standards the Liberals did well in the far West, better than at any time since 1968, Trudeau's first election campaign as party leader.

35 For the story of this set of policy reversals, see E. Greenspon and A. Wilson-Smith, *Double Vision: The Inside Story of the Liberals in Power* (Toronto: Doubleday, 1996).

36 There is a large literature on the impact of the electoral system on Canadian politics. The definitive essay is still Alan Cairns, "The Electoral System and the Party System in Canada, 1921-1965," *Canadian Journal of Political Science* 1, 1 (1968): 55-80. For a series of reflections on electoral reform written in the aftermath of the 1997 election, see the November 1997 special issue of *Policy Options.*

Chapter 5: Representing Interests

1 Gordon Stewart, *The Origins of Canadian Politics: A Comparative Approach* (Vancouver: University of British Columbia Press, 1986), 90.

2 David Elkins, "Parties as National Institutions: A Comparative Study," in *Representation, Integration and Political Parties in Canada,* ed. Herman Bakvis (Toronto: Dundurn Press, 1991), 12-13.

3 Ibid.

4 Paul Pross, *Group Politics and Public Policy* (Toronto: Oxford University Press, 1986).

5 Neil Nevitte, *The Decline of Deference: Canadian Value Change in Cross-National Perspective* (Peterborough, ON: Broadview Press, 1996), 80.

6   Elkins, "Parties as National Institutions," 31.
7   Liberal Party of Canada, "Multicultural Recruitment Manual" c. 1982, National Archives of Canada, MG 28, IV 2, Vol. 646. File: Multiculturalism (1).
8   K.J. Andersen, "New Canadian Program," National Archives of Canada, MG 28, IV 2, Vol. 607. File: Ethnic. Thompson, a one-time provincial party leader, was eventually rewarded with an appointment to the Senate. In 1998, he became the target of widespread criticism for his virtual non-attendance in the Senate and was forced to resign his seat.
9   Daiva Stasuilis and Yasmeen Abu-Laban, "Ethnic Minorities and the Politics of Limited Inclusion in Canada," in *Canadian Politics: An Introduction to the Discipline,* ed. Alain-G. Gagnon and James Bickerton (Peterborough, ON: Broadview Press, 1992), 583.
10   Ibid., 588.
11   See Lisa Young, *Feminists and Party Politics* (Vancouver: UBC Press, 2000).
12   George Ehring and Wayne Roberts, *Giving Away a Miracle: Lost Dreams, Broken Promises and the Ontario NDP* (Oakville, ON: Mosaic Press, 1993), 19.
13   Elaine Bernard, "Labour, the NDP and Social Movements: What Political Parties Do and Why We Need Each Other," paper distributed to NDP Party Renewal Conference, Toronto, December 1994, 3.
14   Ian McLeod, *Under Siege: The Federal NDP in the Nineties* (Toronto: Lorimer, 1994), 116.
15   Ibid., 123-5.
16   See Janet Heibert, "Interest Groups and Canadian Federal Elections," in *Interest Groups and Elections in Canada,* ed. F. Leslie Seidle (Toronto: Dundurn Press/ RCERPF, 1991).
17   Ibid., 21-3.
18   F. Leslie Seidle, "Canadian Political Finance Regulation and the Democratic Process: Established Rules in a Dynamic System" (revised version), paper prepared for the Round Table on Discontent and Reform in Mature Democracies, Tokyo, August 1996.
19   A recent Supreme Court ruling may open the door for Parliament to make another attempt at limiting independent expenditures.
20   Keith Archer and Faron Ellis, "Opinion Structure of Party Activists: The Reform Party of Canada," *Canadian Journal of Political Science* 27, 2 (1994): 277-308.
21   *Alberta Report,* 27 January 1997.
22   National Firearms Association, "What Is the National Firearms Association?" Photocopy, 1997.
23   David A. Tomlinson, e-mail message to supporters, 2 April 1997.
24   For example, see *Toronto Sun,* 26 May 1997, E13.
25   Despite the studied non-partisan stance at the national level, some local volunteers were willing to take a partisan stance. When two of the authors of this book stopped at a FOCB booth in Vancouver Centre during the election campaign to ask how one should vote to support the CBC, the volunteer did not hesitate to advocate voting NDP.
26   Advertisement appearing in *Le Devoir,* 26 May 1997, A2.
27   Richard Johnston, André Blais, Henry E. Brady, and Jean Crête, *Letting the People Decide: Dynamics of a Canadian Election* (Montreal and Kingston: McGill-Queen's University Press, 1992), 163-4.
28   A. Brian Tanguay and Barry J. Kay, "Third-Party Advertising and the Threat to

Electoral Democracy in Canada: The Mouse that Roared," *International Journal of Canadian Studies* 17 (Spring 1998): 59.

29   Ibid., 65.

30   These figures do not include local constituency-contest expenditures. The discrepancy in favour of the parties is even greater at that level.

31   Kathryn May, "PSAC to Try to Elect Federal Candidates that Support Union's Goals" *Vancouver Sun,* 19 April 1997, A18.

32   Terrence Mercer, Testimony to the Standing Committee on Procedure and House Affairs, 11 March 1998.

Chapter 6: Remaking Party Democracy

1   See, for example, Neil Nevitte, *The Decline of Deference: Canadian Value Change in Cross-National Perspective* (Peterborough, ON: Broadview Press, 1996).

2   F. Leslie Seidle, "The Angry Citizenry: Examining Representation and Responsiveness in Government," *Policy Options* 15, 6 (1994): 75.

3   André Blais and Elisabeth Gidengil, *Making Representative Democracy Work* (Toronto: Dundurn Press, 1991), 16.

4   Ibid.

5   Canada, Royal Commission on Electoral Reform and Party Financing, *Reforming Electoral Democracy,* Vol. 1 of the *Report of the Royal Commission on Electoral Reform and Party Financing* (Ottawa: Minister of Supply and Services, 1991), 225. These figures have remained stable since the early 1990s. Figure 2.1, on p. 28 above, charts this process.

6   David Laycock, *Populism and Democratic Thought in the Canadian Prairies, 1910-1945* (Toronto: University of Toronto Press, 1990), 21.

7   As quoted in C.B. Macpherson, *Democracy in Alberta: Social Credit and the Party System,* 2nd ed. (Toronto: University of Toronto Press, 1962), 71.

8   W.L. Morton, *The Progressive Party in Canada* (Toronto: University of Toronto Press, 1950), 121.

9   John C. Courtney, "Leadership Conventions and the Development of the National Political Community in Canada," in *National Politics and Community in Canada,* ed. R. Kenneth Carty and W. Peter Ward (Vancouver: University of British Columbia Press, 1986), 94.

10   Ibid., 98.

11   Desmond Morton, *The New Democrats, 1961-1986: The Politics of Change* (Toronto: Copp Clark Pitman, 1986), 92.

12   Christina McCall-Newman, *Grits: An Intimate Portrait of the Liberal Party* (Toronto: Macmillan, 1982), 17.

13   This process did not turn out to be a deliberative one. Instead of having individual ministers report on their departments and allowing for debate on each report, Trudeau decided to present one report himself on behalf of the government. The result was that any criticism would be interpreted as a direct assault on the party leader: Joseph Wearing, *The L-Shaped Party: The Liberal Party of Canada, 1958-1980* (Toronto: McGraw-Hill Ryerson, 1981), 168.

14   David E. Smith, "Party Government, Representation and National Integration in Canada," in *Party Government and Regional Representation in Canada,* ed. P. Aucoin (Toronto: University of Toronto Press, 1985), 31.

15 Chapter 4 provides an account of the Liberal reform process, which only managed to implement part of the reform agenda.

16 See, for example, Hannah Pitkin, ed., *Representation* (New York: Artherton Press, 1969).

17 Blais and Gidengil, *Making Representative Democracy Work,* 37, 42, and 61.

18 Joseph Wearing, "Guns, Gays, and Gadflies: Party Dissent in the House of Commons under Mulroney and Chrétien," paper presented at the Annual Meeting of the Canadian Political Science Association, Ottawa, June 1998.

19 "We believe in accountability of elected representatives to the people who elect them, and that the duty of elected members to their constituents should supersede their obligations to their political parties": *Reform Party of Canada Constitution (1992),* Schedule A: "Statement of Principles," 15.

20 For full details of these projects, see William Cross, "Teledemocracy: Canadian Political Parties and Communication Technology," in *Digital Democracy: Policy and Politics in the Wired World,* ed. Cynthia Alexander and Leslie Pal (Toronto: Oxford University Press, 1998).

21 "I'll Support Suicide: Manning," *Toronto Star,* 24 April 1994, A12.

22 "Referendum '94 Results Released," press release from the office of MP Ted White, 21 June 1994.

23 Ted White, "The Post Mortem," *North Shore News* (Vancouver), 29 June 1994.

24 F. Christopher Arterton, *Teledemocracy: Can Technology Protect Democracy?* (Newbury Park, CA: Sage, 1987), and Benjamin Barber, *Strong Democracy: Participatory Politics for a New Age* (Berkeley: University of California Press, 1984).

25 William Cross, "The Conflict between Participatory and Accommodative Politics: The Case for Stronger Parties," *International Journal of Canadian Studies* 17 (Spring 1998): 37-55.

26 By contrast, members join the NDP only through its provincial wings, and the Liberals, through riding associations.

27 *Reform Party of Canada Constitution (1992),* Section 5A.

28 See, for example, Tom Flanagan, *Waiting for the Wave: The Reform Party and Preston Manning* (Toronto: Stoddart, 1995).

29 Cross, "The Conflict between Participatory and Accommodative Politics."

30 *The New Constitution of the Progressive Conservative Party of Canada (April 1995),* Section 8.3.

31 Progressive Conservative Party of Canada, *Background Paper on Party Restructuring,* September 1994, 2.

32 Ibid., 3.

33 Progressive Conservative Party of Canada, *Supplementary Notes on Party Restructuring,* October 1994, 12.

34 *The New Constitution of the Progressive Conservative Party of Canada, April 1995,* Section 8.1.3.

35 Ibid., 9.3.1 and 9.3.3.

36 It is ironic that the Bloc was the first federal party to include its membership directly in leadership selection. Just one year earlier, the party limited participation in the choice of Lucien Bouchard's successor to the 158 members of the party's General Council. This body consists of MPs, riding association presidents, regional directors, and executive members of the party's youth wing.

37 Even though the rise of Reform was one of the forces that pushed federal parties towards direct election of party leaders, Reform's first leader (Preston Manning) was elected at the party's founding convention, and not by the membership of the new party.
38 John C. Courtney, *Do Conventions Matter? Choosing National Party Leaders in Canada* (Montreal and Kingston: McGill-Queen's University Press, 1995), 326.
39 Cross, "The Conflict between Participatory and Accommodative Politics."
40 Courtney, *Do Conventions Matter?,* 336-7.
41 Keith Archer and Alan Whitehorn, *Political Activists: The NDP in Convention* (Toronto: Oxford University Press, 1997), 237.
42 For a discussion of provincial party experiences with direct election, see William Cross, "Direct Election of Provincial Party Leaders, 1985-1995: The End of the Leadership Convention?" *Canadian Journal of Political Science* 24, 2 (1996): 295-315.
43 See Courtney, *Do Conventions Matter?,* 112, and R. Kenneth Carty, "Campaigning in the Trenches: The Transformation of Constituency Politics," in *Party Democracy in Canada: The Politics of National Party Conventions,* ed. George Perlin (Scarborough, ON: Prentice-Hall, 1988), 89.
44 R. Kenneth Carty and Donald E. Blake, "The Adoption of Membership Votes for Choosing Party Leaders: The Experience of Canadian Parties," *Party Politics,* 5 (2) 1999: 211-24.
45 See Peter Woolstencroft, "Democracy and the Selection of Party Leaders: The Case of the 1998 Progressive Conservative Leadership Election," paper presented at the 1999 meetings of the Canadian Political Science Association, Sherbrooke, Quebec.
46 Even among direct-election voters, however, the cost of participation has an effect on participation. Telephone votes, normally with a relatively high voting fee for direct-election processes (averaging around $20), have a lower participation rate than those with a minimal or no voting fee.
47 See Cross, "Direct Election of Provincial Party Leaders in Canada," 309.
48 David K. Stewart, "Electing the Premier: An Examination of the 1992 Alberta Progressive Conservative Leadership Election," paper presented at the annual meeting of the Canadian Political Science Association, Calgary, 1994, 12, and Margaret Hunziker, "Leadership Selection: The 1985 Alberta Progressive Conservative Leadership Convention," MA thesis, University of Calgary, 1986, 116.
49 Courtney, *Do Conventions Matter?,* 278.
50 The New Democrats have always been the exception in this regard. The number of convention delegates awarded each constituency depends upon the number of local NDP members.
51 "Bloc Leadership 'Telethon' Will End by Faceoff Time: Party Will Unveil Results of Vote in Elaborate 90 Minute Radio-Canada Show," *Montreal Gazette,* 13 March 1997, A12.

Chapter 7: Paying for Parties

1 W.T. Stanbury, *Money in Politics: Financing Federal Parties and Candidates in Canada* (Toronto: Dundurn Press/RCERPF, 1991), 27-8.
2 Khayyam Z. Paltiel, "Party Finance before World War I," in *Canadian Political Party Systems: A Reader,* ed. R. Kenneth Carty (Peterborough, ON: Broadview Press, 1992), 123-5.

3 André Siegfried, *The Race Question in Canada* (1907; reprint, Toronto: McClelland and Stewart, 1966), 119.

4 Ibid., 122.

5 E.E. Harrill, "Party Finance in the Second Party System," in *Canadian Political Party Systems: A Reader*, ed. R. Kenneth Carty, 258.

6 Ibid., 254.

7 Khayyam Z. Paltiel, "Campaign Financing in Canada and Its Reform," in *Canada at the Polls: The General Election of 1974*, ed. Howard Penniman (Washington, DC: American Enterprise Institute, 1975), 195.

8 An exception to this is the question of independent, or "third party," expenditures during elections. The rules governing such spending have been amended on several occasions, and have been successfully challenged in court. This issue is discussed in some detail in Chapter 5.

9 Corporations are also eligible to claim the tax credit, but a relatively small proportion do so, probably because the value is less, in relative terms. In this sense, the tax credit creates less incentive for corporate donors. See Stanbury, *Money in Politics*, 300.

10 See Lisa Young, "Party, State and Political Competition in Canada: The Cartel Argument Revisited," *Canadian Journal of Political Science* 31, 2 (June 1998): 339-58.

11 Canada, Royal Commission on Electoral Reform and Party Financing [hereinafter RCERPF], *Reforming Electoral Democracy*, Vol. 1 of the *Report of the Royal Commission on Electoral Reform and Party Financing* (Ottawa: Minister of Supply and Services, 1991), 336.

12 Since 1983, spending limits for candidates and parties have been indexed to inflation.

13 Calculated from Elections Canada, *Candidates' Returns Respecting Election Expenses*, October 1998.

14 F. Leslie Seidle, "Canadian Political Finance Regulation and the Democratic Process: Established Rules in a Dynamic System" (revised version), paper prepared for the Round Table on Discontent and Reform in the Mature Democracies, Tokyo, August 1996.

15 It should be noted that Conservative spending in 1993 also included the costs of the party's leadership-selection process that year. The bump in Liberal spending in 1990 reflects that party's leadership-selection expenses that year.

16 The observant reader will note that the NDP has comparatively high levels of expenditure. This finding is misleading, for the party's complex financial integration and reporting practices lead to an overstatement of the real resources expended by the national party. For a detailed discussion of NDP finances, see Stanbury, *Money in Politics*, especially Chap. 6.

17 Calculated from the Canadian Election Study data set.

18 Chief Electoral Officer, *Report of the Chief Electoral Officer Regarding Election Expenses* (Ottawa: Minister of Supply and Services, 1994). The $24.8 million that the Conservatives spent aside from election expenses would reflect normal annual operating costs, any pre-writ spending and polling, as well as costs associated with the leadership convention the party held in the same year.

19 Canada, House of Commons, Standing Committee on Procedure and House Affairs, *Report on the Canada Elections Act*, June 1998, 57.

20 See Richard S. Katz and Peter Mair, "Changing Models of Party Organization and Party Democracy: The Emergence of the Cartel Party," *Party Politics* 1 (1995): 5-28.

21 Canada, RCERPF, *Reforming Electoral Democracy,* 365.

22 Ibid., 368.

23 Preliminary figures released by Elections Canada.

24 Ibid.

25 Stanbury, *Money in Politics,* 361.

26 W.T. Stanbury, "Getting and Spending: The Effect of Federal Regulations on Financing Political Parties and Candidates in Canada," in *Party Politics in Canada,* 7th ed., ed. Hugh Thorburn (Scarborough, ON: Prentice-Hall, 1996).

27 Lori Kittelberg, "Reform Party's Top Fundraisers," *Hill Times,* 20 July 1998.

28 Seidle, "Canadian Political Finance Regulation and the Democratic Process," Table 4. Reported in 1995 dollars. Corporations are also eligible to receive a less-generous tax credit. The cost of that credit to the public treasury is not available for the 1989-93 election cycle, but in previous election cycles its value ranged from $2 million to almost $6 million (1995 dollars).

29 Stanbury, *Money in Politics,* 213.

30 Ibid., 55.

31 Pascale Michaud and Pierre Laferrière, "Economic Analysis of the Funding of Political Parties in Canada," in *Issues in Party and Election Finance in Canada,* ed. F. Leslie Seidle (Toronto: Dundurn Press/RCERPF, 1991), 378. There is no reason to expect the 1985-8 election cycle to be unique.

32 The Canadian Radio-television and Telecommunications Commission's definition of a "network" is fairly narrow, so, as of 1998, it applied only to the CBC and CTV in English-speaking Canada, and to SRC, TVA, and TQS in French-speaking Canada, as well as to the English and French services of CBC Radio/Radio-Canada.

33 *Report of the Broadcasting Arbitrator,* appended to *Report of the Chief Electoral Officer on the 36th General Election* (Ottawa: Minister of Supply and Services, 1997), 87-8.

34 Figures for the 1997 election are based on preliminary numbers from Elections Canada. They may be amended after the release of the report of the Chief Electoral Officer on election expenses.

35 Preliminary figures released by Elections Canada and calculated from Elections Canada, *Candidates' Returns Respecting Election Expenses.*

36 Ibid. Recall the cautionary note concerning interpreting NDP expenditure reports in note 16, above.

37 Ibid.

38 In its 1998 members' direct leadership vote, the Conservative party imposed spending limits of $1.8 million during the period prior to the first ballot, and $500,000 between the first and second ballots. The weak state of the party meant that none of the candidates had much money.

39 Canada, RCERPF, *Reforming Electoral Democracy,* 281, 283.

40 The parties have adopted the practice of channelling contributions to leadership candidates through the national party, and thereby issuing tax receipts to the contributors. In the 1990 Liberal leadership convention, for example, some $1.95 million in contributions to candidates was routed through Liberal party headquarters, where tax receipts were issued. For a detailed discussion of this, see Stanbury, *Money in Politics,* Chap. 5.

41 Reform Party of Canada, "Blue Book." This is available at the Reform Party's Web site at http://www.reform.ca.

Chapter 8: On the Ground

1 André Siegfried, *The Race Question in Canada* (1907; reprint, Toronto: McClelland and Stewart, 1966), 112-13.

2 The mathematics of the electoral system means that it is possible to win more seats, and hence office, with fewer votes than your opponents. Both John Diefenbaker, in 1957, and Joe Clark, in 1979, became prime minister this way, and it has not been uncommon at the provincial level.

3 Some of the argument in the proceeding paragraphs is developed in R. Kenneth Carty, "For the Third Asking: Is There a Future for National Political Parties in Canada?," in *In Pursuit of the Public Good,* ed. Tom Kent (Montreal and Kingston: McGill-Queen's University Press, 1997). In 1921, the Progressives got 22.9 percent of the vote, more than Reform's 18.7 percent in 1993; in 1962, Social Credit got 26 percent of the Quebec vote, as compared with the Bloc's 49 percent in 1993.

4 M. Duverger, *Political Parties* (London: Methuen, 1964), 64, describes a cadre party as "the grouping of notabilities for the preparation of elections, conducting campaigns and maintaining contact with the candidates."

5 For a detailed examination of Canadian parties from the perspective of their local associations, see R. Kenneth Carty, *Canadian Political Parties in the Constituencies* (Toronto: Dundurn Press, 1991).

6 On party association strength in 1988, see ibid., 98-102; on the state of the Ontario Conservatives at the time of the 1997 general election, see Peter Woolstencroft, "On the Ropes Again? The Campaign of the Progressive Conservative Party in the 1997 Federal Election," in *The Canadian General Election of 1997,* ed. Alan Frizzell and Jon Pammett (Toronto: Dundurn Press, 1997), 76.

7 Carty, *Parties in the Constituencies,* 36-9. Reform's early years were characterized by steady membership growth, but after the 1993 election it, too, fell into this election-cycle pattern as its average association membership fell by a third the following year. Details on Reform memberships can be found in W. Cross, "Grassroots Participation in Canadian Political Parties: An Examination of Leadership Selection, Candidate Nomination, Policy Development and Election Campaigning," Ph.D. diss., University of Western Ontario, 1996.

8 Reform also holds internal membership referendums to decide organizational and policy matters.

9 The new system of national membership lists does not appear to be changing this dynamic. The Conservative party had a traditional flood of new members in its "national member" universal-vote leadership contest in 1998 that led to Joe Clark's return as leader: see Peter Woolstencroft, "Democracy and the Selection of Party Leaders: The Case of the 1988 Progressive Conservative Leadership Election," a paper presented to the annual meeting of the Canadian Political Science Association, June 1999.

10 R. Kenneth Carty and Lynda Erickson, "Candidate Nomination in Canada's National Political Parties," in *Canadian Political Parties: Leaders, Candidates and Organization,* ed. H. Bakvis (Toronto: Dundurn Press, 1991), 105; Carty, *Parties in the Constituencies,* 106, 133-5.

11 Nomination processes have become more open than they have ever been. In the decades after Confederation, delegate conventions were typically held to ensure that

all parts of the sprawling, thinly populated constituencies were represented, while, in the second party system, regional bosses often held sway over nominations in areas where a party was strong.

12 Reform Party of Canada, *Candidate Recruitment and Selection Manual* (April 1996), 6. The document's Appendix 6 provides local associations with a suggested form advertisement.

13 Carty and Erickson, *Candidate Nomination*, and Lynda Erickson, "Canada," in *Passages to Power*, ed. P. Norris (Cambridge: Cambridge University Press, 1997), provide comparisons of safe and hopeless settings for the 1988 and 1993 general elections, respectively.

14 Anthony M. Sayers, *Parties, Candidates and Constituency Campaigns in Canadian Elections* (Vancouver: UBC Press, 1998). The discussion in the next few paragraphs follows Sayers's typology of local nomination processes.

15 The situation in 1997 was by no means an exception. In the preceding election, in 1993, prominent examples of the same phenomenon included Jane Stewart (daughter of a former provincial Finance minister and party leader, granddaughter of a premier), Susan Whelan (daughter of a federal minister), and, of course, Reform leader Preston Manning, himself the son of Alberta's longest-serving premier. This route to a political career has been common throughout Canadian history and can be traced back to Confederation. Two of the Fathers, and subsequent prime ministers, Macdonald and Tupper, both had sons follow them into the Commons. In the past, by-elections often provided the mechanism for family succession.

16 The Liberals, Conservatives, and New Democrats ran candidates in all 301 ridings, the Bloc only in Quebec, and Reform only a few in Quebec.

17 Woolstencroft, "On the Ropes Again," 77.

18 A comparison of NDP candidates in Quebec with those in their stronghold of Saskatchewan is instructive. In 1997, in Quebec, the percentage of NDP candidates who were women was 45; in Saskatchewan, it was 0.

19 On the disproportionate media attention given to contested nominations, see Carty and Erickson, "Candidate Nomination," 117-18.

20 Erickson, "Canada," 47.

21 Carty and Erickson, "Candidate Nomination," 123-5.

22 This is an example of the leader's legal power to say who would not be a candidate effectively becoming a political power to indicate who would be.

23 Erickson, "Canada," 53.

24 David C. Docherty, *Mr. Smith Goes to Ottawa: Life in the House of Commons* (Vancouver: UBC Press, 1997), Chap. 2.

25 "Political widow" is a term used to describe women who "inherited" their seat when a husband (or other family relative) died in office and the local party ran them, hoping to exploit their name-recognition and voter sympathy.

26 Reform Party, *Recruitment Manual, 3* .

27 The party has used this power to approve would-be candidates to deny a few individuals the right to present themselves to local constituency nominating meetings. These have typically been notoriously unacceptable individuals or, in a few instances, those involved in legal difficulties.

28 The phrase is Lynda Erickson's. These decisions are typically made by provincial-level campaign chairs, and in the 1990s were most aggressively used by those managing campaign planning in Ontario.

29 "Federal Liberal Officials Defend Favouring Star Candidates," *Vancouver Sun*, 11 February 1997; "Jennings Takes Liberal Nomination in Third Ballot in N.D.G.," *Montreal Gazette*, 21 April 1997.

30 See Carty, *Parties in the Constituencies*, 128-9.

31 Surveys of convention delegates and riding presidents in both the Liberal and Conservative parties indicate that the majority believe the leader ought to accept the local choice.

32 This is the picture provided by the studies coming from successive national election survey projects. See, for example, Richard Johnston, André Blais, Henry E. Brady, and Jean Crête, *Letting the People Decide: Dynamics of a Canadian Election* (Montreal and Kingston: McGill-Queen's University Press, 1992).

33 On the extraordinary volatility, and seat turnover, in Canadian elections, see Donald Blake, "Party Competition and Electoral Volatility: Canada in Comparative Perspective," in *Representation, Integration and Political Parties in Canada,* ed. H. Bakvis (Toronto: Dundurn Press, 1991).

34 In 1988 losing NDP candidates spent about 40 percent of their limit, less than half that of their winning colleagues. These differences between winners and losers were much greater than for candidates in the other parties. See R. Kenneth Carty and Munroe Eagles, "Do Local Campaigns Matter? Campaign Spending, the Local Canvass and Party Support in Canada," *Electoral Studies* 18, 1 (1999): 69-87.

35 Carty, *Parties in the Constituencies,* 209-17. In fact the national parties often take their candidates' election-expense reimbursements from the state, so this probably underestimates the support locals provide the national party. In 1997 Reform's constituency associations contributed about $1.5 million to its national campaign: see Faron Ellis and Keith Archer, "Reform at the Crossroads," in *The Canadian General Election of 1997,* ed. Alan Frizzell and Jon Pammett, 120.

36 NDP candidates do not do as much personal fund-raising as those in other parties. It also appears to be the case that rich associations do not require their candidate to put as much personal effort into fund-raising as do others. This means that, by and large, most MPs have probably not been as deeply involved in fund-raising as have those they defeated.

37 The NDP has been the most aggressive about using paid campaign managers, especially in ridings the national campaign has targeted. In these cases, experienced managers may well be sent in to the constituency by provincial campaign chairs. On the use of paid staff by all the major parties, see Carty, *Parties in the Constituencies*, 162-6.

38 Sayers, *Parties, Candidates and Constituency Campaigns,* passim.

39 Carty, *Parties in the Constituencies,* 172-3.

40 Authors' interviews with the 1997 Liberal and NDP Vancouver Centre campaign managers.

41 Carty and Eagles, "Do Local Campaigns Matter?"

42 See Docherty, *Mr. Smith,* 51-9, or Blake, "Competition and Volatility," for accounts of the high turnover rates among Canadian politicians.

Chapter 9: In the Air

1 See S.J.R. Noel, "Patronage and Entourages, Action-Sets, Networks," in *Canadian Parties in Transition,* 2nd ed., ed. A. Brian Tanguay and Alain-G. Gagnon (Toronto: Nelson, 1996).

2 David E. Smith, "Party Government in Canada," in *Canadian Political Party Systems: A Reader,* ed. R. Kenneth Carty (Peterborough, ON: Broadview Press, 1992), 552.

3 Michael Nolan, "Political Communication Methods in Canadian Federal Election Campaigns, 1867-1925," *Canadian Journal of Communication* 7 (1981): 31.

4 Ibid., 32.

5 Ibid., 30-1, discussing the conclusions of Khayyam Z. Paltiel and Jean Brown Van Loon in "Financing the Liberal Party, 1867-1965," in Committee on Election Expenses, *Studies in Canadian Party Finance* (Ottawa, 1966), 212.

6 Thomas S. Axworthy, "Capital-Intensive Politics: Money, Media and Mores in the United States and Canada," in *Issues in Party and Election Finance in Canada,* ed. F. Leslie Seidle (Toronto: Dundurn Press, 1991), 184.

7 David R. Spencer and Catherine M. Bolan, "Election Broadcasting in Canada: A Brief History," in *Election Broadcasting in Canada,* ed. Frederick J. Fletcher (Toronto: Dundurn Press, 1991), 11.

8 See ibid., 5. The parties played to this by advertising the times and stations.

9 Axworthy, "Capital-Intensive Politics," 186.

10 Dalton Camp, *Gentlemen, Players and Politicians* (Toronto: McClelland and Stewart, 1970), 137.

11 Ibid.

12 Peter C. Newman, *Renegade in Power: The Diefenbaker Years* (Toronto: McClelland and Stewart, 1963), 54.

13 Peter Stursberg, *Diefenbaker: Leadership Gained, 1956-1962* (Toronto: University of Toronto Press, 1975), 53.

14 Reginald Whitaker, *The Government Party: Organizing and Financing the Liberal Party of Canada, 1930-1958* (Toronto: University of Toronto Press, 1977), 249.

15 Noel, "Patronage and Entourages," 242.

16 Spencer and Bolan, "Election Broadcasting in Canada," 28.

17 R. Kenneth Carty, "Three Canadian Party Systems," in *Canadian Political Party Systems: A Reader,* ed. R. Kenneth Carty (Peterborough, ON: Broadview Press, 1992), 577.

18 Guy Lachapelle, *Polls and the Media in Canadian Elections* (Toronto: Dundurn Press, 1991), 10; Daniel J. Robinson, *The Measure of Democracy: Polling Market Research, and Public Life, 1930-1945* (Toronto: University of Toronto Press, 1999). Robinson (p. 68) notes that the first national Gallup poll, in 1941, reported on the highly sensitive issue of conscription.

19 R. MacGregor Dawson, *The Government of Canada,* 5th ed. (Toronto: University of Toronto Press, 1970), 441.

20 Carty, "Three Canadian Party Systems," 582.

21 Much of the data in the remainder of this chapter result from interviews conducted with national and local campaign staff, party pollsters, and media consultants from the Liberal, New Democratic, Progressive Conservative, and Reform parties.

22 At the request of new party leader John Turner, Angus Reid also polled for the Liberals in 1984.

23 While it is the norm today for the art and science of polling to be wedded in a single person, this is not always the case. The Conservatives' Owen conducted the party's 1997 polls and organized the results, while others more experienced in strategy development, and closer personally to the leader (such as Bruce Anderson from Ottawa's Earnscliffe Strategy Group), had principal responsibility for analyzing the data and developing a strategy from it.

24 The Conservatives had several new additions to their national campaign team in 1997. Tom Scott, from Foster Advertising, oversaw Conservative advertising efforts during several previous campaigns. Scott was extremely well regarded within both the industry and the party, but had retired from the advertising industry prior to the 1997 campaign. Miele was part of a younger, less experienced team put together late in the day by the party's leadership.

25 The early use of advertising firms by the Liberal party is well chronicled in Whitaker, *The Government Party,* 216-63.

26 For the first time, in 1997 the Liberals used a Red Leaf type structure for their French-language advertisements.

27 Joseph Wearing, *The L-Shaped Party: The Liberal Party of Canada, 1958-1980* (Toronto: McGraw-Hill Ryerson, 1981), 200.

28 Ibid., 201. Prime Minister Trudeau subsequently appointed Grafstein to the Senate for his troubles.

29 John Laschinger and Geoffrey Stevens, *Leaders and Lesser Mortals: Backroom Politics in Canada* (Toronto: Key Porter Books, 1992), 92.

30 As a stand-alone service, this sort of poll would normally cost about $15,000, but few local candidates could afford that.

31 The Liberals employ a time-buying structure similar to that used for the production of their advertisements. They put together their own dedicated firm made up of time buyers from several different agencies.

32 Robert Mason Lee, *One Hundred Monkeys: The Triumph of Popular Wisdom in Canadian Politics* (Toronto: Macfarlane Walter and Ross, 1989), 260-3.

33 Ibid., 260.

34 Canada, *Report of the Standing Committee on Procedure and House Affairs,* June 1998, 8.

35 An example of this is Manning's appearance on a campaign debate on the CBC television program "The National," 20 May 1997. Manning made reference to International Monetary Fund studies supporting the introduction of tax cuts. When NDP representative Nelson Riis questioned Manning's representation of the studies, Manning promised to post the studies on the party's Web page so that voters could read them directly.

Chapter 10: Rebuilding the Canadian Party System

1 See the description of party constituency politics in Chapter 8 and compare with André Siegfried, *The Race Question in Canada* (1907; reprint, Toronto: McClelland and Stewart, 1966), Chaps. 20-2. Siegfried might have been surprised at the extent to which local individuals now feel free to cross party lines, but much of the rest of our story would be familiar to him.

2 Reginald Whitaker, *The Government Party: Organizing and Financing the Liberal Party of Canada, 1930-1958* (Toronto: University of Toronto Press, 1977).

3 Neil Nevitte, *The Decline of Deference: Canadian Value Change in Cross-National Perspective* (Peterborough, ON: Broadview Press, 1996).
4 For a discussion of continuities in the Liberal party before and after 1993, see Stephen Clarkson, "Straddling Two Party Systems: The Liberal Party of Canada at War, 1974-1997," paper presented to the conference on The Evolution of Canadian Party Systems in the Twentieth Century, Centre for Election Studies, University of Waterloo, June 1999.

Bibliography

Aldrich, John H. *Why Parties? The Origin and Transformation of Party Politics in America.* Chicago: University of Chicago Press, 1995.

Andersen, K.J. "New Canadian Program." National Archives of Canada, MG 28, IV 2, Vol. 607. File: Ethnic.

Archer, Keith. "Leadership Selection in the New Democratic Party." In *Canadian Political Parties: Leaders, Candidates and Organization,* ed. H. Bakvis, 3-56. Toronto: Dundurn Press, 1991.

Archer, Keith, and Faron Ellis. "Opinion Structure of Party Activists: The Reform Party of Canada," *Canadian Journal of Political Science* 27, 2 (1994): 277-308.

Archer, Keith, and Alan Whitehorn. *Political Activists: The NDP in Convention.* Toronto: Oxford University Press, 1997.

Arterton, F. Christopher. *Teledemocracy: Can Technology Protect Democracy?* Newbury Park, CA: Sage, 1987.

Authier, Philip. "Liberals Rip Bouchard's Fund Raising for the Bloc," *Montreal Gazette,* 5 May 1997.

Axworthy, Thomas S. "Capital-Intensive Politics: Money, Media and Mores in the United States and Canada." In *Issues in Party and Election Finance in Canada,* ed. F. Leslie Seidle, 157-234. Toronto: Dundurn Press, 1991.

Barber, Benjamin. *Strong Democracy: Participatory Politics for a New Age.* Berkeley: University of California Press, 1984.

Bartolini, Stefano, and Peter Mair. *Identity, Competition, and Electoral Volatility: The Stabilisation of European Electorates, 1885-1985.* Cambridge: Cambridge University Press, 1990.

Bernard, André. "The Bloc Québécois." In *The Canadian General Election of 1997,* ed. Alan Frizzell and Jon Pammett, 135-48. Toronto: Dundurn Press, 1997.

Bernard, Elaine. "Labour, the NDP and Social Movements: What Political Parties Do and Why We Need Each Other." Paper distributed to NDP Party Renewal Conference, Toronto, December 1994.

Blais, André, and Elisabeth Gidengil. *Making Representative Democracy Work: The Views of Canadians.* Toronto: Dundurn Press, 1991.

Blake, Donald. *Two Political Worlds: Parties and Voting in British Columbia.* Vancouver: University of British Columbia Press, 1985.

−. "Party Competition and Electoral Volatility: Canada in Comparative Perspective." In *Representation, Integration and Political Parties in Canada,* ed. H. Bakvis, 253-73. Toronto: Dundurn Press, 1991.

Blake, Donald, and Lynda Erickson. "Electoral Volatility and Realignment in 1993." Paper presented at the 1998 Annual Meeting of the Canadian Political Science Association.

−. "New Party Insurgency and Party System Change: The 1993 Canadian Election." Unpublished manuscript, 1998.

Bradford, Neil, and Jane Jenson. "Facing Economic Restructuring and Constitutional Renewal: Social Democracy Adrift in Canada." In *Labor Parties in Postindustrial Societies,* ed. Francis Fox Piven, 190-211. New York: Oxford University Press, 1992.

Cairns, Alan. "The Electoral System and the Party System in Canada, 1921-1965." *Canadian Journal of Political Science* 1, 1 (1968): 55-80.

Camp, Dalton. *Gentlemen, Players and Politicians.* Toronto: McClelland and Stewart, 1970.

Canada. Chief Electoral Officer. *Report of the Chief Electoral Officer Regarding Election Expenses.* Ottawa: Minister of Supply and Services, 1994.

−. Elections Canada. *Candidates' Returns Respecting Election Expenses.* Ottawa: Minister of Supply and Services, 1998.

−. Elections Canada. *Report of the Broadcasting Arbitrator,* appended to *Report of the Chief Electoral Officer on the 36th General Election.* Ottawa: Minister of Supply and Services, 1997.

−. House of Commons, Standing Committee on Procedure and House Affairs. *Report on the Canada Elections Act. Record of Proceedings,* June 1998.

−. Royal Commission on Electoral Reform and Party Financing. *Reforming Electoral Democracy.* Vol. 1 of *Report of the Royal Commission on Electoral Reform and Party Financing.* Ottawa: Minister of Supply and Services, 1991.

Carty, R. Kenneth. "Campaigning in the Trenches: The Transformation of Constituency Politics." In *Party Democracy in Canada: The Politics of National Party Conventions,* ed. G.C. Perlin, 84-96. Scarborough, ON: Prentice-Hall, 1988.

−. *Canadian Political Parties in the Constituencies.* Toronto: Dundurn Press, 1991.

−. "The Electorate and the Evolution of Canadian Electoral Politics." *American Review of Canadian Studies* 26, 1 (Spring 1996): 7-29.

−. "For the Third Asking: Is There a Future for National Political Parties in Canada?" In *In Pursuit of the Public Good,* ed. Tom Kent, 144-55. Montreal and Kingston: McGill-Queen's University Press, 1997.

−. "Three Canadian Party Systems." In *Canadian Political Party Systems, 1978-1984,* ed. R. Kenneth Carty, 563-86. Peterborough, ON: Broadview Press, 1992.

−. "Transforming the Politics of Leadership Selection." Paper presented to the annual meeting of the Atlantic Provinces Political Science Association, October 1994.

−, ed. *Canadian Political Party Systems, 1978-1984.* Peterborough, ON: Broadview Press, 1992.

Carty, R. Kenneth, and Munroe Eagles. "Do Local Campaigns Matter? Campaign Spending, the Local Canvass and Party Support in Canada." *Electoral Studies* 18, 1 (1999): 69-87.

Carty, R. Kenneth, and Lynda Erickson. "Candidate Nomination in Canada's National Political Parties." In *Canadian Political Parties: Leaders, Candidates and Organization,* ed. H. Bakvis, 95-189. Toronto: Dundurn Press, 1991.

Chambers, William Nesbet, and Walter Dean Durnham, eds. *The American Party Systems: Stages of Political Development.* New York: Oxford University Press, 1967.

Clarke, Harold D., and Allan Kornberg. "Evaluations and Evolution: Public Attitudes towards Canada's Federal Political Parties, 1965-1991." *Canadian Journal of Political Science* 26, 2 (1993): 287-311.

Clarkson, Stephen. "Democracy in the Liberal Party: The Experiment with Citizen Participation under Pierre Trudeau." In *Party Politics in Canada,* 4th ed., ed. H.G. Thorburn, 154-60. Scarborough, ON: Prentice-Hall, 1979.

–. "Straddling Two Party Systems: The Liberal Party of Canada at War, 1974-1997." Paper presented to the conference on The Evolution of Canadian Party Systems in the Twentieth Century, Centre for Election Studies, University of Waterloo, June 1999.

Cornelier, Manon. *The Bloc.* Toronto: Lorimer, 1995.

Courtney, John C. *Do Conventions Matter? Choosing National Party Leaders in Canada.* Montreal and Kingston: McGill-Queen's University Press, 1995.

–. "Leadership Conventions and the Development of the National Political Community in Canada." In *National Politics and Community in Canada,* ed. R. Kenneth Carty and W. Peter Ward, 94-111. Vancouver: University of British Columbia Press, 1986.

Cross, William. "The Conflict between Participatory and Accommodative Politics: The Case for Stronger Parties." *International Journal of Canadian Studies* 17 (Spring 1998): 37-55.

–. "Direct Election of Provincial Party Leaders, 1985-1995: The End of the Leadership Convention?" *Canadian Journal of Political Science* 24, 2 (1996): 295-315.

–. "Grassroots Participation in Canadian Political Parties: An Examination of Leadership Selection, Candidate Nomination, Policy Development and Election Campaigning." Ph.D. diss., University of Western Ontario, 1996.

–. "Teledemocracy: Canadian Political Parties and Communication Technology." In *Digital Democracy: Policy and Politics in the Wired World,* ed. Cynthia Alexander and Leslie Pal, 132-48. Toronto: Oxford University Press, 1998.

Dawson, R. MacGregor. *The Government of Canada,* 5th ed. Toronto: University of Toronto Press, 1970.

Dobbin, Murray. *Preston Manning and the Reform Party.* Toronto: Lorimer, 1991.

Docherty, David C. *Mr. Smith Goes to Ottawa: Life in the House of Commons.* Vancouver: UBC Press, 1997.

Duverger, M. *Political Parties.* London: Methuen, 1964.

Ehring, George, and Wayne Roberts. *Giving Away a Miracle: Lost Dreams, Broken Promises and the Ontario NDP.* Oakville, ON: Mosaic Press, 1993.

Elkins, David. "Parties as National Institutions: A Comparative Study." In *Representation, Integration and Political Parties in Canada,* ed. H. Bakvis, 3-62. Toronto: Dundurn Press, 1991.

Ellis, Faron, and Keith Archer. "Reform at the Crossroads." In *The Canadian General Election of 1997,* ed. Alan Frizzell and Jon Pammett, 111-33. Toronto: Dundurn Press, 1997.

Flanagan, Tom. *Waiting for the Wave: The Reform Party and Preston Manning.* Toronto: Stoddart, 1995.

Fraser, G. *Playing for Keeps: The Making of the Prime Minister, 1988.* Toronto: McClelland and Stewart, 1989.

Gagnon, Lysianne. "The Bloc Is a Very Versatile Power Tool." *Globe and Mail,* 15 March 1997, D3.

Glassford, Larry A. *Reaction and Reform: The Politics of the Conservative Party under R.B. Bennett, 1927-1938.* Toronto: University of Toronto Press, 1992.

Graesser, M. "Leadership Crises in an Opposition Party: The Liberal Party of Newfoundland." In *Leaders and Parties in Canadian Politics: Experiences of the Provinces,* ed. R. Kenneth Carty, Lynda Erickson, and Donald Blake, 32-52. Toronto: Harcourt Brace Jovanovich, 1992.

Greenspon, Edward, and Jeff Sallot. "Pragmatic McDonough Nudges NDP to Centre." *Globe and Mail,* 21 September 1998.

Greenspon, Edward, and A. Wilson-Smith. *Double Vision: The Inside Story of the Liberals in Power.* Toronto: Doubleday, 1996.

Harrill, E.E. "Party Finance in the Second Party System." In *Canadian Political Party Systems: A Reader,* ed. R. Kenneth Carty, 252-64. Peterborough, ON: Broadview Press, 1992.

Heibert, Janet. "Interest Groups and Canadian Federal Elections." In *Interest Groups and Elections in Canada,* ed. F. Leslie Seidle, 3-76. Toronto: Dundurn Press/ RCERPF, 1991.

Hunziker, Margaret. "Leadership Selection: The 1985 Alberta Progressive Conservative Leadership Convention." MA thesis, University of Calgary, 1986.

Johnston, Richard, and J. Ballantyne. "Geography and the Electoral System." *Canadian Journal of Political Science* 10 (1977): 857-66.

Johnston, Richard, André Blais, Henry E. Brady, and Jean Crête. "The Electoral Basis of the Canadian Party Systems, 1978-1984." In *Canadian Political Party Systems: A Reader,* ed. R. Kenneth Carty, 587-623. Peterborough, ON: Broadview Press, 1992.

–. *Letting the People Decide: Dynamics of a Canadian Election.* Montreal and Kingston: McGill-Queen's University Press, 1992.

Johnston, Richard, André Blais, Elisabeth Gidengil, and Neil Nevitte. *The Challenge of Direct Democracy: The 1992 Canadian Referendum.* Montreal and Kingston: McGill-Queen's University Press, 1996.

Katz, Richard S., and Peter Mair. "Changing Models of Party Organization and Party Democracy: The Emergence of the Cartel Party." *Party Politics* 1 (1995): 5-28.

Kittelberg, Lori. "Reform Party's Top Fundraisers." *Hill Times,* July 20, 1998.

Lachapelle, Guy. *Polls and the Media in Canadian Elections.* Toronto: Dundurn Press, 1991.

Laghi, Brian. "Manning's Big Gamble." *Globe and Mail,* 29 May 1999, A1.

Laschinger, John, and Geoffrey Stevens. *Leaders and Lesser Mortals: Backroom Politics in Canada.* Toronto: Key Porter, 1992.

Laycock, David. *Populism and Democratic Thought in the Canadian Prairies, 1910-1945.* Toronto: University of Toronto Press, 1990.

Lee, Robert Mason. *One Hundred Monkeys: The Triumph of Popular Wisdom in Canadian Politics.* Toronto: Macfarlane Walter and Ross, 1989.

Liberal Party of Canada. *Multicultural Recruitment Manual* [c. 1982]. National Archives of Canada, MG 28, IV 2,Vol. 646. File: Multiculturalism (1).

Lovink, J.A.A. "On Analysing the Impact of the Electoral System on the Party System in Canada." *Canadian Journal of Political Science* 3 (1970): 497-516.

McCall-Newman, Christina. *Grits: An Intimate Portrait of the Liberal Party.* Toronto: Macmillan, 1982.

McIvor, Heather. "The Politics of Revival: The Progressive Conservative Party of Canada, 1993-1998." Unpublished ms.

McLaughlin, David. *Poisoned Chalice: The Last Campaign of the Progressive Conservative Party?* Toronto: Dundurn Press, 1994.

McLeod, Ian. *Under Siege: The Federal NDP in the Nineties.* Toronto: Lorimer, 1994.

Macpherson, C.B. *Democracy in Alberta: Social Credit and the Party System,* 2nd ed. Toronto: University of Toronto Press, 1962.

Mair, Peter. *Party System Change: Approaches and Interpretations.* Oxford: Clarendon Press, 1997.

Manning, Preston. "Leadership for a New Generation." Address to the Reform Assembly '98, 29 May 1998.

May, Kathryn. "PSAC to Try to Elect Federal Candidates that Support Union's Goals." *Vancouver Sun,* 19 April 1997, A18.

Martin, P., A. Gregg, and G. Perlin. *Contenders: The Tory Quest for Power.* Scarborough, ON: Prentice-Hall, 1983.

Mercer, Terrence. Testimony to the House of Commons Standing Committee on Procedure and House Affairs. *Record of Proceedings,* Wednesday, 11 March 1998.

Michaud, Pascale, and Pierre Laferrière. "Economic Analysis of the Funding of Political Parties in Canada." In *Issues in Party and Election Finance in Canada,* ed. F. Leslie Seidle, 369-98. Toronto: Dundurn Press/RCERPF, 1991.

Morton, Desmond. *The New Democrats, 1961-1986: The Politics of Change.* Toronto: Copp Clark Pitman, 1986.

Morton, W.L. *The Progressive Party in Canada.* Toronto: University of Toronto Press, 1950.

National Firearms Association. "What Is the National Firearms Association?" Photocopy, 1997.

Nevitte, Neil. *The Decline of Deference: Canadian Value Change in Cross-National Perspective.* Peterborough, ON: Broadview Press, 1996.

Newman, Peter C. *Renegade in Power: The Diefenbaker Years.* Toronto: McClelland and Stewart, 1963.

Noel, S.J.R. "Patronage and Entourages, Action-Sets, Networks." In *Canadian Parties in Transition,* 2nd ed., ed. A. Brian Tanguay and Alain-G. Gagnon, 238-51. Toronto: Nelson, 1996.

Nolan, Michael. "Political Communication Methods in Canadian Federal Election Campaigns, 1867-1925." *Canadian Journal of Communication* 7 (1981): 28-46.

Norton, Roy. "The P.C. Leadership Selection Process: A New Model for National Political Parties." Paper presented to the Canadian Political Science Association annual meeting, June 1999.

Pal, Leslie A. *Interests of State: The Politics of Language, Multiculturalism and Feminism in Canada.* Montreal and Kingston: McGill-Queen's University Press, 1993.

Paltiel, Khayyam Z. "Campaign Financing in Canada and Its Reform." In *Canada at the Polls: The General Election of 1974,* ed. Howard Penniman, 181-208. Washington, DC: American Enterprise Institute, 1975.

–. "Party Finance before World War I." In *Canadian Party Systems: A Reader,* ed. R. Kenneth Carty, 122-7. Peterborough, ON: Broadview Press, 1992.

Paltiel, Khayyam Z., and Jean Brown Van Loon. "Financing the Liberal Party, 1867-1965." In Committee on Election Expenses, *Studies in Canadian Party Finance,* 147-256. Ottawa, 1966.

Perlin, George C. "Leadership Selection in the PC and Liberal Parties: Assessing the Need for Reform." In *Party Politics in Canada,* 7th ed., ed. H.G. Thorburn, 196-212. Scarborough, ON: Prentice-Hall, 1996.

–. *The Tory Syndrome: Leadership Politics in the Progressive Conservative Party.* Montreal and Kingston: McGill-Queen's University Press, 1980.

Pitkin, Hannah, ed. *Representation.* New York: Artherton Press, 1969.

Progressive Conservative Party of Canada. *Background Paper on Party Restructuring.* September 1994.

–. *The New Constitution of the Progressive Conservative Party of Canada (April 1995).*

–. *Supplementary Notes on Party Restructuring.* October 1994.

Pross, Paul. *Group Politics and Public Policy.* Toronto: Oxford University Press, 1986.

"Referendum '94 Results Released." Press release from the office of MP Ted White, 21 June 1994.

Reform Party of Canada. "Blue Book." Available at the Reform Party's Web site, at http://www.reform.ca.

–. *Candidate Recruitment and Selection Manual.* April 1996.

–. *Reform Party of Canada Constitution (1992).*

Robinson, Daniel J. *The Measure of Democracy: Polling Market Research, and Public Life, 1930-1945.* Toronto: University of Toronto Press, 1999.

Russell, Peter. *Constitutional Odyssey: Can Canadians Become a Sovereign People?* 2nd ed. Toronto: University of Toronto Press, 1993.

Sayers, Anthony M. *Parties, Candidates and Constituency Campaigns in Canadian Elections.* Vancouver: UBC Press, 1998.

Seidle, F. Leslie. "The Angry Citizenry: Examining Representation and Responsiveness in Government." *Policy Options* 15, 6 (1994): 75-80.

–. "Canadian Political Finance Regulation and the Democratic Process: Established Rules in a Dynamic System" (revised version). Paper prepared for the Round Table on Discontent and Reform in Mature Democracies, Tokyo, August 1996.

Shafer, Byron E., ed. *Postwar Politics in the G-7: Orders and Eras in Comparative Perspective.* Madison: University of Wisconsin Press, 1996.

Sharpe, Sydney, and Don Braid. *Storming Babylon: Preston Manning and the Rise of the Reform Party.* Toronto: Key Porter, 1992.

Siegfried, André. *The Race Question in Canada.* 1907. Reprint, Toronto: McClelland and Stewart, 1966.

Simeon, Richard. *Federal-Provincial Diplomacy: The Making of Recent Policy in Canada.* Toronto: University of Toronto Press, 1972.

Smith, David E. "Party Government in Canada." In *Canadian Political Party Systems: A Reader,* ed. R. Kenneth Carty, 531-62. Peterborough, ON: Broadview Press, 1992.

–. "Party Government, Representation and National Integration in Canada." In *Party*

Government and Regional Representation in Canada, ed. P. Aucoin, 1-68. Toronto: University of Toronto Press, 1985.

Spencer, David R., and Catherine M. Bolan. "Election Broadcasting in Canada: A Brief History." In *Election Broadcasting in Canada,* ed. Frederick J. Fletcher, 3-38. Toronto: Dundurn Press, 1991.

Stanbury, W.T. "Getting and Spending: The Effect of Federal Regulations on Financing Political Parties and Candidates in Canada." In *Party Politics in Canada,* 7th ed., ed. Hugh Thorburn, 72-95. Scarborough, ON: Prentice-Hall, 1996.

—. *Money in Politics: Financing Federal Parties and Candidates in Canada.* Toronto: Dundurn Press, 1991.

Stasuilis, Daiva, and Yasmeen Abu-Laban. "Ethnic Minorities and the Politics of Limited Inclusion in Canada." In *Canadian Politics: An Introduction to the Discipline,* ed. Alain-G. Gagnon and James Bickerton, 580-608. Peterborough, ON: Broadview Press, 1990.

Stewart, David K. "Electing the Premier: An Examination of the 1992 Alberta Progressive Conservative Leadership Election." Paper presented at the annual meeting of the Canadian Political Science Association, Calgary, 1994.

Stewart David K., and R. Kenneth Carty. "Does Changing the Party Leader Provide an Electoral Boost? A Study of Canadian Provincial Parties, 1960-92." *Canadian Journal of Political Science* 26, 2 (1993): 313-30.

Stewart, Gordon. *The Origins of Canadian Politics: A Comparative Approach.* Vancouver: University of British Columbia Press, 1986.

Stursberg, Peter. *Diefenbaker: Leadership Gained, 1956-1962.* Toronto: University of Toronto Press, 1975.

Thorburn, Hugh. "Interpretations of the Canadian Party System." In *Party Politics in Canada,* 7th ed., ed. Hugh Thorburn, 117-27. Scarborough, ON: Prentice-Hall, 1996.

Wearing, Joseph. *The L-Shaped Party: The Liberal Party of Canada, 1958-1980.* Toronto: McGraw-Hill Ryerson, 1981.

Whitaker, Reginald. *The Government Party: Organizing and Financing the Liberal Party of Canada, 1930-1958.* Toronto: University of Toronto Press, 1977.

White, Ted. "The Post Mortem." *North Shore News* (Vancouver), 29 June 1994.

Whitehorn, Alan. "The NDP Election Campaign: Dashed Hopes." In *The Canadian General Election of 1988,* ed. Alan Frizzell, Jon H. Pammett, and Anthony Westell, 43-53. Ottawa: Carleton University Press, 1988.

Woolstencroft, Peter. "Democracy and the Selection of Party Leaders: The Case of the Progressive Conservative Leadership Election." Paper presented to the Canadian Political Science Association annual meetings, June 1999.

—. "On the Ropes Again?: The Campaign of the Progressive Conservative Party in the 1997 Federal Election." In *The Canadian General Election of 1997,* ed. Alan Frizzell and Jon Pammett, 71-90. Toronto: Dundurn Press, 1997.

—. "Reclaiming the 'Pink Palace': The Progressive Conservative Party Comes in from the Cold." In *The Government and Politics of Ontario,* 5th ed., ed. G. White, 368-75. Toronto: University of Toronto Press, 1997.

Young, Lisa. *Feminists and Party Politics.* Vancouver: UBC Press, 2000.

—. "Party, State and Political Competition in Canada: The Cartel Argument Revisited." *Canadian Journal of Political Science* 31, 2 (1998): 339-58.

Young, Walter D. *The Anatomy of a Party: The National CCF.* Toronto: University of Toronto Press, 1969.

Index

An italic page number indicates a figure or table.

Set in Bembo by Brenda and Neil West, BN Typographics West
Printed and bound in Canada by Friesens
Copy editor: Beverley Endersby
Proofreader: Susan Broadhurst
Indexer: Heather Ebbs

Visit the UBC Press web site at

UBC Press · Vancouver · Toronto

www.ubcpress.ubc.ca
for information and detailed descriptions of other UBC Press books

If you liked this book, look for these related titles:

R.K. Carty, ed., *Politics, Policy, and Government in British Columbia*

David Docherty, *Mr. Smith Goes to Ottawa: Life in the House of Commons*

David Stewart and Keith Archer, *Quasi-Democracy?*
Parties and Leadership Selection in Alberta

Lisa Young, *Feminists and Party Politics*

Ask for UBC Press books in your bookstore or contact us at
info@ubcpress.ubc.ca.

You can order UBC Press books directly from Raincoast
telephone 1-800-663-5714
fax 1-800-565-3770